MW01618440

Human Relations FOR THE EDUCATOR

Meeting the Challenges for Today and Tomorrow

SECOND EDITION

Scott L. Arnett
Morningside College
Susie L. Lubbers
Morningside College
Susan R. Burns
Morningside College

Kendall Hunt
publishing company

Book Team

Chairman and Chief Executive Officer Mark C. Falb
President and Chief Operating Officer Chad M. Chandlee
Vice President, Higher Education David L. Tart
Director of Publishing Partnerships Paul B. Carty
Senior Developmental Editor Lynnette M. Rogers
Vice President, Operations Timothy J. Beitzel
Assistant Vice President, Production Services Christine E. O'Brien
Senior Production Editor Mary Melloy
Permissions Editor Tammy Hunt
Senior Cover Designer Suzanne Millius

Kendall Hunt
publishing company

www.kendallhunt.com
Send all inquiries to:
4050 Westmark Drive
Dubuque, IA 52004-1840

ISBN 978-1-4652-1368-6

Printed in the United States of America
10 9 8 7 6 5 4 3 2 1

Brief Contents

Contents

Acknowledgments

We would like to thank our families for their encouragement and patience throughout the development of this book. We would also like to acknowledge our mentors for their sustained guidance and support. We greatly appreciate the institutional support given by Morningside College's Administrations. We wish to personally thank Brenda Lussier for her art-work. Without all of the above, this project would not have been possible.

About the Authors

Scott L. Arnett graduated from the University of Oklahoma in 1997 with a Ph.D. in special education. He has expertise in intellectual disabilities, transition, severe/profound disabilities, and assistive technology. Dissertation and research interests involve assisting individuals with intellectual disabilities to increase their self-determination. Dr. Arnett was promoted to associate professor of education at Morningside College during the 2003 academic year, where he was awarded the First Year Teaching/Advising Award for 2005. He was also awarded the Lucille and Charles Wert Faculty Excellence Award, May 2005.

Susie L. Lubbers is an assistant professor of education at Morningside College in Sioux City, Iowa. Her focus areas are effective pedagogy and emotional intelligence. Prior to Morningside, Susie spent 15 years as a high school language arts teacher in a large Iowa school district. She has facilitated workshops both regionally and nationally. Her degrees are from the University of South Dakota and Southwest Minnesota State University.

Susan R. Burns, association dean for academic affairs and associate professor of psychology at Morningside College, received her B.S. and M.S. in experimental psychology from Emporia State University and her Ph.D. in personality/social psychology with an emphasis in child development from Kansas State University. Although Dr. Burns' responsibilities are primarily administrative in nature, she continues to teach a Psychology of Gender course each academic year. She, with a colleague in computer science, co-founded the Video Game Institute for Education and Research (VGIER) lab on Morningside College's campus, researching the psychological and physiological effects of playing videogames. Susan actively encourages students to become engaged in the research process as assistants in the VGIER lab. Dr. Burns was selected as a recipient of the 2004 and 2008 Sharon Walker Faculty Excellence Award, the 2006 state of Iowa, American Association of University Women Distinguished Faculty Award recipient, and the Omicron Delta Kappa Honor Society 2006 Faculty Person of the Year.

ABOUT THE ARTIST

Brenda Lussier is a graduate of Morningside College with a bachelor's degree in art education. Her mother said she was drawing before she could talk. Brenda hopes to one day become a full-time illustrator.

Introduction

Those entrusted with preparing future teachers find themselves in the midst of an evolution in the field of education. Preservice teaching institutions must recognize as their primary task to prepare new teachers with the skills and resources necessary to meet the demanding professional challenges of today *and* tomorrow. We can no longer focus only on the skills needed to teach in today's world, but we must now prepare teachers with the skills to meet tomorrow's world. We have not attempted to communicate through an oracle, nor can we begin to describe what the future will look like. Nevertheless, we feel strongly that the preservice teacher equipped with skills in human relations will be in the best position to conquer the challenges of tomorrow's world, whatever the challenges may look like.

An area in teacher preparation that is presently underexamined and is potentially the most essential for educator professional development is the field of human relations. The most important challenges facing any teacher, at any time, are in the human exchange and relationship-building areas with those he or she works *under* (e.g., administrators, principals, superintendents, etc.), works *with* (e.g., faculty, colleagues, paraprofessionals, etc.), and works *for* (e.g., students, parents, the community, etc.). This text is designed to give the preservice teacher the essential skills to promote productive interactions and build on existing relations.

The overriding emphasis of this text is on being *applied*. This applied approach is not only intentional on our part, but, we believe, essential for the new teacher. We have been very selective in the materials used in this text. Whether we are examining the historical contributors to the field of human relation, theories, concepts, or best practices, all information presented has an applied nature.

The first step in becoming an exceptional teacher is to know who you are and how you became who you are. The text begins with a discussion on how the self, or who we are, is developed; then, future teachers are asked to examine themselves in a chapter called "Who Is This Person People Call An Exceptional Teacher?" This section is designed for educators to see the importance of self-reflection in everything they do, how values, beliefs, and attitudes play a major role in building relationships, the significance of being ethical in the many decisions a teacher makes throughout the day, and the importance of being an encouraging teacher.

The second section of the text addresses the prerequisite background knowledge the new teacher must possess in order to establish and maintain productive relationships. This information includes the understanding of perceptions, communication skills (including active listening, verbal, and nonverbal communication), and conflict management.

The last section of the text includes the understanding, development, and maintenance of relationship building with supervisors, colleagues, faculty, paraprofessionals, and parents. We then spend the bulk of this section looking at establishing and maintaining productive relationships with students.

There is only a conscious motivation for writing this text; an emphasis must be placed on creating a continuous dialogue on the training needs of preservice teachers in the context of human relations. Without continuous discussions and the recognition of the relationship-building skills needed, preservice teachers will find themselves at a great disadvantage when confronted with the new challenges of tomorrow.

BIOGRAPHIES

The appendix presents biographical information on each contributor to this text. The preservice teacher should visit these biographies, which often offer events and insight into the thinking of the theorists and practitioners highlighted.

The self is not something one finds; it is something others create.
—Anonymous

1 The Development of Self

OBJECTIVES

After completing this chapter you should be able to:

- Define human relations;
- Explain the importance of others' perceptions in the development of the self;
- Discuss how teachers' perceptions and treatment of students influence children's development of selves;
- Describe how who we are is shaped by internalized conversations within ourselves.

KEY TERMS

Human relations
Internalized conversation
Looking glass self
Self-fulfilling prophecy
The self

HUMAN RELATIONS DEFINED

Human relations
Systematic study of the ongoing process of shared interactions that occur among people in all aspects of their lives

Human relations is the systematic study of the ongoing process of shared interactions that occur among people in all aspects of their lives (Arnett & Burns, 2008). An interesting view of human relations is given to us by Swensen (1973): "To put it simply, the field of interpersonal relations is now characterized by widely diverse groups of people from varying disciplines, working as individuals or as small groups, all pursuing their own problems in their own way, with occasional and sometimes extensive interaction between two or more groups, but with no generally agreed upon theory or research strategy for the field" (p. 11). Swensen would later state that human relations is characterized by many competing schools of thought rather than by one model or paradigm that is accepted by most of those working within the field. Gallese (2003) agrees with Swensen, noting that "various modalities of normal and pathological interpersonal relations are the focus of many different disciplines such as neuroscience, cognitive and developmental psychology, philosophy of mind, and psychiatry" (p. 517). Notice that three decades after Swensen's comments, little has changed and our understanding of human relations still is dependent on multiple and various disciplines.

The self
That central inner force, common to all beings and yet unique in each.

The Self

What is this thing we call the self? The self is that central inner force, common to all human being and yet unique in each. The self is also defined as the essential qualities that make a person distinct from all others. Shakespeare says we have only one self: "To thine own self be true." Have you ever heard yourself say, "I'm not myself today," implying that you believe you have two selves? William James says we have three selves: the material self, the social self, and the spiritual self. Burton White says we have four selves: the physical self, the mental self, the emotional self, and the social self. George Herbert Mead (1934) says we have a self for each person we know (determined by roles we play). Diane Ackerman (2005) says the mind has the capacity to render the often multiple contradictory selves into a stable and coherent self. How many selves do you have?

THE DEVELOPMENT OF SELF

Chapter 2 examines the foundations of exceptional teachers. Exceptional teachers know who they are, how they will behave ethically, and the importance of encouragement. Chapter 1 focuses on *how the self is developed*, which will benefit the discussion of *who we are* in the next chapter.

The founders of the study of human relations shared certain beliefs that continue to be influential today. They spent a great deal of time examining the development of the self, or who we are. Specifically, they "saw human beings as being social in their basic nature and as having no existence apart from existence in relationship to other human beings"

(Swensen, 1973, p. 8). Similarly stated, Manis and Meltzer (1978) noted, early theorists thought the individual becomes humanized through interaction with other persons. In its extreme form, we are not born human, but through interactions with others, we become human. In other words, human beings construct their realities of who they are in a process of interaction with other human beings.

Spend a moment trying to identify who you are. We usually do this by the labels we use for ourselves: athlete, musician, scholar, Christian, republican, democrat, independent, etc. Take a moment to identify some of your values about the following: pro-choice, pro-life, gay rights, death penalty, assisted suicide, the National Rifle Association, American Civil Liberties Union. How did you acquire these labels and values? Were you born with these? The founders of the field of human relations believe we learned who we are through the interactions with others.

An appropriate place to begin the examination of the development of the self, or who we are, is in the works of **Charles Horton Cooley** (1864–1929). Cooley's most influential work is the concept of the **looking glass self** (LGS). He first discussed the LGS in *Human Nature and the Social Order* (1902) but extended this concept in the text *Social Organization* (1909). Swensen (1973) gives us the most pointed and clearest understanding of Cooley's looking glass self. Basically, Cooley's idea is that *our selves, or who we are, develop out of our perceptions of the reactions of others to us. We are who we perceive other people think we are.* In this sense, no self exists or could exist apart from other people. Our perceptions of ourselves are seen as being mirrored, as in a looking glass, in the reactions of other people to us. Thus, who we are is a construction from the information that people around us reflect back to us. From this perception of the reaction of others to us, we *gradually* develop a general idea, a kind of consensus, of what other people think of us and thus develop an idea of our selves, or who we are. Thus, what we think of ourselves is decisively influenced by what others think of us. By internalizing our perception of what others think about us, in *time*, we gain our image of our self. Cooley (1909) suggested that an individual forms an opinion of how he or she appears to the other person and reacts with a positive or negative *self-feeling* to the imagined judgment.

Looking glass self
Cooley's belief that our "self" develops out of our perceptions of the reactions of other to us

> "I am not who you think I am, I am not who I think I am, I am who I think you think I am." —Max Webber

Theories of self-development emphasize the individual's perception of how other persons see him or her. *All* are concerned with the expectations they believe other people have concerning what they should be like. As Kinch (1968) noted, the more frequently people perceive a particular type of response directed toward them, the more likely they are to use that response in changing their own self-concept. Brown, Von Bank,

Figure 1.1 Adolescence is a time of self-exploration and understanding, and much of how adolescents define themselves comes from their peers.

and Steinberg (2007) experimentally illustrated the power of the looking glass self to adolescents. Adolescence is a time of self-exploration and understanding, and much of how adolescents define themselves comes from their peers. These authors describe how peers serve as "identity markers" for adolescents. In fact, "Crowds offer identity prototypes against which young people can measure themselves and through which they can grasp their reputation among peers" (Brown, Von Bank, & Steinberg, 2007, p. 1163).

Preservice teachers must start their professional journey with the recognition of how powerful the LGS is. Think back to the very first thing you remember. What if your very first memory was of someone calling you stupid, then the day after he did it again, and this was to continue? Is this going to affect who you are? Cooley believes it will.

Cooley might argue that Tiger Woods is a great golfer, not because of his athletic abilities or that he shoots under par and wins tournaments, but he is great because *he had perceived* that others thought he was great since he was a young boy. What if from the age of 7 until Tiger was 21, everyone told him he was a terrible golfer? Would this affect who he is? If you *repeatedly perceive* that others think you are very intelligent, you will indeed see yourself as very intelligent. If your *continued* perception is that others think you are clumsy or a troublemaker, you will indeed see yourself as being clumsy or as a troublemaker.

It is imperative that preservice teachers experience the LGS first hand. In one class, a professor gives his midterm exams in the mall (Visa card is always an option, but not required). For part of the exam, the students are required to find the LGS.

In one of many experiences at the mall, two heterosexual female students held hands and pretended to be in love with each other. They entered a jewelry store and asked to see engagement rings. A female salesperson described by the students as being "a lot older" looked shocked and refused their request, leaving the showroom and entering a back room. Both students were amazed at her reaction and felt that they had done something "very bad" and felt "ashamed" of their behaviors. Soon thereafter a male salesperson entered the showroom and offered to help the students choose the right rings. The students began to feel okay with the situation they were presenting (being gay and in love) but now began to feel that they were looked at only as customers for the salesperson to profit from and not as real people that the salesperson wanted to get to know.

One student arrived at the mall early for the exam. He was of drinking age and went into a sports bar and ordered a drink. (This behavior is *not* recommended prior to a midterm exam!) The waitress looked "put out," perhaps thinking he was not of legal age, demanded to see his ID and made it clear to him he was not welcome. The student noted that the waitress's reaction made him feel not only unwelcome but also that he was a "criminal," doing something wrong. Once the waitress recognized that he was of drinking age, a smile came over her face and she began treating him well, most likely hoping he would tip well and return again in the future.

One student, known for being a leader, organized a tour of the mall. The student created a sign that read "ACME TOUR COMPANY." He led other students through the mall, stopping at individual stores, and noting what year the store had opened and what products the store sells. At first the "tourists" found this activity to be fun, but as other shoppers began to stare, point, and laugh, the student "tourists" began to drop off the tour. The tour dwindled until only the guide was left. Amazingly, with only the tour guide left, the tour continued.

A favorite activity of my male athletes is to venture into a Victoria's Secret store, asking to purchase underwear for themselves. I can only image what the salesperson is thinking.

It is important to note that for this exam the student does not have to contrive a situation to find the LGS. All that is required is that a student greet another person, then perceive the reaction from the other person (a welcoming smile, an avoiding frown, etc.), and the LGS has been located.

In the next class following the midterm exam, students are encouraged to discuss how their "self" would be affected if these feelings (e.g., being ashamed of who they were, treated as if they were the "town idiot," constantly stared at, embarrassed, etc.) were to accompany them *every day of their lives*. It is one thing to contrive a situation and get strange looks; it is completely different to perceive that people think of you that way *every* time you enter the mall. Imagine every time you enter a store you are looked at as being a shoplifter; or if every time you greet a stranger, you are seen as weird. Experiencing these continuous feelings, day after day, will no doubt affect your perception of your self.

Factors influencing the development of the self depend on the frequency of these perceived responses, the perceived importance from others, and how consistent these perceptions present themselves. By noting how others perceive us, we can see ourselves as others see us (as in looking into a mirror) and recognize the responses that we facilitate in others.

Some may disagree with Cooley's LGS, believing that they have more control over who they are. Some may even feel they can dismiss entirely others' perceptions of themselves, but, in truth, we cannot overlook the impact of others on our self-esteem, self-worth, or self-confidence. ***More importantly, as a teacher, you cannot overlook the influence of others on the development of your students' self.***

Name: ______________________________

Charles Horton Cooley's Looking Glass Self

Cooley (1902) proposed that our self, or who we are, develops out of our perceptions of the reactions of others to us. Basically, we are who we perceive other people think we are. Our perceptions of ourselves are seen as being mirrored, as in a looking glass, in the reactions of other people to us. From this perception of the reaction of others to us, we *gradually* develop a general idea, a kind of consensus, of what other people think of us and thus develop an idea of ourselves, or who we are.

Describe two observations.
Make your observations relevant to the definition.

---

(1) Observation: (e.g., trip to the mall or cafeteria)

Relevance to the definition: If *every time* I went to the mall (or cafeteria), people made me feel _______________, this would *gradually, over time, affect who I am.*

(2) Observation: (e.g., trip to the mall or cafeteria)

Courtesy of Brenda Lussier.

Relevance to the definition: If *every time* I went to the mall (or cafeteria), people made me feel ______________, this would *gradually, over time, affect who I am.*

____

In reaction to Cooley's looking glass self, **George Herbert Mead** (1863–1931) made us aware that the choices and decisions one makes eventually come from the self and are not just determined by external influences.

Mead offers a naturalistic account of the origin of the self and explains this notion in terms of social behavior. According to Mead, the individual can look at his or her own behavior from the point of view of the *other*. When people can view their own behavior from the perspective of another, Mead believed, at that point, they have a self. Individuals must be in both their own perspective and in the perspective of the other.

Mead agrees with Cooley that the self develops out of interactions with other people. Swensen (1973), in describing this concept, notes that to exist as a person, to have a self, to be a personality, one must have others to interact with. If there is no one around to interact with, no self, no personality, no human being, as we usually think of the concept, can exist.

But Mead disagrees with Cooley's ideas about the reactions of others to him. Mead (1934) teaches that the essence of self is cognitive and that it exists in the **internalized conversation** a person carries on within him- or herself, which constitutes thinking. Mead believes it is this internal interactive process that constitutes a self. Although we may have a general concept of what others think of us, and that this "generalized other" forms a basis for the unity of the self, we are nonetheless different selves to different people.

Internalized conversation
The conversation a person has with him- or herself. This interactive process constitutes the "self" according to Mead.

Many would agree with Mead's perspective of the development of the self over Cooley's LGS. Most preservice teachers prefer to believe that they themselves have a say in who they are. We, as individuals, are more than just how we are perceived by others; and furthermore, we have a say in this process of developing the self. Mead offers us an internal dialogue or conversation with oneself, and it is in this process of that conversation that our self is developed. Also of interest, through internalized conversations, an individual assesses the value of the looking glass self.

This internal dialogue offers choices in a person's development of self. Individuals are capable of modifying influences and of creating and changing their own behavior. Mead recognizes the great influences others have on individuals. He also sees the participants' part in creating their own destinies. At times this internal dialogue may be seen as a vital conflict in the development of the self. Circumstances may put pressure on people to change, but this active dialogue may maintain stability of the self regardless of others' perceptions. We all know individuals who have accomplished things that others believed they could not. Mead would credit their internal dialogue for the accomplishments.

Cooley reminds us to be aware of the influence others have on the development of the self. Mead acknowledges the external influences on the self but makes us aware that the choices and decisions we make (after engaging in internal dialogue) eventually come from the self and are not just determined by external influences.

Preservice teachers should examine Mead's internal conversations prior to becoming a practitioner. Teachers should be aware of and be willing to discuss events in which internal conversations went against what others wanted them to do or thought they should do. There are times when teachers perceive that others want them to go one way, but these teachers must professionally, ethically, or morally choose to go another way.

This exercise of examining Mead's internal conversations has many implications for the teacher. One implication of internal dialogues is to examine our use of ethical decision making (revisited in chapter 2) versus being pressured into doing something that you later may deem as wrong. It is an interesting dilemma when a principal asks a teacher to lie to a parent for the "best interest" of the school. Another way this exercise is beneficial is for teachers to examine ways to encourage this internal dialogue in their students. One major goal of the education process is to instill and increase self-determination into all students. Self-determination can only be exercised through a conversation one has with oneself, about an individual's desires, values, beliefs, preferences, interests, and those things meaningful to him or her (Arnett, 1997). Teachers should promote and include the use of internal conversations in their daily curriculum.

Name: ____________________

George Herbert Mead's Internalized Conversation

In reaction to Cooley's concept of the looking glass self, Mead (1934) makes us aware that the choices and decisions one makes eventually come from the self and are not determined just by external influences. Mead believed that the essence of self lay in the internalized conversation people carry on within themselves.

Offer three internalized conversations you have had with yourself.

(1) ____________________

____

____

____

(2) ____________________

____

____

____

(3) ____________________

____

____

____

Courtesy of Brenda Lussier.

Cooley's looking glass self and Mead's internalized conversation are best revealed in the classroom through **Robert K. Merton's** (1910–2003) **self-fulfilling prophecy.** The phrase *self-fulfilling prophecy* (SFP) was first used by Merton in 1948. As part of the explanation of the SFP, Merton states that if persons define situations as real, they are real in their consequences. The basis of the SFP is that once a student has been pegged ahead of time as, say, a troublemaker, a nonscholar, or likely to be self-centered, the chances are increased that our treatment of this student will, in effect, help our negative prophecies or expectations come true.

Self-fulfilling prophecy
The ultimate function of SFP is not to *predict* the future, but *make* the future.

Here the SFP would work to the detriment of the student. On the other hand, we could peg a student as cooperative, scholarly, or likely to be a self-starter, thus increasing the chances that our treatment of him or her will convey these expectations and, in turn, contribute to the student living up to our positive prophecy. In these cases, the SFP would work to the student's benefit.

The SFP works like this (notice how the SFP ties into the looking glass self): the teacher forms impressions and expectations (troublemaker, scholar, or student athlete, who only wants to play sports and not crack a book); based on these expectations, the teacher acts in a certain manner (expects trouble, A papers, or the athlete to not read his or her assignments); the teacher's treatment tells each student what behavior and what achievement the teacher expects; if this treatment is consistent, *gradually, over time*, it will tend to shape the student's behavior and achievement; with time, the student's behavior and achievement will conform more and more closely to that which is expected of him or her (the troublemaker makes trouble, the B+ paper becomes an A paper, the student athlete is never called on and, because he or she is never called on, stops reading the assignments).

Each time a teacher sizes up or sizes down a student, the teacher is, in effect, influencing this student's future behavior and achievement. If a teacher believes a student is incapable of learning, the teacher is less likely to spend time working with the student. And, since the teacher is spending little or no time working with the student, the student is likely to fail, thus living up to the teacher's expectations. Wagar may have described it best in his statement, "The ultimate function of a prophecy is not to predict the future, but to *make it*" (Wagar, 1963, p. 66).

Expectation and Performance

One of the most widely read and cited research studies that illustrates the impact of the self-fulfilling prophecy comes from researchers Robert Rosenthal and Lenore Jacobson (1968). Rosenthal and Jacobson administered an intelligence test to students in grades kindergarten through fifth grade. The teachers were not told that the test was an intelligence test, but that the test was being developed as a measure for students' potential to "bloom" (i.e., showing sudden growth in intelligence) in the coming year. The teachers were also told which students were likely to be "growth spurters" (students selected at random, not dependent on test performance). Researchers readministered intelligence assessments one and two years later. Results demonstrated the presence of the self-fulfilling prophecy. That is, growth spurters gained more IQ points than the control group of students in the one- and two-year follow-up. These authors conclude that high teacher expectations led to intelligence growth in the children who were identified as having potential for growth. More recently, Jussim and Harber (2005) reviewed roughly 30 years of research that followed Rosenthal and Jacobson's (1968) original students. Based on their extensive review, Jussim and Harber suggest that although self-fulfilling prophecies do exist, the effects are typically small and do not accumulate "across perceivers or over time, and they may be more likely to dissipate than accumulate" (p. 131). These authors do, however, acknowledge that students who are from "stigmatized social groups" are more likely to experience influential self-fulfilling prophecies from their teachers. Jussim and Harber additionally argue that teachers' expectations may accurately predict behavior or performance because the teachers are accurate in their assessment of students. Although there may be controversy over the extent to which teachers' expectations affect students' intelligence, there is little doubt that self-fulfilling prophecies can impact the behavior of others. Thus, teachers need to be aware of the perceptions and expectations (factual or not) they have of students, and how those expectations affect their behavior toward their students.

If our perceptions of what others think influence who we are, according to Cooley's looking glass self, the SFP would offer that others' behavior or expectation of us will influence who we will become. When students perceive that their teacher sees them as being self-confident, with high self-esteem and self-worth, and then the teacher's behavior reflects this attitude, along with an expectation that matches this attitude, according to the LGS and the SFP, the students will have the best opportunity to become self-confident, with high self-esteem and self-worth.

Mead might argue that if a teacher's impressions, expectations, and behaviors are that certain students are not college material, and the students become aware of these impressions, expectations, and behaviors, the students would have an internalized dialogue with themselves. If the internalized dialogue results in the students' disagreeing with their teacher's view, the students may be motivated to prove the teacher wrong. Hence, when the students obtain their college degree, the **students** *have made their future.*

Name: Katee Prefer

Robert K. Merton's Self-Fulfilling Prophecy

The basis of the self-fulfilling prophecy is that once a student has been pegged ahead of time as, say, a troublemaker, the chances are increased that our treatment of this student will, in effect, help our expectations (or prophecy) come true.

Offer an example in your life where you (or another) "made" your (or his or her) self-fulfilling prophecy come true.

When I was in high school, my teacher believed me to do extremly well in school. There was an expectation of straight A's. Therefore, I graduated close to straight A's and try to keep the pattern going in college.

Courtesy of Brenda Lussier.

SUMMARY

This chapter shows the importance others have played in the development of the self. Cooley's looking glass self places a total emphasis on others' perspectives in the determination of who a person will become. Mead's internalized conversation allows for the emphasis of others' influences to remain, but these influences are accompanied by an internal dialogue within the individual that *together* constitute the development of the self.

Through *self-reflection*, which is a major focus throughout this textbook, preservice teachers must take the time to recognize the role others have played in the manifestation of who they are. After we have taken the time to recognize how others have influenced who we are, we then must turn our attention to the task of recognizing how we, as teachers, will influence the development of the self in our students, as described by Merton's self-fulfilling prophecy. For many students this self-reflection may turn out to be the most important task a teacher has.

CASE 1.A

John had struggled with high school until he had Mrs. Stinger in eleventh-grade government class. Every teacher he had in high school, until Mrs. Stinger, believed that he was like his older siblings; they were troublemakers who never took school seriously and were expelled frequently from classes because of their lack of respect for the teacher. In fact, they never graduated from high school, choosing to drop out instead when they turned sixteen. Mrs. Stinger, however, was a new teacher in the building, transferring from another school in the district. She had heard about John from the other teachers in her department, but she refused to form an opinion of the boy until she had the chance to get to know him in her class. On the first day of class, he came into her room with a chip on his shoulder, almost daring her to believe everything she had heard about him and his siblings. She introduced herself to him and told him she was looking forward to having him in class. He was perplexed. Granted he had never been disrespectful to his teachers, nor had he been expelled, but he couldn't remember the last time a teacher had told him that she was looking forward to having him in class. It took a few weeks, but soon Mrs. Stinger had John looking forward to coming to class and seeing her and talking with her for a few moments before class started. A few more weeks and John was doing his work, actually believing that he had something to contribute to the class. Other teachers began asking Mrs. Stinger what she had done to turn John around; she would smile at them and then tell them that she had let him know that he was part of her community in the classroom, and she knew he would be productive member of the community.

QUESTIONS

1. What does this example say about the power of a teacher's expectations on a student?

When the teacher believes that their student can do something, they will treat that student like they will achieve something. Expectations of teacher's of their students can affect them for good or for bad.

2. How could this situation with John and Mrs. Stinger have turned out differently?

Mrs. Stinger could have considered John like his siblings and expect trouble. She could have ignored him in class and isolated him from the rest of the class.

3. Could his success in her class carry over to other classes? Why or why not?

Yes, his attitude in this class will raise his hopes that other teachers will treat him the same.

CASE 1.B

Cindy is a student in Mr. Martinez's first-grade classroom. When school started in September, she was a happy child, excited about starting first grade. She quickly became one of his "favorite" students. She was always willing to run errands to the office for him; she raised her hand politely in class when she had an answer to a question; her reading was taking off and she was starting to read chapter books by November. She was truly a joy to have in class. After winter break, however, Mr. Martinez noticed a change in Cindy. She started picking minor fights with students in class, always quick to blame the other person. When Mr. Martinez would ask her to do a favor for him, she would look past him and ignore him. When he would ask her a question in class, she would not answer it. It seemed as though she were a different child in his classroom. Not having any children of his own and being a new teacher, Mr. Martinez thought that she might be going through "a phase," and so he let her behaviors go. This continued through to the end of the year, which saw Cindy's progress in school almost halt. He tried to talk with her, but she would not tell him anything. When he found out that Cindy would have Mrs. Smithson as her second-grade teacher, he talked to Mrs. Smithson about Cindy's behaviors in his class. He was astounded when Mrs. Smithson told him that Cindy's parents had gotten a divorce in March, which in hindsight explained much of her behavior change.

QUESTIONS

1. What should Mr. Martinez have done when Cindy's behavior changed in January?

2. How could that have changed the outcome of her first-grade year?

CASE 1.C

Ms. Daniels is having a phenomenal year with her fifth-grade students. When they come into her room in the morning, they are quick to sit down and start the day. When she assigns work for them in groups, they come together and work quietly and collaboratively. Not all of her students are "A" students; in fact, some are struggling learners, but they turn to each other and learn from one another. In her 10 years of teaching Ms. Daniels has not had a class like this. They are inquisitive and resemble "learning sponges"; at times she thinks she may be dreaming and hopes never to wake up from the dream. She encourages their efforts in class, and in return, they work harder. Ms. Daniels had the students keep a journal, which chronicled their learning in fifth grade. In the journal, she asked them to write about how they learned, what they learned from others in class, and how important it is to work with others in class.

QUESTIONS

1. What might Ms. Daniels have done at the beginning of the year and throughout the year to get the class working together as a community of learners?

2. What does this say about her personality and the personalities of her students?

3. Is this attainable with every group of students? Why or why not?

SUGGESTED ACTIVITIES

1. Create an "I Am" poem. Because each of us is not who we were yesterday or who we will be tomorrow, creating an "I Am" poem helps us to create our perception of who we are. Visit http://ettcweb.lr.k12.nj.us/forms/iampoem.htm to create an "I Am" poem.

2. I am not who you think I am
   I am not who I think I am
   I am who I think you think I am.

   German sociologist and political economist, Max Weber, is credited with this quotation. Brainstorm how this quotation by Weber fits the overall meaning of chapter 1: The Development of Self.

3. Create your own "River of Life." This is an excellent way to introduce oneself to others because every person has a rich life story that reflects moments of celebration as well as hard times. Like a river, your life has a certain flow. There are times when a river is rushing and flowing over the banks. At other times, the river goes over rapids and rocks or moves slowly and peacefully. Visit http://knowledgecafe.care2share.wikispaces.net/River+of+Life for directions.

It is important that we constantly remind ourselves that to know thyself is the most difficult lesson in the world.
—Miguel de Cervantes

2

Who Is This Person People Call an Exceptional Teacher?

OBJECTIVES

After completing this chapter you should be able to:

- Describe the difference between autocratic, permissive, and democratic teachers.
- Discuss the importance of self-reflection in professional and personal development.
- Explain the value of understanding personal ethical stances prior to entering the classroom.
- Explain Lawrence Kohlberg's theory of moral development as a means to help understand teachers' and students' moral reasoning.
- Distinguish between different types of thinking/reasoning used to face the dilemma of students' conflicting interests in the classroom.
- Describe the difference between values and beliefs.
- Describe the code of ethics for teachers developed by the National Education Association.
- Discuss the value of being an encouraging teacher.

KEY TERMS

Autocratic teacher
Beliefs
Care-based thinking
Conventional
Democratic teacher
Encouragement
Ends-based thinking
Ethics
Hypocrisy
Moralizer
Permissive teacher
Postconventional
Preconventional
Principle-based ethics
Rule-based thinking
Self-reflection
Values
Virtue-based ethics

FOUNDATION OF ALL EXCEPTIONAL TEACHERS

Chapter 1 offered an explanation of how the self is developed through the interactions with others. In this chapter we are concerned with what kind of teacher you will become.

The *foundation of all exceptional teachers* must consist of knowing who they are, knowing how they will behave ethically in the classroom, and knowing the importance of encouraging all students. This chapter begins by examining who the teacher is, and the importance of self-reflection in this examination, followed by ethical practices in the classroom. Students will examine belief systems, values, morals, and how they are obtained. And last, the importance of being an encouraging teacher cannot be overstated.

Rudolf Dreikurs (1897–1972), a world-renowned Austrian psychologist, offers us a place to begin the question, who is this person people call an exceptional teacher?

Autocratic teacher
A teacher who teaches by force and punishment, not allowing students to demonstrate creativity in their efforts

Is this teacher an autocratic boss? According to Dreikurs and Cassel (1972), an **autocratic teacher** "is committed to making pupils do as they are told, forcing them to learn, berating them when they don't, punishing any misdemeanor and denying any creative freedom of expression" (p. 15). According to these authors, this autocratic teacher is a relic of the feudal past, and sooner or later will be defeated.

Permissive teacher
A teacher who believes students can do no wrong, and that ultimately they will be valuable members of society without unnecessary guidance

Or maybe the teacher is too **permissive**? According to Dreikurs and Cassel, to this teacher no child is ever wrong; every action is condoned because eventually the student will turn out to be a good and worthwhile member of society. The teacher allows the students to select their own topics or lessons for the day. "You may wonder at the end of the day what you have taught and why your head aches so much, but you know that a noisy classroom indicates that children are communicating and learning from each other," and "At the end of the term . . . [t]hey disrespect the rights of others, are tired, bored, one-track minded and unable to cope with any routine at all" (p. 17). Dreikurs and Cassel describe this teacher as a "laissez-faire anarchist." Elstad (2006) suggests that this laissez-faire approach to the use of technology in the classroom (e.g., Internet, games, chatting) can cause major disruption for both the teacher and students. Students are perceptive to empty threats given by permissive teachers (in classrooms with or without technology), and Elstad (2006) explains that it is not rational to assume that students will alter their behavior. The integration of technology into classrooms is very beneficial and essential in today's society; however, teachers must consider how they facilitate its use.

Democratic teacher
A teacher who allows students to be active members of the education process, who has reasonable expectations for his or her students, and takes responsibility for the education process

Another option is a **democratic teacher**. These teachers see their role as a *"responsible guide"* (pp. 20–24). The responsible guide takes a more democratic approach to education than the previously described approaches. When using this style of teaching, educators take responsibility for their actions and expect students to do the same. The responsible guide holds students accountable for meeting set expectations, but the expectations are within reason.

SELF-REFLECTION

Dreikurs and Cassel's (1972) descriptions of approaches to teaching (e.g., autocratic, permissive, and democratic) are just three examples of the various styles professionals in education find themselves using. Introducing and describing these styles is not the main purpose of this chapter; rather, our hope is to have every teacher continually **self-reflect** and examine and reexamine what kind of teacher he or she is or wants to become. As stated throughout this text, knowing who you are and what kind of teacher you wish to become will have a beneficial impact on relationships with your students, and *good relationships will produce good academic achievement.*

Self-reflection Requires a continual analysis and critical examination of what is going on around a teacher and involves an internal conversation on how the teacher might improve his or her teaching

Of the multitude of questions teachers should ask themselves, one is if they are comfortable in a certain teaching style (e.g., autocratic, permissive, democratic). Just because a teacher is comfortable in a certain style doesn't necessarily indicate *effectiveness*, rather, only an indication of a *desire to resist change*. To state this again, if a teacher is comfortable being autocratic, the comfort that accompanies this approach is not an indication of the teacher being effective, but that he or she is less likely to change, for example, to a democratic style of teaching. This type of self-reflection is essential to becoming the best educator the teacher can be.

Other questions that teachers should reflect on include: Are students learning what I intend them to learn from my lesson plans? Or, what areas do I need to change to become a more effective teacher? These questions and reflections should continue to follow teachers into the classrooms *every* day they teach.

Preservice teachers may not yet have the classroom experiences with which to answer some of the above questions. Nevertheless, they should ask themselves, "Am I going to use this teaching style because I was taught this is the way to do things, or am I preparing myself to offer a variety of different teaching styles and strategies that will aid me in determining what is the most effective for my students?" Determining the effectiveness of any teaching style can be accomplished only through the dedication of self-reflection.

Figure 2.1 The importance of being an exceptional teacher cannot be overstated.

Another important question in this process of self-reflection is, How do I, as a teacher, interact with others? Do I interact with everyone the same way, or do I interact differently with different people? (e.g., Do I interact one way with my students, another way with my principal, and a different way with support staff, and parents?). Teachers must become conscious of their interaction styles and then reexamine the question of why they interact in this fashion, as well as whether this interaction style is the most effective for accomplishing those difficult tasks that lie ahead.

Without teachers having an understanding of who they are, it becomes a difficult task to know and understand who their students are. For example, if teachers believe in strictly following all rules and allowing no excuses, and teachers, through self-reflection, have examined their beliefs and believe that this style is the *most effective* (versus most *comfortable*) for their students, these teachers are now in a position to enlighten students on the importance of their beliefs and thus, give credibility to their position. Although not every student may learn best from a teacher with an autocratic style, every student can learn and benefit from a teacher's self-reflection and commitment to a position.

If, on the other hand, teachers believe in students' taking responsibility for their own educational program, encouraging input from students regarding the rules, knowing that there are always exceptions to these rules, and as with the other scenario, examine, through self-reflection, their beliefs and feel that this style is the *most effective* for students, the teachers are now in a position to clarify these different beliefs. Again, every student can benefit from a teacher's self-examination and commitment. If we have an understanding of who we are and have revisited our beliefs regarding teaching styles and believe our chosen style is the *most effective* teaching style from which our students can benefit, we are in a position to convey these beliefs to our students. By knowing ourselves and self-disclosing (e.g., our beliefs about teaching styles) to students, *they are in a position to offer feedback to our beliefs and actions*. The end result of this two-way communication is a better understanding of students as persons. We may learn from this two-way communication that Johnny wants/needs more structure, while Susie wants/needs more freedom of expression. By investing time in learning about ourselves, we are now capable of learning about others.

EFFECTIVE VERSUS COMFORTABLE

Previously, we made the distinction between an *effective* teaching style and a teaching style that is *comfortable* for the teacher. When teachers confess to being comfortable in a certain teaching style, they are only admitting to being resistant to change. If teachers state that they are more comfortable being permissive, this only signals a resistance to being authoritarian. This misses the point. Teachers should concern themselves with being effective, not with being comfortable. Learning where you are comfortable, for most, comes easily and naturally. Learning where you are most effective can be a lifelong struggle, and can only be accomplished through self-reflection.

Without continuous self-reflection, teachers may use a certain style only because they *have been taught to do it that way*. This response will be our answer when asked why we teach in that style. We will have little understanding of why we do what we are doing, and students will have even less of an understanding of us. Sadly, when revisiting this classroom 10 years later, the teacher will still be teaching the same way he or she was taught to teach. People are often reluctant to look inside of themselves, but self-reflection is instrumental in personal maturity and in professional growth. This growth, to the professional teacher, should be seen as ongoing.

In future chapters of this text, the discussions established will assist in illuminating some of these questions with some direction, but ultimately, professional growth will come from self-examination and reflection, not from authors or any text. Later, in chapter 7, Carl Rogers will offer an excellent example of a lifelong examination of self.

Identity Statuses

Self-reflection, interestingly, is seen as a process that most often takes place during the adolescent years, the time during which most individuals begin to question their beliefs and values and start committing to those values as part of their identity. Although self-reflection and identity-formation are critical to the adolescent years, the authors, and others, argue that this process is something that often occurs throughout the life span, whenever individuals are examining important areas of their lives and making (or attempting to make) commitments to certain beliefs, values, and decisions. James Marcia (2002) notes four different "identity statuses" that we often see when individuals discuss their beliefs, values, and identity.

The first status, Identity Diffusion, is often the most unfortunate status for individuals in the identity formation process. These individuals "often lack not just an identity, but also a secure sense of self" (p. 204). Persons in this identity status, unfortunately, neither actively question their beliefs and values, nor commit to any particular beliefs or values, and thus, as Marcia states, lack a clear sense of self.

The second status, Identity Foreclosure, is used to describe individuals who have not thoroughly examined their beliefs and value systems, but rather have committed to (without question) the beliefs and values of others (e.g., parents and teachers). People with this identity status tend to be "solid in their identities, although not very flexible" (p. 203). Identity foreclosures in the educational setting would best be described as the teacher previously mentioned, who, in response to the question "Why do you teach this way?" answers "Because that is how I was taught to teach."

The third status, Identity Moratorium, as described by Marcia, "struggles to find occupational and ideological paths suitable for themselves. In their struggle, we find them to be alternately engaging, irritating, especially morally perceptive, challenging, and finally sometimes

(*Continued*)

exhausting" (p. 203). Marcia notes that it is important to recognize "that the process in which they are engaged is a necessary and positive one" (p. 203). These individuals are actively questioning their beliefs and values and are seeking to find a fit for themselves. The preservice and newly employed teachers may find themselves in this type of an identity status, seeking to find the teaching style that not only works best for themselves, but also for their students. Thus, a person in this identity status may try many new and different approaches, not necessarily committing to one or another, but rather remaining open to examination.

The last status, Identity Achievement, is seen as the ideal state of identity formation. In this status, individuals have been through the identity moratorium stage and have "found themselves." Once people find their goals, values, beliefs, and in this case, teaching style, and have committed to them, they can be identity-achieved. Of important note, these individuals, having been through the moratorium and achievement process, understand that, in life, other issues may arise that would cause them to requestion their beliefs, values, and goals, and they are prepared to do so.

For you to put this theory to best practice, actively question what your goals and beliefs are as a preservice teacher. What skills and knowledge do you hope to share with your students? What teaching style or approach do you hope to use with your students? What teaching style worked for you as a student? These are just a few questions to consider. The key is for you to actively question, or experience, a moratorium as Marcia (2002) would suggest, and then once you have considered the issues important to you as a future educator, attempt to find your teaching self. That is, commit to your beliefs, values, and goals as an educator. Marcia and others have suggested that once people have achieved Identity Achievement, they are able to reconsider their beliefs and values. Although we support the process of making decisions and committing to elements of your teaching approach, to be an effective educator, the ongoing process of self-reflection is also encouraged.

ETHICS AND THE TEACHER

Ethics
The moral principles, beliefs, and values by which we determine what is right or wrong

It is important for all preservice teachers to examine and become familiar with their ethical stances prior to entering the classroom. **Ethics** are the moral principles, beliefs, and values by which we determine what is right or wrong (Beebe, Beebe, & Redmond, 2008). Morals are closely related to values, in that they are our standards for good behavior, but they are more specific in nature than values.

In reviewing the history of human relations, the most colorful personality is, without a doubt, **Harry Stack Sullivan** (1892–1949). Sullivan, more than any one person, turned the attention of social and behavioral sciences toward the study of human relations. According to Swensen (1973), Sullivan anticipated and outlined most every development in the field of human relations. He applied the concepts of Cooley and Mead to his work and developed a theory of interpersonal relations that served as a basis for and anticipation of much subsequent research.

His influence had major impacts in many varying disciplines. Sullivan's most significant contributions were not written by him but by his students, who used lecture notes and seminars after his death. Like Cooley and Mead, Sullivan exerted his influence by his personal teaching.

In many ways, the story of Sullivan should end as stated above. But the contradictions, fabrications, and attempted concealments in his life are difficult to overlook, even by authors who wish to be kind. Chapman (1976) notes, "Sullivan unfortunately was sometimes dishonest in talking about events of the first three decades of his life. He concealed many things and invented others to fill the gaps" (p. 26). Sullivan concealed academic failures and his homosexuality, fabricated his professional training, contradicted his own stories when professionally convenient, and hid his lack of training. Chapman tells the story of Sullivan running afoul of the law and, after being apprehended, he "pretended he was crazy" in order to avoid imprisonment.

Chapman also notes Sullivan "was a poor writer and he knew it" (p. 12). Sullivan "wrote awkwardly" and his "lectures and seminars, though impressive to those who heard them, are often rambling, unorganized, and obscure when printed" (p. 12). He used inaccurate and outdated terminology that often misled his readers. His book *Personal Psychopathology* "is so disorganized and badly written that in some sections it is difficult to see what the author is driving at" (p. 15). Chapman says that Sullivan had gaps in his knowledge that he describes as "flabbergasting," his terminology was "clumsy" and "self-instructed," and he was "culturally ignorant."

Sullivan's life story is enlightening, entertaining, at times depressing, and often insightful into the thinking of his ideas. Readers may take his life story as they may, but students must not overlook his significant contributions to the field of human relations. His lectures and seminars (although reportedly disorganized) were often original and inspiring. He took the foundations that Cooley and Mead offered and contributed to them by integrating multiple disciplines and ideas.

In Sullivan, we learn (1) the value of integrating others' thoughts and ideals, (2) the anticipation of things to come, and (3) how to inspire the young to learn. Through his weaknesses, we are reminded of the importance of staying on top of our field and of the need for teachers to remain open and honest, and to treat ethically all with whom they come in contact.

Discussions on ethical practices should include the work of **Lawrence Kohlberg** (1927–1987), best known for his theory delineating the stages of moral development. He was more interested in the reasoning behind the moral decisions people make than the decisions themselves. For Kohlberg, the "why" is key. In his research, Kohlberg presented short stories with moral dilemmas to individuals and then asked them what they thought the characters should do. One of his classic stories is as follows: In Europe, a woman was near death from a rare kind of cancer. There was one drug that the doctors thought might save her. It was a form of radium that a druggist in the same town had recently discovered. The drug was expensive to make, and the druggist was charging 10 times what the drug cost him to make it. The sick woman's husband, Heinz, went to everyone he knew to borrow money, but he could get together only $1,000, which is half of what the druggist was charging. He told the druggist that his wife was dying and asked him to sell the drug cheaper or let him pay the rest later. But the druggist said, "No, I discovered the drug, and I am going to make money from it." So Heinz got desperate and broke into the man's store that evening to steal the drug for his wife.

Another story is about a man who had a seriously injured son and wanted to rush him to the hospital. The man had no car, so he approached a stranger, told him about the situation, and asked to borrow his car. The stranger refused, saying he had an important appointment to keep. So the father took the man's car by force.

Preconventional
Moral reasoning based on rewards, punishment, or exchange of favors

Based on his research, Kohlberg (1976) identified three levels of moral development; each level includes two stages. The first level is **Preconventional**, when rewards, punishment, or an exchange of favors are most impressive in the decision of right and wrong. In stage 1, *Obedience Orientation*, the decision of right and wrong is left to be determined by an authority, as well as whether the behavior will result in punishment. For example, students, when asked why they should not steal may say "because my teacher (or parent) says that stealing is wrong" or "because if you steal you go to jail." Stage 2, *Instrumental Orientation*, is guided by the exchange of favors when determining right from wrong. Individuals at this stage are able to recognize that stealing is wrong but may deem it acceptable if they benefit from the behavior. For example, a student at this level may not turn in a classmate for cheating because the cheater has promised some favor in return.

Kohlberg's Levels of Moral Development

First Level: **Preconventional**
- *Stage 1*: Obedience Orientation
- *Stage 2*: Instrumental Orientation

Second Level: **Conventional**
- *Stage 3*: Interpersonal Norms
- *Stage 4*: Social-Order Orientation

Third Level: **Postconventional**
- *Stage 5*: Social-Contract Orientation
- *Stage 6*: Universal Ethical Principles Orientation

Conventional
Moral reasoning based upon social approval or disapproval from peers or authorities

The second level Kohlberg identifies is **Conventional**. This is where people conform because of social disapproval from peers or authorities. For example, students may laugh at a racial joke because they want to be a part of the group. According to Kohlberg, there is evidence that most people never progress beyond this level. Stage 3, found in the Conventional level is *Interpersonal Norms* (also called the "good boy–good girl stage"). An individual in this third stage is concerned with others' opinions when deciding right from wrong. For example, a student who consistently helps others, treats others nicely, and behaves well in the classroom at this stage does so to make a good impression. When asked why she behaves so well, she may answer, "because I am a good person, and I want others to know how good I can be." Stage 4, *Social-Order* (also called Social Systems) *Orientation*, is recognizable by the individual's desire to uphold laws as a way to protect order and prevent chaos in society. Individuals who reason at this stage believe it is every member of society's responsibility to follow the established laws. If asked why people should not steal, a person at this stage would respond with something like, "Stealing is bad because if one person steals, then another person will, and then another, and another, and then there will be absolute anarchy."

Kohlberg's last level is **Postconventional** and is based on a set of internal moral principles. If people at this level see the law as unfair, they usually work to change the law. At times, certain individuals recognize that ethical ideas can supersede a law (for example, the works of Gandhi and Martin Luther King). In stage 5, *Social-Contract Orientation*, individuals believe that it is important to have laws in society and members should follow those laws as long as they are beneficial to the members of the group (or society). For example, most people believe stealing is wrong, but their opinions often change if they find out that a young child stole food because he was not fed at home. Stage 6 is *Universal Ethical Principles Orientation*, whereby moral reasoning is guided by a personal belief system or set of values that are not governed by concrete rules or laws.

Postconventional
Moral reasoning based on self-chosen ethical principles

In his research, Kohlberg offered empirical evidence that people do not revert to lower stages of reasoning or skip stages as they mature. Interestingly, according to Kohlberg, people cannot understand the moral reasoning that occurs at stages higher than their own. He also noted that each successive stage of moral reasoning offered a more satisfying philosophical solution to moral problems than its predecessor.

Teachers are faced with moral dilemmas every day in their classrooms, from minor choices to be made, to larger, more difficult situations. Researchers Kidder and Born (1998) discuss another type of moral dilemma that teachers often must face in their career. What if the needs of one student conflict with another (or the needs of the overall class)? Kidder and Born describe this situation as a right-right moral dilemma, meaning that it is right to meet the needs of one student but also right to consider the needs of other students in the class. These authors offer three approaches of thinking to help teachers make decisions in those situations: ends-based thinking, rule-based thinking, and care-based thinking. **Ends-based thinking**, according to Kidder and Born, has teachers consider the dilemma in terms of "the greatest good for the greatest number" (p. 40).

Ends-based thinking
Considering moral dilemmas in terms of the greatest good for the greatest number

The second form, **rule-based thinking**, asks teachers to consider, "If everyone in the world were to do what I am about to do—follow the rule I am to follow—is that the kind of world I would want to live in?" (p. 40). For example, if the teacher decides to dismiss the needs of one student for the sake of the larger class, the teacher must ask him- or herself, "If every teacher in the world were to decide to dismiss one student's needs,

Rule-based thinking
Consideration of what the world would be like if everyone acted in the same manner

what kind of world would this be?" Taking this approach challenges teachers to consider their principles and ultimately to take responsibility for their decisions.

Care-based thinking Thinking and behaving that requires you to do what you would want others to do to us

The third form, **care-based thinking**, "commands that we do what we would want others to do to us" (p. 40). Commonly known as the Golden Rule, this form requires the teacher to consider the perspective from the student's point of view when making decisions about the student's actions.

Principle-based ethics Principles that individuals should voluntarily follow

Murdock, Gartin, and Crabtree (2002) additionally note two types of ethics. The first type they describe is **principle-based ethics**. These are recognized by the individual's *desire to uphold laws as a way to protect order and prevent chaos in society*. Principle-based ethics are seen as principles that individuals should voluntarily follow, for example, to "promote and maintain a high level of competence and integrity in practicing their profession" (Code of Ethics, Council for Exceptional Children, 1983). These principles are attempts to maximize the good through impartiality.

Virtue-based ethics Ethics determined by considering how a caring, virtuous person would behavior

A second type of ethics Murdock et al. (2002) discuss is **virtue-based ethics**, also called the *ethics of care*. A person using the virtue-based ethics would first consider the potential actions that a caring and honorable person would take and then evaluate those actions in light of how in line those actions are with what the virtuous person would do. Murdock and colleagues note, "The focus would be one of concern emphasizing personal connections with others and *protecting others from harm*" (p. 187). In Kohlberg's moral dilemma described previously, a person who uses virtue-based ethics (ethics of care) would have no problem with Heinz's behavior. However, an individual using principle-based ethics would consider Heinz's behavior criminal and unethical. If a person sees the law as unfair, he or she usually works to change the law. At times, certain individuals recognize that ethical ideas can supersede a law (e.g., the works of Gandhi and Martin Luther King).

According to Murdock et al. (2002), actions based on either orientation (virtue-based or principle-based) are usually compatible, but problems and conflicts arise when they are not. When such situations occur, educators could be asked to choose between their belief in the ethics of care or principle-based ethics. Preservice teachers must prepare as much as possible today for ethical situations that may occur in their futures. Without this self-examination, the teacher may make a decision without fully considering all the ramifications. For example, how would you handle the following situation?

A principal calls you into the office and explains that the school needs your help. It seems that a student with a disability "fell through the cracks" and did not get the services that the school promised to provide. The child's parent is angry over the situation and the principal asks you to lie to the parent about what actually happened. The principal tells you that if you don't lie the school will be liable for a large lawsuit, and the school as a whole will suffer.

How you will deal with the above ethical situation needs to be fully considered prior to your becoming a practitioner. While forming your reply to the principal, it is necessary for you to understand what your own beliefs and values are with regard to this fictitious situation. **Beliefs**, according to Beebe and colleagues (2008), are ways in which you structure your understanding of reality. Beliefs designate what is true and what is false. They consist of thoughts, opinions, and attitudes. **Values**, according to the same authors, are those things identified by you as being good and bad, right and wrong. Values are directly related to the kind of person you are and will become. People are not born with values; we learn values from others. In the early years of our youth, the family instills in us our most basic values. Later, others, such as our peers and teachers, will contribute to our overall value system. Thus, when considering whether you would lie for the principal of your school, you need to decide if that action would go with or against your beliefs and values.

Beliefs
Ways in which you structure your understanding of reality

Values
Things identified by you as being good and bad/right and wrong

Hanna (2000) offers a discussion on how to determine if the values you have are really yours or if they are values you have borrowed from others. She uses the Transactional Analysis model (refer to Berne, discussed in chapter 5) to make this determination. According to Hanna, borrowed values (e.g., from your parents) need to be reexamined because they were developed during an earlier time, in a different environment and situation. This is not to say borrowed values are wrong, but because they were borrowed, they need to be reexamined. It should be clear to the readers that these values (borrowed or your own) play an instrumental part in our ethical behaviors. This reexamination of values fits clearly with the previous section on self-reflection and identity formation.

MORAL EDUCATION

Today, teachers are encouraged to teach values. Even if teachers think that this is not their role, the teachers still remain very influential in value formation. Hanna (2000) offers ways to teach values without being a **moralizer**. Moralizers tell others what they should value and believe in. We should praise and reinforce those values that are close to our own. According to Hanna, we should teach and guide. Ask questions often and encourage students to express their opinions. And at times, the teacher should stand back and let a person's own experiences teach. We know that we learn the best through our errors. Hanna tells us to instill a value of self. Students must learn to value themselves so that they can better value others. It is important to encourage a value on thinking for oneself. Students must be encouraged to be critical and creative thinkers, without the fear of being criticized and having negative reactions toward their opinions.

Moralizer
A person who tells others what they should value and believe in

Of interest, many preservice teachers offer as the reason for going into the teaching profession to "teach their good values to their students." An often agonizing question that these preservice teachers must eventually ask themselves is *"Do I want another teacher teaching my children their values, which may or may not be the same as mine?"* When we share the same values, the dilemma is nonexistent, but what of the family who does not share the values of the teacher?

TEACHER'S ROLE

The teacher's role is to *educate* and *create good citizenry* but *not to instill values.* Look first at the teacher's role to create good citizenry. Preservice teachers should become aware of why their state and the nation are so interested and invested in a student's education. Simply put, the role of education is to produce good citizens. Our country has a vested interest in creating citizens who can read, write, solve problems, think for themselves, vote, and be law-abiding. Many of the behaviors that are exhibited by good citizens are seen by others as being good values. For example, honesty, hard work, helping others, patriotism, being a good neighbor, protecting the weak, volunteering in the community, treating others the way you wish to be treated, and so on, all can be arguably noted as values. These arguably good values for the sake of our argument should be seen only as characteristics of good citizens.

The guidelines offered assume that the teacher's role is to educate everyone he or she comes in contact with (e.g., students, parents, colleagues, supervisors, board of education members, members of the community, etc.), and, in this education, examine both sides of an issue and the consequences of actions (e.g., unprotected sex, abuse of alcohol and drugs, a life of crime).

A teacher may encounter students who share (or have assumed) their parents' belief that the Holocaust did not happen. The role of the teacher is to educate the students in historical evidence (e.g., documentaries, transcripts of the Nuremburg trials, books and articles by survivors or objective historians, etc.), while not discounting the right of the students (and their parents) to believe as they wish to believe.

It should be obvious to the teacher that both sides of an argument are needed in order for students to develop their own opinions and beliefs (versus borrowing opinions and beliefs from the teacher). Whether we like it or not, there are two sides to the issues on abortion, gun control, the death penalty, and gay rights. If teachers present only one side, they are guilty of what Hanna (2005) refers to as being a moralizer (as discussed previously). Moralizing is the direct, although subtle, transmission of the adults' values to young people. It takes away individuality, and students are hindered from thinking for themselves.

The teacher is to leave to the parents their right to instill values in their children as they (not the teacher) see best. Parents may choose to raise their children as agnostics, atheists, Protestants, Republicans, Democrats, or communists, to believe in education, missionary work, or crime, and that the use of alcohol, tattoos, and vulgarity is acceptable. They may instill into their children a view on abortion, gun control, the death penalty, and gay rights that is in opposition to your views.

You, as a teacher, may choose to *change* (this term is used in contrast to *educate*) your students' beliefs, but in doing so, you are doing a disservice to your students and your community. Abraham Maslow noted that it is the teacher's role to "help a person find out what's already in him rather than to reinforce him or shape or teach him into a prearranged form, which someone else has decided upon in advance" (1968, p. 686).

Values should not be seen as being good or bad but only different. For example, in one family a value that may be passed on to their children is that you support your government, right or wrong. In another family a value that may be passed on is that it is the responsibility of every citizen to hold the government responsible for its actions. All values, beliefs, and opinions must be dealt with by teachers in a respectful and professional manner, regardless of the teachers' own personal stances.

In summary, the teacher should go about the task of educating everyone they come in contact with, making sure not to moralize, and develop and encourage good citizenry, while allowing parents their right to instill values as they see best. Teachers who continue to struggle with their desire to teach values (in contrast to citizenry) to their students, need only to ask themselves, who do *they* wish to instill values in their children, themselves or other teachers?

CODE OF ETHICS

Teachers should become very familiar with their schools' policies on ethics. These documents will clarify what the school expects and what is permissible. Along with these policies, teachers should always be engaged in *self-reflection*. Teachers should think before they act. Ask, "Why am I doing what I am doing? Is this for the right reasons?" Teachers should consider all consequences of their behaviors and any alternatives that may exist. They should seek advice from others and benefit from others' experiences. We wish to offer this guideline: Ask if this action is *in the best interest* of your student(s)? If it is, do it; if it is not, then don't.

Not only should teachers be familiar with school policies, all teachers should be knowledgeable of their professional code of ethics. The following are the National Education Association (NEA, 1975) code of ethics that all teachers should exemplify:*

The educator, believing in the worth and dignity of each human being, recognizes the supreme importance of the pursuit of truth, devotion to excellence, and the nurture of democratic principles. Essential to these goals is the protection of freedom to learn and to teach and the guarantee of equal educational opportunity for all. The educator accepts the responsibility to adhere to the highest ethical standards.

The educator recognizes the magnitude of the responsibility inherent in the teaching process. The desire for the respect and confidence of one's colleagues, of students, of parents, and of the members of the community provides the incentive to attain and maintain the highest possible degree of ethical conduct. The Code of Ethics of the Education Profession indicates the aspiration of all educators and provides standards by which to judge conduct.

*Reprinted by permission of National Education Association.

Principle 1: Commitment to the Student. The educator strives to help each student realize his or her potential as a worthy and effective member of society. The educator therefore works to stimulate the spirit of inquiry, the acquisition of knowledge and understanding, and the thoughtful formulation of worthy goals.

In fulfillment of the obligation to the student, the educator:

- Shall not unreasonably restrain the student from independent action in the pursuit of learning.
- Shall not unreasonably deny the student access to varying points of view.
- Shall not deliberately suppress or distort subject matter relevant to the student's progress.
- Shall make reasonable effort to protect the student from conditions harmful to learning or to health and safety.
- Shall not intentionally expose the student to embarrassment or disparagement.
- Shall not on the basis of race, color, creed, sex, national origin, marital status, political or religious beliefs, family, social or cultural background, or sexual orientation, unfairly.
  - Exclude any student from participation in any program.
  - Deny benefits to a student.
  - Grant any advantage to a student.
- Shall not use professional relationships with students for private advantage.
- Shall not disclose information about students obtained in the course of professional service, unless disclosure serves a compelling professional purpose or is required by law.

Principle 2: Commitment to the Profession. The education profession is vested by the public with a trust and responsibility requiring the highest ideals of professional services. In the belief that the quality of the services of the education profession directly influence the nation and its citizens, the educator shall exert every effort to raise professional standards, to promote a climate that encourages the exercise of professional judgment, to achieve conditions that attract persons worthy of the trust to careers in education, and to assist in preventing the practice of the profession by unqualified person.

In fulfillment of the obligation to the profession, the educator:

- Shall not in an application for a professional position deliberately make a false statement or fail to disclose a material fact related to competency and qualifications.
- Shall not misrepresent his or her professional qualifications.
- Shall not assist entry into the profession of a person known to be unqualified in respect to character, education, or other relevant attribute.
- Shall not knowingly make a false statement concerning the qualifications of a candidate for a professional position.
- Shall not assist a noneducator in the unauthorized practice of teaching.

- Shall not disclose information about colleagues obtained in the course of professional service unless disclosure serves a compelling professional purpose or is required by law.
- Shall not knowingly make false or malicious statements about a colleague.
- Shall not accept any gratuity, gift, or favor that might impair or appear to influence professional decisions or actions.

We adapted behaviorists' Bailey and Burch (2005) core ethical principles for this discussion. These ethical principles should be in the forefront of consideration while relating to others.

- Do no harm.
- Abstain from behavior that is detrimental.
- Earn your reputation.
- Treat everyone with respect and dignity.
- Promote independence.
- Accept responsibility for your actions.
- Always seek input and opinions from parents and guardians.

It is important to note that having a code of ethics does not assure ethical behavior. We offer the following advice:

- Teachers must be prepared to act ethically in the absence of guidelines and even when their actions are in conflict with guidelines or instructions. Rules allowed for the incarceration of Japanese Americans during World War II, pushed Native Americans off their lands, and institutionalized (and in some cases sterilized) people with disabilities.
- Ethical dilemmas are best resolved in a public forum.
- Teachers, involved in ethical issues with students, should always seek opinions of parents or guardians.
- If confronted with the question, should the student have input regarding an ethical issue that impacts his or her life, only ask yourself, how important is it for you to have input with an ethical issue that impacts your life?

Before we leave this section on ethical behavior, we would like to remind the teacher that the Family Education Rights and Privacy Act (FERPA), also known as the Buckley Act, requires teachers to treat all information as confidential and to disclose it only with the consent of the student's parents. Parents see this as an issue of trust and expect teachers to act with the utmost professionalism when it comes to their children's right to privacy.

THE ENCOURAGING TEACHER

Currently, many are concerned with the need to reform our school systems. This concern has to do with the educational failure of so many of our students. Students who drop out feel that the school has nothing to offer them, coupled with the feeling of being left behind. Many advocate the need for more teachers. Many advocate that our teachers are underpaid, overworked, and asked too much of. "If we only paid our teachers more, there would be more teachers available to take the pressure off those practitioners in the field." Many note the need to rebuild the school's infrastructure. Often schools lack the basic needs to create an environment conducive to learning. Some school days are shortened or canceled because of the lack of air conditioning. Many classrooms could use a coat of paint. It is very common for teachers to reach into their own pockets to buy teaching supplies. Many advocate the need for new technologies; these would bridge the gap in our education inadequacies.

While few can find fault with any of these arguments, these are not issues related to the reforming of our schools. The above-mentioned issues are problems that every U.S. citizen should be concerned with, not just teachers. Unfortunately, in some counties citizens have voted against raising taxes to benefit our schools. These "nay voters" are often not fully aware of what life is really like in schools today. Everyone is needed to resolve these changes. One important role of teachers is to educate the community on the needs of our schools. The real concern with reforming our school systems is not the "nay voters" but the teachers themselves. The problem with our school systems is that teachers offer too little encouragement to their students.

As Dreikurs and Cassel (1972) note, "A child needs encouragement like a plant needs sun and water. Unfortunately those who need encouragement most, get it the least because they behave in such a way that our reaction to them pushes them further into discouragement and rebellion" (p. 49). Failures by our students are often a result of a lack of encouragement by our teachers. Encouragement improves relationships with students, offering the teacher the opportunity to develop the rapport needed to *guide* students (previously discussed as the democratic style). Encouraged students feel they can be accepted for who they are. "Encouragement produces courage" (Dreikurs & Cassel, 1972, p. 49); whereas discouragement affects a student's self-worth, self-esteem, self-respect, renders the student vulnerable, and makes him or her fearful. "We know that when children are discouraged, they misbehave, have no respect for order, and learn very little" (Dreikurs & Cassel, 1972, p. 12). "Only one who has faith in a child, who can see the good in him as he is, can encourage" (Dreikurs & Cassel, 1972, p. 50). Patterson (2009) finds through teachers' encouragement, compliments, and engaged conversation, there was a decrease in disruptive student behavior. Encouragement is a very powerful tool to the educator. Likewise, discouraging educators lack faith in human nature (Gazda, Asbury, Balzer, Childers, Phelps, & Walters, 1999). Dreikurs and Cassel (1972) note that teachers should be constantly on the lookout for opportunities to encourage students. These authors offered the following suggestions to become the encouraging teacher:

- We should mark only correct responses instead of pointing out mistakes, and use those mistakes as positive learning (not as failures or as a critical evaluation of the child).
- Avoid criticism.

- Appreciate and commend effort, efforts being more important than results.
- Appreciate and promote students' opinions.
- Separate the deed from the doer; one may disapprove of a behavior without rejecting the student.
- Encourage thoughtful risk-taking for students to meet their objectives.
- Show faith in every student.
- Stimulate and lead, but do not push.
- Find ways to integrate the student into the group.
- Do not create an environment of competition.
- Offer opportunities for responsibilities.
- Celebrate and share successes and provide support and encouragement through difficult times.

HOW SHOULD WE GO ABOUT ENCOURAGING?

- Focus on what has been achieved (for example a grade of C–); when appropriate show genuine appreciation for their effort.
- Focus on what can be achieved with hard work (a grade of B–).
- Avoid criticism and blame. ("If you had only studied more.")
- Offer specific suggestions for improvement. ("Keep hitting those books, all good students do.")

HOW SHOULD WE GO ABOUT ENCOURAGING WHILE DISCIPLINING?

- Separate the person from the behavior (Carl Roger's work, chapter 7).
- Be gentle, respectful, and supportive to the person.
- Be firm and direct with the undesirable behavior.
- Don't allow students to refocus or blame others, teach and *model* responsibility for one's own behavior.
- Be constructive in your comments.
- Use specific language to combat misunderstandings.
- Define the issue in broad enough terms that your explanation covers future challenges.
- Be encouraging about their future behaviors.

A distinction should be made between **encouragement** and *praise*. The teacher must offer and emphasize encouragement, but not necessarily praise. Encouragement is a way of showing that we respect the student's efforts and improvements, and that we have faith in the student. Unfortunately, praise can only be given at the completion of a project, and only to a select few. Often, praise is given to the students who need it least and is absent from those who need it most. At any time during the day, and this should be on the forefront of every teacher's mind, encouragement may be given, even when a student does poorly on an exam. Whereas praise is usually offered to only a select few, encouragement

Encouragement
Support that can be given to anyone at any time.

can be offered to anyone (students, parents, colleagues, supervisors, board members, etc.) at any time. Teachers should not praise a student for doing poorly, but rather, encourage the student to do better. Encouraging students, even the most excellent of students, may be the most important job a teacher has. Real school reform will be measured in the amount we, as teachers, encourage our students.

Hypocrisy
Expecting from your students that which you are unwilling to do yourself

This chapter was designed for preservice teachers to examine the foundations of exceptional teachers: knowing who they are, knowing how they will behave ethically, and knowing the importance of being encouraging. Other issues must be addressed as well. The first involves an issue that can cause teachers' foundations to decay: **hypocrisy.** Preservice teachers should ask themselves, who are hypocritical teachers? Hypocrisy is when preservice teachers do not read their textbooks but later become upset when their students don't read theirs. Hypocrisy is not participating in classroom discussions but becoming upset when their future students don't participate in discussions. Hypocrisy is showing up late for classes and then becoming upset when their students show up late. Teachers do not go into the teaching profession with the intention to be hypocritical. Preservice teachers need to be aware that it is what they are doing today that may label them as hypocritical tomorrow (we refer the reader to the story of Sullivan).

A second issue involves doubt. This topic comes from a very unexpected source, the revered Mother Teresa. *Time* magazine (November 2008) reports on the two contradicting lives Mother Teresa lived. The one with which we are most familiar has her being described as a "Saint of the Gutters," Nobel Peace Prize recipient, global beacon for the poor, sick, and dying, with an inextricable closeness to God. The other life of which we are most unaware was described as an "arid landscape from which the deity had disappeared." She revealed in letters the absence of God for nearly a half-century. The public life portrayed her as cheerful, whereas her private life was characterized by spiritual pain, loneliness, and torture. Her pain was so great that at one point she doubted the existence of heaven and even of God. Throughout this torture, Mother Teresa found ways to live with her doubt and never abandoned her work or her faith.

As previously discussed, the exceptional teacher is self-reflecting. Unfortunately, with this self-reflection often comes doubt. It is typical for professionals at one time or another to doubt themselves, their work, and their causes. Many of the people we have looked up to have doubted their paths in life, their contributions to their fields, and their commitments to making the world a better place. However, as we struggle with our professional doubts, we need only to draw encouragement from Mother Teresa's life to remind us of why we struggle. We, as a society of plenty, may choose to ignore Mother Teresa's contributions, but those sick, dying, lonely, unloved, and forgotten people she touched will never forget her, *nor will the students who come through the exceptional teachers' doors.*

SUMMARY

In summary, who is this person we call an exceptional teacher? Exceptional teachers will continually self-reflect. They will devote time to getting to know who they are and why they do the things they do. They will convey this knowledge of themselves to their students in an effort to assist in learning about their students. Exceptional teachers will practice ethical behaviors every day of their professional career. Ethical decisions will be guided by what is in the best interest of their students. Exceptional teachers will feel the obligation to educate everyone they come in contact with, teach students to become good citizens, not moralize their students, and leave the formation of values to the families. Exceptional teachers will recognize how their encouragement will allow their students to face and conquer the multitude of challenges that lie ahead of them. If this can be accomplished, the never-ending chant for school reform may finally be laid to rest.

Preservice teachers should recognize that what they do today will determine how they will be viewed in the future. Preservice teachers should also recognize that all great teachers have experienced doubt, but what made them great was the determination to push aside their doubt and become exceptional teachers.

CASE 2.A

As Mr. Daniels straightened his room at the end of the year after the students were finished, he started reflecting on his first year of teaching at Smith Elementary School. He had been told that he should come in with a strong presence and not give the students too much latitude. Although that kept things orderly in his room, he wished he would have had a less authoritarian style of discipline. He thought back on the times when, had he not been so strict with the students, they might have been able to learn from their mistakes on their own instead of his direct involvement in everything that happened in the classroom.

QUESTION

- How could Mr. Daniels have approached discipline in different ways for the best interests of the students as well as himself?

CASE 2.B

Mrs. Jacobson is a high school home economics teacher whom most students find very approachable. Every morning, students are in her room before the first period, talking to each other and sharing what has been going on in their lives. She enjoys the easy conversations with her students. One morning, one of her students came in extra early and sat in a desk across from Mrs. Jacobson. She started to cry and told Mrs. Jacobson she was pregnant and was planning on getting an abortion. She felt that she could not talk to her parents, but she knew she could count on Mrs. Jacobson to be there for her. Mrs. Jacobson, a strong pro-life activist, listened while she talked.

QUESTIONS

1. What should Mrs. Jacobson tell her student?

2. Should she allow her personal beliefs to enter the conversation?

3. What should she do?

CASE 2.C

Zach just failed his first American history exam. His teacher, Mrs. Gates, although very disappointed in his performance, knows that Zach was really trying when he took the test. After class the next day, Mrs. Gates asked Zach to stay after class to talk about his test. Zach stays, but it is clear that he doesn't want to have this conversation with his teacher.

QUESTIONS

1. How should Mrs. Gates approach the conversation?

mrs. Gates needs to approach Zach with a mindset of love and encouragement. She already knows that he is trying his best, so she should not go into the conversation with frustration or anger.

2. What should she ask Zach?

She should ask him what he doesn't understand or what she can help him with. She should also ask what in the test didn't make sense and what studying he did.

4. What advice should she give him?

If he didn't study, she should suggest better study habits or study guides. She should give him praise and then encouragement to contince to work hard.

5. Why is it important that Mrs. Gates have the conversation with her student?

Zach seems to be struggling with something in the class. It is Mrs. Gates' job to figure out what is wrong and how to solve the problem.

SUGGESTED ACTIVITIES

1. Take the quiz entitled "What Is Your Classroom Management Profile?" Answer 12 questions to determine which style of classroom management you prefer. Visit http://www.cbv.ns.ca/sstudies/gen3.html to access the document created by Indiana University.

2. Read "Fluttering Butterflies," an entry in *Random Thoughts* by Louis Schmier, professor of history at Valdosta State University. Reflect on his blog and analyze the connection with chapter 2: Who Is This Person People Call an Exceptional Teacher?

There is no truth. There is only perception.
—Gustave Flaubert

3

Understanding Perceptions and Drawing Conclusions

OBJECTIVES

After completing this chapter you should be able to:

- Discuss the value in understanding the student as a whole person rather than considering only specific behaviors.
- Explain the mutual relationship between the students and their environment, using the ecological systems perspective.
- Describe how misperception can occur when propaganda is used.
- Distinguish among the types of propaganda that is used to mislead people.
- Explain the role of balance theory and attribution theory in our perceptions of ourselves and others.
- Describe how selective perception, context dependence, cognitive dissonance, hindsight bias, and memory bias affect our perceptions of others.
- Discuss the importance of being other-oriented in interactions with students.
- Identify the role of stereotypes in misperceptions.

KEY TERMS

Attribution theory
Balance theory
Cognitive dissonance
Context dependence
Ecological perspective
Gestalt
Hindsight bias
Johari window
Memory bias
Other-oriented
Propaganda
Selective perception
Stereotyping

One amazing thing about people is that often, after having a conversation, each participant in the conversation leaves with an understanding of the topic discussed that is *potentially different* from what the other individuals understand. This may be true even though each person believes that he or she is walking away with the *same* understanding of the conversation and a common and shared meaning. These misperceptions are much more common than we suspect. In fact, we might suggest that they are a way of life that often goes unnoticed.

To explain this phenomenon better, we should start by examining "instant replay" on the football field. The audience sees a play where a flag is thrown by the referee, indicating a violation of the rules has been committed. Often, half of the stadium sees the violation and the other half rejects the call. Upon review, via instant replay, the audience is given the opportunity to see the play from various viewpoints (literally), in slow motion, cameras often pausing the motion, reversing and forwarding again and again. After examining the play from various viewpoints, a consensus is often collected. But without the different viewpoints, only individual perceptions exist. These individual perceptions are too often misperceptions.

Because our view is different from another's view, we never perceive the same thing in exactly the same way. Eleanor Roosevelt was once talking with a women's group in which she noted that no one can see all of an elephant from any one view. She pointed out the need to move around the elephant to get a complete picture of the elephant. One strategy the teacher can use to move around the elephant is to take the **Gestalt** perspective.

Gestalt
The whole is greater than the sum of the parts.

Max Wertheimer (1880–1943), a German psychologist, was interested in people's perception of reality. He suggested it was the relationship among things perceived that was important rather than the things themselves. He noted that people tend to perceive things in an organized fashion so that what is seen or heard is different from merely the parts that compose it. He labeled an organized perception a Gestalt.

In 1910, he and colleagues Kurt Koffka and Wolfgang Köhler began to formulate the theoretical position of Gestalt psychology. In the Gestalt perspective, cognition is viewed as a unitary experience that cannot be explained by an analysis of its constituent parts. What humans perceive is organized wholes, not sets of separate stimuli. Our perceptions, according to the Gestaltists, are inextricably interwoven with our thoughts and feelings. Human behavior is best conceived and perceived in holistic terms. Human thoughts, feelings, and actions are meaningfully interrelated into wholes that are more than the sum of their parts.

Gestalt psychologists hold that every experience is an unanalyzable whole that cannot be understood by breaking it down into parts. A home is not merely lumber, shingles, windows, and doors: it is a distinct perception or experiences, with a quality all its own, including family memories, events, and personal feelings. One may note the parts of the whole, but the parts exist in definite relationships to each other. Disturb the relationship of the parts, and the quality of the whole changes.

Simply put, teachers need to know and understand the whole student, not just a behavior that is being exhibited by the student or a label that has been passed on in the teacher's lounge. The student is more than a label or a behavior; these are only singular parts that constitute the whole student. Students cannot be understood by examining only parts of behaviors; the parts must be analyzed in the content of the whole student.

When examining the whole student, the teacher should utilize the **ecological perspective**, in which the teacher assumes a mutual relationship exists between the students and their environment. The physical environment has a major effect on interpersonal behavior and should be considered when examining the whole student. Bronfrenbrenner (1994), well known in developmental psychology for his ecological systems approach to understanding development, describes five "socially organized subsystems that help support and guide human growth" (p. 37). The subsystems consist of the *microsystem* (i.e., the persons and objects within the individual's immediate environments—parents, teachers, home, school), *mesosystem* (i.e., the connections between an individual's microsystems or immediate environments—parents are actively involved with a child's school), *exosystem* (i.e., events or experiences that have an indirect affect on the developing individual—parent had a stressful day at work and

Ecological perspective Assumes a mutual relationship exists between the student and the environment

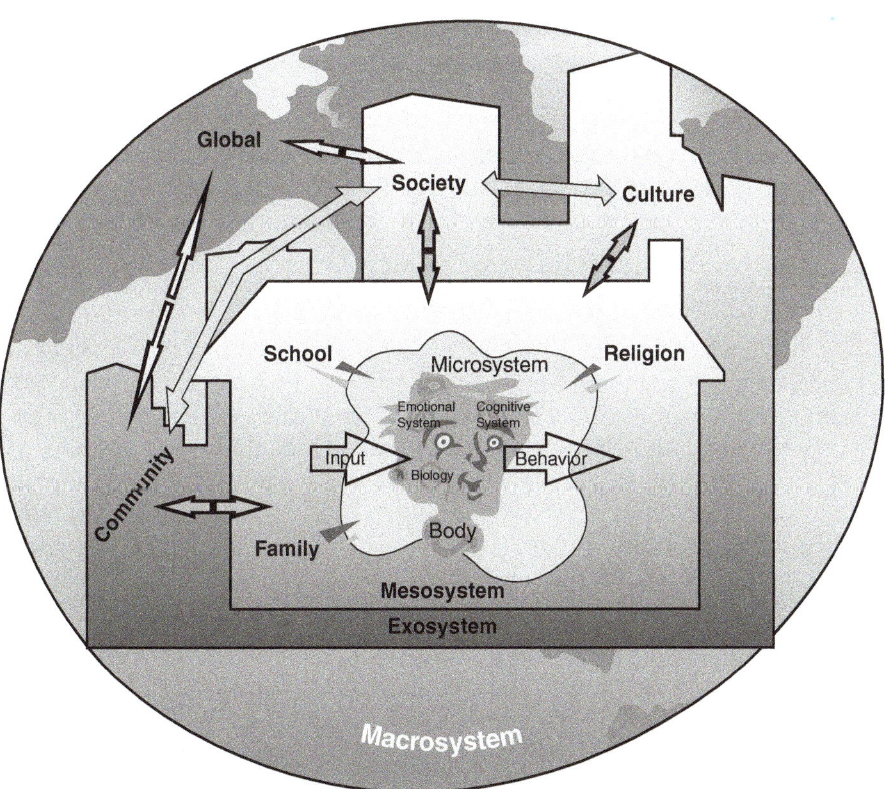

Figure 3.1 Bronfrenbrenner's ecological systems approach.

bring their stress home and take it out on the family), *macrosystem* (i.e., institutionalized beliefs, culture, values—laws that govern our society), and finally the *chronosystem* (i.e., a recognition that your other systems evolve and change with time—individuals' systems change as the age).

An excellent example that exemplifies the Gestalt perspective is the work of Elizabeth Farrell (1870–1932). She is credited with being the first special educator to tie social work, psychology, medicine, mental testing, assessment, and instruction to the needs of her students. Along with Maria Montessori (discussed later), Farrell was keenly aware that students do not learn when their thoughts are occupied with being hungry or cold. Farrell knew that a student was more than a grade on an exam or a particular behavior being expressed. She was aware that the whole student was an intersection of the home life (whether or not the student was being unconditionally accepted for who he or she was, being encouraged to take risks, learning the benefits of an education, etc.), health (physical and emotional), and teachers who were competent in the content and the skills needed to encourage their students.

SHARED MEANING

Although human perceptions are often in error, often a consensus or *shared meaning* can be met. The varying perceptions of how and why the events and tragedies of September 11, 2001, happened are numerous, but few Americans would disagree with the consensus that this was a terrible event. These consensuses, or shared meanings, allow us to make sense out of the world we live in, a world with far too many misperceptions.

Even with the most complete information available, we can never completely understand another's action. Tim McVeigh's bombing of the Murrah building in Oklahoma City, or the Columbine high school shooting, will never be completely understood because we are not those individuals. All we can do is hope to come to a shared meaning of the events.

We must become aware that sometimes people *intend* for us to misperceive. The chairman and CEO of the Enron Corporation, prior to the company folding, put out a press release noting that Enron had been named the most "Innovative Company in America" for the sixth consecutive year by *Fortune* magazine. The release also noted that Enron ranked among the top five in "Quality of Management." Meanwhile, the chairman and other associates were selling their stock in the company, knowing that the company was going to fold, and yet at the same time, they were encouraging their employees to buy more stock in an attempt to keep the value of the stock from falling.

Propaganda
Ideas, facts, or allegations spread deliberately to further one's cause or to damage an opposing cause

This intentional misperception often comes in the form of **propaganda**. Propaganda consists of ideas, facts, or allegations, spread deliberately to further one's cause or to damage an opposing cause. Another definition offers propaganda as an expression of opinion or action by individuals or groups deliberately designed to influence opinions or actions of other individuals or groups with reference to predetermined ends. It is important to note that what determines if information is propaganda is not whether the information is the truth or a lie, but whether or not the information is intended to be used to further or damage one's cause.

Perhaps the most famous propagandist was Dr. Joseph Goebbels, who served Adolph Hitler during World War II. When Germany was winning the war, Goebbels exaggerated the truth to get the German people to support Hitler's war. When the war began to go badly for Germany, Goebbels used lies in order to get the German people to continue to support the war. His sole intent was to further Hitler's cause; whether the information he used was the truth or lies was immaterial.

By declaring that American troops were not in Baghdad, as American tanks rolled in the background, Saddam Hussein's minister of information intended to keep Hussein's loyalists fighting the American troops. The minister of information used both the truth and lies in his attempts to further Hussein's cause.

Some suggest that only dishonest messages can be considered propaganda. Those who argue that the truth is not propaganda often overlook the intent of the message, which is to persuade someone to go along with their agenda. Note how often politicians claim that they speak the truth while their opponents preach propaganda. The politicians are counting on support because of the claim that their information is the truth and hoping the intent of their message is overlooked.

The goal of the propagandist is to shape the attitudes of many individuals simultaneously, while leading everyone to believe that their response was their own decision. Propagandists with their verbal communication typically appeal to the heart, not to the mind. According to Delwiche (2002), tricks of the trade that propagandists use include name calling, glittering generalities, euphemisms, transfer, testimonials, plain folks, logical fallacies, band wagon, and fear. It is important that teachers become aware of these strategies being used to influence our attitudes and behaviors.*

1. ***Name Calling.*** This has ruined reputations, sent people to prison, and made people mad enough to enter battle and slaughter their fellow human beings. The name calling technique links a person or idea to a negative symbol. This form of propaganda is done in the hope that the audience will reject the person or the idea on the basis of the negative symbol, rather than look at the available evidence. Name calling evokes a negative emotional charge. How should we deal with the propagandist's use of name calling? We must ask ourselves, is this idea being dismissed through giving it a name that is connected to something I don't like? If I leave the name out of consideration, what are the merits of the idea itself?
2. ***Glittering Generalities.*** These are virtue words (e.g., Christianity, democracy, patriotism, honor, etc.). These words mean different things to different people. When we hear a word of virtue (e.g.,

*Reprinted by permission of propagandacritic.com.

democracy or freedom), our first reaction is to assume that the speaker is using the word in our sense, that the speaker believes as we do on this important topic. Glittering generalities is name calling in reverse. Although both attempt to arouse vivid, emotionally suggestive words, name calling seeks to make us form a judgment to reject and condemn without examining the evidence, whereas glittering generalities seek to make us approve and accept without examining the evidence. How should we deal with glittering generalities? In this situation, we must ask ourselves if an idea that does not serve our best interests is being sold to us merely through a name that we like. If we leave the virtue word out of consideration, what are the merits of the idea itself?

3. ***Euphemisms.*** Euphemisms are words used to pacify the audience in order to make an unpleasant reality more palatable. In World War I the War Department changed its name to the Department of Defense. Reagan renamed the MX missile the Peace Keeper. In war, civilian casualties are referred to as collateral damage. Referring to a war as a police action may sound more appealing, but it does not make the trauma any less significant. In World War I, traumatized veterans were said to suffer from "shell shock" (a term that conveys the horrors of war). In World War II, the term used was "combat fatigue." During the Vietnam War, the term "post-traumatic stress disorder" was used, a euphemism completely disconnected from the realities of war.

4. ***Transfer.*** This is a device by which the propagandist carries over the authority, sanction, and prestige of something we respect and revere (e.g., church, nation, etc.) to something the propagandist would have us accept. If the church approves of the campaign, it transfers its authority to the propagandist. In transfer, symbols are constantly used (e.g., the Cross, Old Glory, Uncle Sam, the Bible in hand, etc.). Symbols stir emotions. When we see Uncle Sam, we assume all Americans think that way and approve of the message. It is not at all surprising that American presidents give speeches standing in front of the U.S. flag. When a propagandist closes a speech with a prayer, the speaker is attempting to transfer religious prestige to the ideas that he or she is advocating. When a cough drop slogan reads "Visit the halls of medicine," or "Brand X is the best pain reliever that can be bought without a prescription," they are transferring the reputation of science or medicine. What would we think of gay rights if the church accepted this lifestyle? What would we think of assault rifles if the American Rife Association spoke out against them? How do we deal with transfer? We must ask ourselves if there are any legitimate connections between the proposal of the propagandist and the revered thing, person, or institution. Ideas should not be accepted or rejected simply because they have been linked to a symbol, such as a church, medicine, science, democracy, and so forth. We must leave the propagandist's trick out of the picture and ask what the merits of the proposal viewed alone are.

5. ***Testimonial.*** The most common misuse of testimonial involves citing individuals who are not qualified to make judgments about a particular issue. An example would be the endorsements of Michael Jordan or Tiger Woods on a TV commercial. Is the reason we buy Hanes underwear because we believe Jordan is an expert in this area? It would be more convincing (and much cheaper) to have Tiger Woods's chauffer discuss the advantages of owning a Buick than Tiger himself. Often these testimonials are unfair and misleading. Interestingly, if we like the celebrities, we are more likely to believe them; if we don't like them, we don't believe them. How should we deal with testimonials? Why do we regard this person as having expert knowledge or trustworthy information? What does the idea amount to on its own merits, without the benefit of the testimonial?
6. ***Plain Folks.*** Propagandists attempt to convince their audiences that they and their ideas are "of the people." Bill Clinton ate at McDonald's, George H. W. Bush often went fishing, Ronald Reagan chopped firewood, Jimmy Carter presented himself as a humble peanut farmer, and George W. Bush played golf. They often campaigned as political outsiders, aligning themselves with ordinary Americans. How do we deal with plain talkers? What are the propagandist's ideas worth when divorced from his or her personality? What is trying to be covered up with the plain talk approach?
7. ***Bandwagon.*** The propagandists hire a hall, rent airtime on radio stations, fill stadiums, and march in the streets. They use symbols, colors, music, and the arts because they want us to follow the crowd in masses. They direct their appeal to groups held together already by common ties of nationality, religion, race, sex, and vocation. They use flattery to harness the fears, hatred, prejudices, biases, convictions, and ideals common to the group. This approach is an emotional plea to pull us as a group onto a bandwagon. The bandwagon's plea is, "Everyone else is doing it and so should you." Naturally, no one wants to be left behind. We should remember, however, that there is never quite the rush to get on the bandwagon as the propagandist wants us to think. How should we deal with bandwagoneers? Regardless of the fact that others are supporting this program, should we support it? Does the program being promoted serve or undermine individual and collective interests?
8. *a. **Logical Fallacies–Bad Logic.*** An example of bad logic would be, all Christians believe in God, all Muslims believe in God, thus, all Christians are Muslims. We deal with bad logic by translating the basic terms and seeing if the conclusion still makes sense. Note that a message can be illogical without being propagandistic—the difference is that the propagandist deliberately manipulates logic in order to promote the cause.

b. ***Logical Fallacies–Unwarranted Extrapolation.*** This type of propaganda is the tendency to make huge predictions about the future on the basis of a few small facts. For example, if Congress passes legislation limiting the availability of automatic weapons, America will slide down a slippery slope which will ultimately result in the banning of all guns, the destruction of the Constitution, and a totalitarian police state. How do we deal with these fallacies? Is there enough data to support the speaker's prediction about the future? Are there other ways that things might turn out? Why is the speaker painting such an extreme picture?

9. ***Fear.*** "The streets of our country are in turmoil. The universities are filled with students rebelling and rioting. Communists are seeking to destroy our country. Russia is threatening us with her might, and the Republic is in danger. Yes—danger from within and without. We need law and order! Without it our nation cannot survive." The speaker was Adolf Hitler, 1932. When a propagandist warns listeners that disaster will result if they do not follow a particular course of action, he or she is using an appeal to fear. The propagandist hopes to redirect attention away from the merits of a particular proposal and toward steps that can be taken to reduce the fear. For example, insurance companies portray a terrible automobile accident and then remind people that they can never have enough insurance. A letter from a pro-gun organization begins by describing a lawless America in which only criminals own guns. When politicians create fear in the minds of the public and offer themselves as an alternative to the fear, they are using this technique. Lyndon Johnson, in 1964, effectively linked a well-known TV commercial portraying a young girl being annihilated in a nuclear blast to Barry Goldwater's bid for the presidency. Albert Einstein once stated, fear has always been the basis of most human actions. How do we deal with fear? Is the speaker exaggerating the fear or threat in order to get my support? How legitimate is the fear? Will the proposed recommendations actually reduce the supposed threat?

Father Coughlin (1939) offered one additional trick: *card stacking*. Card stacking involves the selection and use of *facts or falsehoods*, illustrations or distractions, and logical or illogical statements in order to give the best or the worst possible case for an idea, program, person, or product. Of interest, an editorial writer for the *New York Times* (September 1, 1937) wrote: "What is truly vicious is not propaganda but a monopoly of it."

Good citizens (this being the primary goal of education) should be able to *recognize the intent* of the strategies being used to persuade. Once we learn to think independently for ourselves, then we can take on the hardest challenge of learning to think together, referred to by the Institute for Propaganda Analysis (IPA) as the art of democracy.

In *The Fine Art of Propaganda*, the IPA stated:

It is essential in a democratic society that young people and adults learn how to think, as well as learn how to make up their minds. They must learn how to think independently, and they must learn how to think together. They must come to conclusions, but at the same time they must recognize the right of other men [people] to come to opposite conclusions. So far as individuals are concerned, the art of democracy is the art of thinking and discussing independently together.

Name: ______________________________

Propaganda

Propaganda consists of ideas, facts, or allegations, spread deliberately to further one's cause or to damage an opposing cause. It is important to note that what determines if information is propaganda is not whether the information comprises *truth or lies*, but whether or not the information is intended to be used to further or damage one's cause.

Describe some propaganda you have witnessed. Identify the trick being used (name calling, glittering generalities, euphemisms, etc.) and offer the intent of the message.

(Propaganda)

____

____

____

____

____

____

____

(Trick being used)

____

(Intent of message)

____

____

INTERPRETATION OF PERCEPTIONS

To understand the process that occurs when we make interpretations of perceptions, we begin by examining Heider's *balance theory* and *attribution theory*. **Fritz Heider** (1896–1988) observed that an attitude toward a person and the attitude toward an act by that person were interrelated and that these attitudes influenced each other. If the attitude toward the event and the attitude toward the person are not similar, then an imbalance exists. In other words, observers seek congruence between the person they are observing and the acts they are observing. The imbalance produces tension, which the observer tends to reduce by changing his or her cognitive structure to reestablish **balance**. For example, when a "good" person is seen doing something "bad" (let's say kicking a dog), this produces tension in the observer, who is then motivated to reestablish balance because good people do not do bad things. The observer returns to balance by seeking congruence. The observer may change the structure of the situation by noting that the dog must have attacked the good person, thus reestablishing balance.

Balance theory
Observers seek cognitive congruence between the person they are observing and actions the person exhibits.

In 1958 Heider introduced the **attribution theory**. According to Heider, the attribution theory describes how we attribute attitudes or causes to other people's actions. Individuals must assign some cause to behaviors because we desire to make sense out of what has happened. We tend to attribute the attitudes and actions of others to the other person (internal attribution); conversely, we tend to attribute our own attitudes and actions to the situation (external attribution).

Attribution theory
Explanation of how we attribute attitudes or causes to other people's actions; either internal (person-centered) or external (situation-centered).

So, the question must be asked, "Why don't we cut others the same 'slack' we cut ourselves?" We explain the things we do that people like about us because of who we are (internal attribution): "I aced the exam because I'm a good student." The things we do that are undesirable, we attribute to external circumstances: "I failed the exam because it was an unfair test or I had the flu on the day of the exam." However, we tend to deal with others' undesirable actions by attributing them to their personality (not the external circumstances that we would attribute to ourselves). For example, he dropped out of school because he is not smart or dedicated enough. Why we do not cut others the same slack we cut ourselves is because *we are too lazy to look for the external circumstances.* For example, the student may have a sick mother who needs caring for, or his school funds have run out, and so on (all external circumstances). Exceptional teachers spend time gathering all the information necessary prior to making judgments regarding their students' actions and, in doing so, cut their students the same slack they give themselves.

Interestingly, if we know the individual, we tend to attribute the cause of the problem to external factors or the situation (as we would do for ourselves). For example, we know Johnny dropped out of school because his mother has terminal cancer and he wants to be with her (external attribution). If we don't know the individual, we tend to attribute the action to the person's personality. Thus, Johnny dropped out of college because he couldn't "cut it" or he is lazy (internal attribution).

Another distinction that is made when understanding attributions is whether the behavior observed is global (i.e., seen in many different situations) versus specific (i.e., witnessed in isolation). If a behavior is global, we again tend to attribute that behavior to the person. For example, if a professor trips or stumbles while lecturing on several different occasions, a student is more likely to assume the professor is clumsy (make an internal attribution) than if the student had witnessed it only once. If a professor trips only once, then it can be assumed there must have been something in his or her path causing the stumble (making an external attribution).

In summary of this section, attribution theory and balance theory give insight into the perceptions we make and conclusions we draw based on other people's actions. We attribute the actions of another either to the situation in which the people find themselves (external) or the people themselves (internal). It is essential for the teacher to remember that knowledge of and previous experiences with the student will heavily influence the conclusions we draw about the student and the situation. Teachers need to be aware of their natural tendency to attribute their students' behaviors to internal dispositions (being lazy, unmotivated, etc.) if they do not know the students. Sometimes it is difficult for teachers to get to know every student with whom they work, but prior to assigning causality to a personality trait, the teacher must look beyond the behavior and into the lives of the students (refer to the discussion on Gestalt psychology).

Another way in which we can understand misperception is explained in decision-making terms by Rick Dove. Dove (2005) states that misperceptions are more likely to occur in the process of gaining *new knowledge* than in the refining of *old information*. During the information-gaining process, there are certain risks for distortion of knowledge: selective perception, context dependence, cognitive dissonance, hindsight bias, and memory bias.

Selective perception
Our expectations influence our perceptions. We give extra attention to information consistent with our expectations.

First, **selective perception** simply put means that we encounter all new circumstances with expectations, and those expectations result in us giving extra attention to information that fits with our expectations (i.e., we selectively perceive information that fits our expectations). Dove states that selective perception can lead us to mold our interpretations of experiences to fit our expectations. Thus, if students have the expectations that a teacher is a nice person, they will attend to the nice things the teacher does and perhaps even interpret ambiguous gestures (i.e., gestures that do not clearly fit in the categories of nice or not nice) into their expectation of the teacher's niceness.

Context dependence
The effect of first impressions and last impressions are very important and sway how we perceive a person or situation.

Cognitive dissonance
Occurrence when people behave in a way that is conflicting with their beliefs and values. In response to this conflict, they change their beliefs to decrease psychological discomfort.

Next, Dove describes **context dependence** as a factor influencing misperceptions. Specifically, Dove notes that first impressions (i.e., primacy effect) and last impressions (i.e., recency effect) are very influential in drawing conclusions about people and experiences. The third influencing factor in misperception is **cognitive dissonance**. Cognitive dissonance refers to humans desiring consistency in information, attitudes, ideas, and beliefs. In some instances, if we receive new information that does not fit our old knowledge, we might change either our perception of the new information *or* change our old knowledge to have consistency, thereby reducing our psychological discomfort. The work of **Leon Festinger** (1919–1989), whose work in cognitive dissonance has generated interest and enthusiasm both inside and outside of social psychology, is a good example of this.

Fourth, **hindsight bias** occurs when we, after the fact, interpret an outcome as expected and obvious all along. For example, students may interpret their grades (once grades have been assigned) as what they "knew they would get" even though they may have had no clear idea of what grade they were going to be assigned.

Hindsight bias
The occurrence of interpreting outcomes as expected and obvious all along.

Finally, according to Dove, **memory bias** occurs when we falsely recall information to fit our misperceptions. Dove notes that "we appear to store memories of new information as related fuzzy concepts without all the original detail; however, upon recall, the mind reconstructs a detailed remembrance" (2005, p. 47). For example, if five people witness a fight in the hallway, the details of that occurrence may be somewhat unclear to each. However, upon recalling the witnessed event later, they may unintentionally fill in the blanks of their memory with detailed information.

Memory bias
False recall of information to fit our misperceptions.

All five of the risks for distortion as presented by Dove combine to add to the likelihood of the presence of misperceptions.

When attempting to understand misperceptions, we must not ignore the power of our *past experiences* in shaping our present perceptions. For example, if we are in a car in which the driver is intoxicated and we are involved in a car wreck, this experience inevitably affects whether we choose to combine drinking and driving behaviors. If on numerous occasions we have ridden in a car with a driver who has been drinking but have not experienced an accident, or possibly an arrest, this too affects our participation in this potentially reckless activity. These experiences, with or without an accident, offer individuals different perceptions of drinking and driving. When relating these different perceptions to an educational setting, Cennamo (1989) notes that past experiences and perceptions may contribute to the preconceptions students bring to a situation of instruction, and in turn may impact (positively or negatively) the amount of mental investment they bring to that learning.

Not only do teachers rarely see the whole picture, but their past experiences influence their perceptions of the whole picture. Clearly, the question of why two teachers have different teaching styles could be answered, at least partially, by their past experiences. If a teacher is raised in a very structured and disciplinary home and the teacher sees the benefit of this lifestyle, this past experience may affect his or her classroom management style. If, on the other hand, a teacher rebels against his or her structured and disciplinary lifestyle, this situation may also affect the teacher's management of the classroom. The scenarios obviously are endless; nevertheless, the teacher's past experiences influence his or her present behaviors and attitudes.

As teachers, we must not only be aware of the impact of our own personal experiences in shaping our attitudes and behaviors, but also be knowledgeable of the experiences of our students, which in turn affect their attitudes and behaviors. Obviously, the teacher will experience those times when he/she does not have complete information of a student's background and thus lacks a full understanding of why the student may have behaved in a certain way. This lack of information places the teacher at risk of misperceiving the student's behavior. It is crucial that

Bullying

An interesting and very serious situation where misperception and drawing conclusions in the classroom can occur is the situation of bullying. Bullying occurs on many different levels (e.g., between students, between teachers, teacher to student, supervisor to teacher, parent to teacher, etc.). Although there are many different types (physical, verbal, psychological) and reasons for bullying to occur, one potential way to deal with bullying is by analyzing the situation from diverse perspectives. From a bully's perspective, the behavior, at least according to the bully, may have been nonthreatening and considered a joke, but from the victim's perspective, the bullying experience can be quite detrimental, both physically and emotionally. Researchers (e.g., Rock, Hammond, & Rasmussen, 2002) suggest that helping bullies take the perspective of their victims can actually decrease the likelihood that they will continue to bully.

For specific recommendations to put this research into practice, Piotrowski and Hoot (2008) suggest that the first step is to identify the bully. Teachers must be on the lookout for emotional immaturity and exaggerated confidence according to Piotrowski and Hoot, but these authors also note that it is difficult to "profile" a bully because they come in all shapes and sizes. They do suggest that the previous research for operational definitions of bullying will help identify bullying behavior. "Such definitions generally describe bullying as a specific type of aggressive behavior that causes distress or harm, demonstrates an imbalance of power, and is repeated over time" (Piotrowski & Hoot, 2008, p. 357).

The specific suggestions Piotrowski and Hoot give include the following: teachers must establish clear rules and consequences for misbehavior; children who bully need to be encouraged to understand the reasons for their own behavior while at the same time being helped to develop empathy for their victims. To prevent bullying, teachers must offer frequent opportunities for discussions about social relationships with clear guidelines of how to handle bullying behavior. Teachers also can equip children by giving sample phrases of how to respond to being bullied. The more children are attuned to what bullying is and how to handle the situation, or how to not themselves bully, the less likely bullying will occur.

Teachers also need to be aware of their own potential misperceptions with regard to bullying behavior. The lack of background knowledge concerning the situation or the individual who is doing the bullying can be detrimental in the conclusions drawn about the situation. Perhaps a student is bullying others because he or she is being bullied (or, even worse, physically abused) at home. Before conclusions can be drawn, the teacher must attempt to look at the whole situation with an objective eye, as difficult as that may be.

teachers learn to see the world through the eyes of their students. Teachers should consider the needs, thoughts, desires, attitudes, motives, feelings, goals, and beliefs (referred to as being **other-oriented**, Beebe et al., 2008), while still maintaining their own integrity, or risk continually misperceiving their students' behaviors.

Other-oriented
Considering the needs, thoughts, desires, attitudes, motives, feelings, goals, and beliefs of others.

It is natural for the teacher to take a little bit of information and attempt to draw conclusions based on this incomplete information. For example, the Gestalt principle of closure has a powerful impact over perception. The mind perceives information in such a way to "fill in the blanks." Often teachers take a little bit of information that they have on a student and fill in the blanks until they feel they have a complete picture, but in truth, they often only have many misperceptions. For example, if we are given a little information, say we have learned that a parent of one of our students has spent 15 years in prison, would this knowledge influence how we will react to that student? This knowledge offers very little information about the student, but the conclusions we might draw based on this little information are very real and encompassing.

An example of how a little bit of information is used to fill in the blanks and result in misperceptions that can directly affect a person's quality of life is the following: The story begins with a man who was fascinated with trains. At lunch, he would take his food to the train tracks in hopes of seeing a train go by. After work and on his days off, he took short walks along the train tracks in hopes of spotting a train. His family and neighbors began to worry about him and consulted a family doctor. At the insistence of the family, the doctor agreed to visit with the man. After the visit, the doctor assured the family that everything was fine, but his coworkers, hearing that he had to leave his work to visit a doctor, began to discuss his obsessive behavior with trains. Together with the family and friends, they decided to keep a close eye on him, and often followed him around town. The man eventually returned to

Figure 3.2 Because our view is different from another's view, we never perceive the same thing in exactly the same way.

the doctor with paranoid tendencies, claiming that everywhere he went he saw people following him and even hiding behind trees. While this may be an extreme example to relate to the classroom, the teacher must become aware that misperceptions can become life-altering if they don't recognize and manage them properly.

Stereotyping
Placing unique people into inflexible categories.

One of the most common misperceptions and part of daily life is **stereotyping.** Students seem to buy into the definition but not the fact that stereotyping is a wrong thing to do. Stereotyping is placing unique people into inflexible categories (Beebe et al., 2008). We place the same judgments on anyone placed into a given category. Stereotyping focuses on similarities among people of one group when, in fact, not all people within that group are the same. Once we have stereotyped, we have assigned a label to that person, who may deserve it or not. Students often feel that being stereotyped as a "scholar," "veteran," or the "clergy" is a good thing. However, it is important to note that it is not the category in question but rather the *act of placing a person into that category* that makes stereotyping wrong. When we place a person into a category, we are doing the person and ourselves a disservice. First, we now see the person as being the same as all of the others in this category. A student in class may have a parent who is a police officer. We now act as if we know something about this person, but in truth, we know very little about this person. It is a harsh reality, but there are those police officers, scholars, veterans, and clergy with whom we do not wish our students to interact, but those individuals are rarely part of our vision in our stereotypes. Again, it is not a question of the category in which we place people; the concern is in the *action* of placing a unique individual who is different from others we know into an inflexible, unchanging category.

One explanation for why we stereotype that most people do not want to hear is that we, as human beings, are lazy. We do not take the time to get to know a person for who that person really is. It is more convenient, and requires much less energy, to assign a label and place this person in an inflexible category. Once a person is assigned to a category, we act as if we know something about this person, but this information is too often only a misperception.

JOHARI WINDOW

The **Johari window** was developed by two individuals, **Joseph Luft** and **Harry Ingham**, thus we have **Johari**. Luft and Ingham (1950) designed the window to reflect various stages of relational development, degrees of self-awareness, and others' *perceptions* of us.

The first thing that needs to be noted, even though the first figure offered is in equal sizes, it would be *very rare* to find any Johari window actually looking like this. In reality, how well we know ourselves and how well others know us determine the actual size of each quadrant of the window.

Johari Window

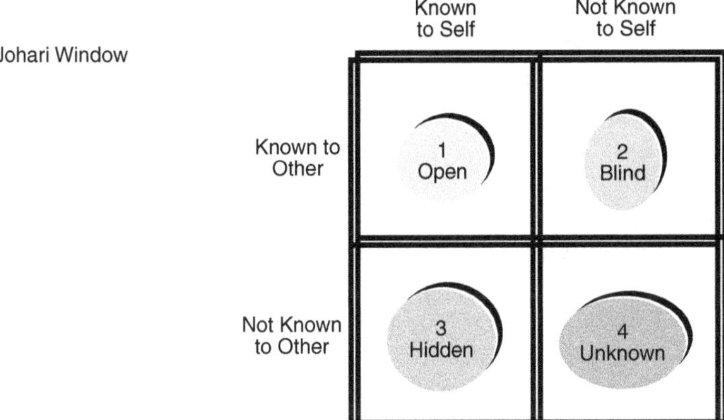

Variations on Johari Window

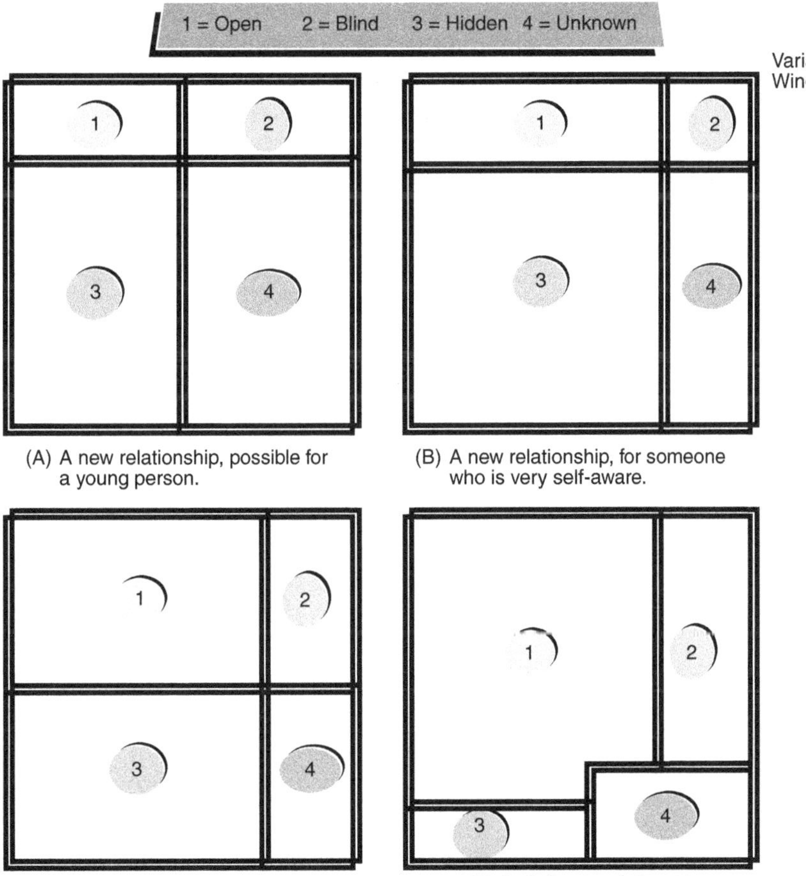

(A) A new relationship, possible for a young person.

(B) A new relationship, for someone who is very self-aware.

(C) A good friendship.

(D) An intimate relationship.

The four-quadrant window represents yourself and others' perceptions of you. The *Open* quadrant represents what you know about yourself and what others know about you. As you disclose more about yourself to others and as others learn more about you, the Open quadrant grows larger.

The *Hidden* quadrant is information you know about yourself but have not disclosed to others. This quadrant is fairly large at first, but as you disclose to others and as others learn things about you, it shrinks as the Open quadrant grows.

The *Unknown* quadrant is the part of yourself that you and others have yet to discover or realize. As we learn and self-disclose more about ourselves, or as others learn and disclose to us, this quadrant becomes smaller and smaller. Because there will always be some things about ourselves that we will never know, we can only guess at the size of the Unknown quadrant.

However, sometimes others observe things about us that we do not realize or perceive about ourselves. This information is found in the *Blind* quadrant. The Blind quadrant is small when someone doesn't know us very well, and it grows larger as others observe us more. However, as relationships develop and more information is revealed and disclosed by others the Unknown and Blind quadrants shrink.

The Johari window shows that intimate relationships play an important role in the growth of self-knowledge. The Johari window can also disclose a great deal about your general approach to relationships.

Have students do the following worksheet.

Name: ______________________________

Johari Window

Draw three Johari windows. Include the Open, Blind, Hidden, and Unknown quadrants in each.

1. You and your best friend of at least three years.

2. You and a family member.

3. You and the professor of this course.

How can the Johari window be relevant to the teacher?

The windows, representing your relationships with students, should change as the semester progresses. As more information is disclosed and relationships develop, the Open quadrant should be larger at the end of the semester as compared to the beginning of the semester.

SUMMARY

The teacher must have an awareness of how common misperceptions are in daily life. The implications of these misperceptions as the teacher goes about drawing conclusions have been shown. As stated throughout this chapter, the process for creating misperceptions is a natural human experience; however, without the awareness of these errors in perceptions, we cannot attempt to avoid them.

The first thing a teacher must do to reduce misperceptions is to walk around the elephant, or at least get input from people who have seen the other side of the elephant. Teachers must recognize that their view is only of a single and individual perception. Without the benefit of instant replay, teachers are not getting the complete picture and may react to events in a way that is detrimental to their students. Those teachers who practice gathering more complete information before reacting to an issue will make far fewer errors in their perceptions and develop more trusting and respectful relationships with their students. To combat misperceptions, the teacher must get to know and understand the whole student (the Gestalt perspective). Students cannot be fully understood by examining only their behaviors or labels. We must examine, through the ecological perspective, students' home life, issues of health, instructional needs, and so on.

Using the balance theory and the attribution theory, others' behaviors influence our attitudes, beliefs, and misperceptions are shown. Many variables come into play, whether we use internal attributions or external circumstances to explain others' behaviors. It is easy to misperceive behaviors if teachers do not have a full understanding of the situation surrounding the students.

Teachers must educate their students to recognize the purpose for certain specific information and the various strategies used to further someone's cause. This intentional misperception often comes in the form of propaganda. Propaganda is information spread intentionally and deliberately to further one's cause or to damage an opposing cause. The goal is to have students recognize persuasive information when they hear it, learn to think for themselves, then learn to think together.

New information versus old information can contribute to misperceptions. Dove (2005) outlined five risks for distortion when using new information (selective perception, context dependence, cognitive dissonance, hindsight bias, and memory bias). The teachers' past experiences and the past experiences of their students, when left undisclosed, will negatively influence relationship building and add to misperceptions.

A very common reason for misperception is stereotyping. The act of placing unique individuals into an inflexible category in which assumptions about the persons often leads to misperceptions should be avoided. Teachers should intentionally identify and model the nonuse of stereotypes and continually remind their students that everyone is a unique individual.

Finally, when all else fails, teachers should ask students if the teachers have an accurate perception of the events in question. Often, by taking the time to discuss events and perceptions with students, teachers find themselves more informed about the students and the way in which they think and learn.

CASE 3.A

On the first day of class, Mr. Hill explained the expectations that he had of his freshmen algebra students. He told them that they were not in middle school any longer, and that he expected them to do all of their homework, study for tests, and come to class prepared each day. Unlike middle school where students who failed classes were still socially promoted, he said, students who fail in high school will need to take the class again the following year to get the credit for graduation. He wanted the students to know that they needed to put forth effort in order to pass algebra. After the first day of class, he overheard some of his students talking to each other about how he was a mean teacher.

QUESTIONS

1. What should he do about the conversation he heard?

2. Should he call the students into his room and talk to them about it?

3. Is it a negative thing to be firm in your expectations as a teacher?

CASE 3.B

Ella is a fifth-grade student who had Mrs. Simpson as a teacher last year in fourth grade. Mrs. Simpson's room was very chaotic, with the students doing pretty much whatever they wanted without much discipline from the teacher. Now Ella has Mrs. Thompson, and she is completely opposite in her classroom management style. Students are expected to be in their seats and raise their hands when they have questions. They are not allowed to do whatever they want in the classroom. Ella wondered how two teachers could be so different from each other.

QUESTIONS

1. How can two teachers have such different styles of classroom management?

2. What repercussions does this have on students?

3. How is learning impacted in the two styles?

CASE 3.C

Jack is a second-grader who constantly picks on other students in his class. He makes fun of those students who aren't as fast as he is; he picks on those students who are shy; he laughs at students who get in trouble. All in all, Jack doesn't discriminate whom he ridicules. One day his teacher, Mr. Miller, kept him inside for recess to talk to him about the behaviors he had been observing. When Mr. Miller asked Jack why he acts the way he does, Jack told him that he thought he was being funny and that the others students laughed when he picked on kids in the room, so they must think he is being funny, too. It is clear to Mr. Miller that Jack doesn't feel bad about his behavior.

QUESTIONS

1. How should Mr. Miller address this problem? What should he say?

2. Whom should he contact?

3. Is it a problem even worth tackling?

Name: ____________________________

Quiz

How Best to Reduce Our Misperceptions

1. Walk around the ____________________________ (Eleanor Roosevelt)

2. Be O ____________________ O ____________________

3. Recognize the intent of the message, known as ____________________________

(Answers)

Thus far we have discussed the need to reduce misperceptions by "*walking around the elephant*" in order to get a more complete picture, *being other oriented* and focusing on others' needs, and recognizing *propaganda* or the intent of the message. In future chapters we will be examining other strategies for reducing misperceptions, for example, transactional analysis (chapter 5), the balcony view (chapter 7), and stereotyping (chapter 8).

Courtesy of Brenda Lussier.

SUGGESTED ACTIVITIES

1. Watch the movie *Crash* (2005, Best Picture Oscar winner). Use the following questions as a guide for debriefing after the film.
   a. Did you view the film with a racially diverse audience? What was the group's reaction?
   b. How do you think someone of another race would perceive this film? Would they call it biased? Your own opinion?
   c. At the film's beginning, which character seemed the most racist? Did your feelings change by the end? Was there one character with whom you most identified?
   d. Rick, the district attorney, did not seem racist. What did you think of this politicizing of race?
   e. Have you ever been discriminated against because of your race? Have you ever treated someone differently or poorly because of race?
   f. Were you surprised the shopkeeper's gun was loaded with blanks? Do you think this was an accident?
   g. How did this film affect your own feelings about race relations?

   Visit http://szetohistory.tripod.com/CrashUnits.pdf to access a curriculum guide for the movie. Choose one of the lessons to complete a creative project on the movie.
2. Watch the PBS program *A Class Divided*. The program presents Jane Elliot's experiment to teach her students about racial discrimination at http://www.pbs.org/wgbh/pages/frontline/shows/divided. Write a reaction to the documentary.

Listening

OBJECTIVES

After completing this chapter you should be able to:

- Explain the physiological process of hearing.
- Identify and provide examples of techniques used to become better listeners.
- Discuss strategies teachers can use to create an atmosphere for encouraging students to be better listeners.
- Explain various types of ineffective listening that teachers should avoid when interacting with others.

KEY TERMS

Ambushing
Attention
Concentration
Defensive listening
Empathy
Eye contact
Insensitive listening
Insulated listening
Listening
Objectivity
Pseudo listening
Receptive body language
Restatement of the message
Selective listening
Stage hogs-conversational
Strategic pauses

The process of listening is both physiological and psychological. This chapter will discuss the various contributing factors that influence effective and non-effective listening with regard to teaching.

PHYSIOLOGICAL PROCESSES OF HEARING

To better understand the hearing process, which influences how well we listen, a brief explanation of what occurs physically while we are hearing is necessary. The process of hearing begins with the outer ear receiving sound waves that are then funneled through the auditory canal (also called the ear canal). Once through the ear canal, the sound waves activate the eardrum by causing it to vibrate. This vibration then extends to three bones within the middle ear (the hammer, anvil, and stirrup). Combined, these three bones are known as the ossicles, which operate in a chainlike reaction with the eardrum vibrating the hammer, which strikes the anvil, and thus activating the stirrup. The stirrup, or last part in the chain reaction of the ossicles, is connected to the oval window. The oval window serves as a connector for the middle ear to the inner ear through the cochlea. The striking of the stirrup on the oval window causes fluid inside the cochlea to move. This motion of fluid in the cochlea causes vibration in the basilar membrane, and in turn causes the organ of Corti, which rests on the basilar membrane, to rise and fall. The organ of Corti has hair cells projecting from it that brush against the tectorial membrane located above it. These hair cells serve as auditory receptors that, when sufficiently activated, send messages through the auditory nerve, and finally send auditory information to higher brain centers for processing.

The sound waves we hear that create this chainlike physiological reaction are measured in two ways: frequency and amplitude. Frequency, measured by hertz, determines the pitch of a noise. High-frequency pitches are recognized as higher tones, whereas low-frequency pitches are heard as low tones. Amplitude, measured in decibels, is the intensity or energy produced by the sounds we hear—the stronger the amplitude, the louder the noise.

Why this quick lesson in physiology? Because without the knowledge of this physiological process, we would not be able to discuss the process of hearing or listening. Obviously, if a student has damage to any of the structures or neural pathways for auditory processing, the process of listening will be impaired. In the United States alone, more than 13 million people communicate with some degree of hearing impairment and on a given day, one fourth to one third of the students in a typical classroom don't hear "normally" (Adler & Towne, 1999). Although these astounding statistics are worthy of much further investigation, throughout this chapter, we will assume students have unimpaired hearing so that we can focus on psychological and environmental factors that influence the listening process.

PSYCHOLOGICAL FACTORS OF LISTENING

For the purposes of this chapter, **listening** is a complex process that entails the physiology of hearing, paying attention, developing understanding, responding to information provided, and remembering the interaction. Teachers are forced on a continual basis to interact and listen to individuals on many different levels (i.e., students, colleagues, parents, and administrators). Here are some guidelines that will assist the teacher in that process.

Listening
Process that entails hearing, attending, understanding, responding, and remembering

BECOMING A BETTER LISTENER

Campbell (2003) offers the following attributes as characteristics of good listening. There is overlap, but obviously all of these attributes work together to contribute to effective listening skills.

1. ***Concentration.*** Although this is not the easiest task, concentration is the beginning process of good listening. Campbell suggests focusing attention on the verbal message (words being said), and nonverbal messages being sent (e.g., posture, eye contact, tone of voice) during the conversation. When analyzing the content, it is best to concentrate on the main ideas or points being presented.

Concentration
Focus on verbal and nonverbal messages being sent during a conversation.

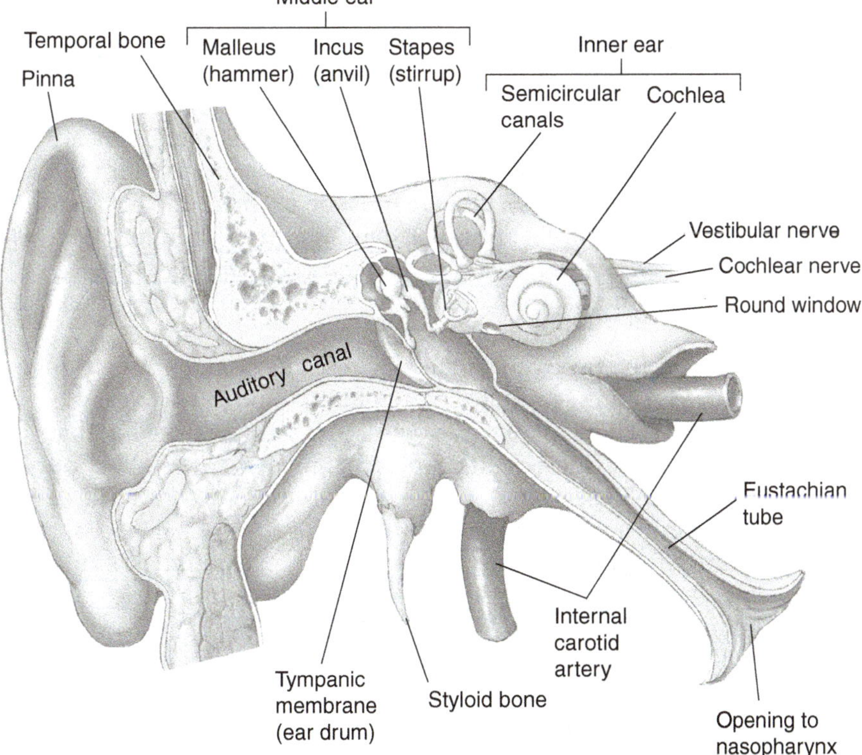

Figure 4.1 Ear anatomy

Attention
Visual portion of attention; including eye contact and receptive body language.

2. ***Attention.*** Campbell defines attention as the visual portion of concentration on the speaker. Through eye contact (discussed below) and other body language, we communicate to the speaker that we are paying close attention to his or her messages. Unfortunately, we are often forced to divide our attention among many demands in our lives, but when teachers listen to their students, it is important to give them their undivided attention. The preservice teacher needs to be aware that *the greatest compliment you can give to your students is your full attention.*

Eye contact
Means for eliminating distracting visual information and attending to facial cues during conversation

3. ***Eye contact.*** Quality eye contact is essential in the listening process for several reasons: First, strong eye contact can eliminate potential competing visual information. Second, although it often occurs without us knowing, when engaging in eye contact, we are also reading the individual's lip movement. This lip reading can assist in the understanding of verbal messages. This process is especially true for students with hearing impairments. Third, nonverbal communication is often easier to read when focusing on a person's face. Campbell notes that by watching the eyes and face of a person we also become aware of unspoken clues to the content. Finally, eye contact with the person speaking sends a clear message to that person that we are listening and paying attention. Teachers should teach students to *listen with their eyes as well as with their ears.*

Receptive body language
Body posture that communicates attentiveness to the speaker

4. ***Receptive body language.*** The listener's body posture and positioning also send messages about how attentive you are being to the speaker and his or her message. For example, crossing the arms and legs may be perceived (correctly or not) to mean a closing of the mind and attention. Nodding of the head vertically can be read by the speaker as agreement or assent to the message. Campbell notes that we must be aware of the messages sent through nonverbal cues. Teachers should be cognitive that students *are always in the process of nonverbally communicating.* Often this communication is unintended, or even unconscious, but nevertheless, the communication is present.

Objectivity
Open and unbiased listening process

5. ***Objectivity.*** To effectively listen, one must be open to the message the other person is sending. This openness is not always easy because we each have our own biases and past experiences that we draw from (discussed in chapter 3); however, if we allow our own personal biases to enter into the listening process, we have put ourselves into a position to misinterpret the message the speaker is sending. Teachers can be instrumental in teaching their students to quiet their internal dialogues that distract the listener from the message being sent.

Restatement of the message
The process of paraphrasing a speaker's message in an attempt to fully understand the speaker.

6. ***Restatement of the message.*** A technique that is sometimes used in humanistic therapeutic practices is to restate the speaker's verbal content as part of feedback. This restating of the content can enhance the effectiveness of good communications. Campbell suggests making comments such as "I want to make sure that I have fully understood your message . . ." and then paraphrasing

the message. Restating the message can allow for more effective communication through clarification of what is heard. This process can involve asking questions for clarification as well.

7. ***Empathy—not sympathy.*** Campbell notes that empathy is "the action of understanding, being aware of, being sensitive to, and vicariously experiencing the feelings, thoughts, and experience of another . . ." whereas sympathy is "having common feelings. . . ." While a listener can take the perspective of another in the communication process, trying to understand where the individual is coming from, he or she does not have to share the same perspective to be an effective listener.

Empathy
Understanding the thoughts, feelings, and experiences of another

8. ***Strategic pauses.*** Silence can be very powerful in the communication and listening process. These pauses not only allow the listener to process the information being sent but also send the message to the speaker that the listener is offering consideration to the message. When dealing with a complex issue, a few well-chosen, deliberate words with a pause for contemplation is much more effective than a room full of words that add to the complexity.

Strategic pauses
Silence in conversation that allows for comprehension and consideration of the message

9. ***Interjections.*** Although tempting, especially when working with students who may take longer to formulate what they are attempting to say, it is crucial to not complete sentences or over-speak a person who is trying to communicate. This interjection sends the message to the students that not only is the teacher not interested in hearing them fully speak their mind, but also the teacher is rushing them in the process.
10. ***You cannot listen while you are talking.*** This may seem obvious, but in the process of communication and listening, one must strive to find a balance of appropriate give and take. Larry King, a notable news talk show host, is known for saying, "I've never learned anything while I was talking."

HELPING YOUR STUDENTS BECOME BETTER LISTENERS

Jones (2007) states that the "teacher's role in developing speaking and listening is crucial" (p. 570). Jones explains that there are four different techniques that teachers can use to promote effective speaking and listening. The interactive approaches include dialogical teaching, developing metacognitive awareness, planning, and assessing. She believes that most classroom interactions consist of teacher initiation through questioning, student response, and feedback from the teacher closing the interaction. These exchanges tend to be brief and focused on correctness in answers. In place of these brief interactions, Jones cites suggestions by Alexander (2003) that assist teachers creating a classroom with dialogical teaching to increase the effectiveness of speaking and listening in the classroom: collective (i.e., focusing on learning as a collaborative purpose rather than working alone), reciprocal (i.e., interactions between teachers and students should be a sharing process and exchange of ideas), cumulative (i.e., it is important to build upon each others ideas), and supportive (i.e., the classroom should be an environment where children can express their ideas without risk of judgment, but with an opportunity for understanding). Additionally, Jones suggests that by increasing the student's metacognitive processes, or acknowledgement and awareness of one's own thought processes, helps them to become more self-reflective, which in turn can increase students' attentiveness and listening to others. In the planning process, Jones proposes that teachers consider the "nature" of the speaking and listening interchange. Teachers should plan for developing relationships, sharing meaning in communication, understanding that meanings come with different understandings (often bound by culture), and using the spoken word as a means for learning. Finally, teachers need to develop some kind of assessment to examine the effectiveness of improving students' speaking and listening abilities. Jones (2007) also notes that students should be a part of the assessment process as well.

Thompson, Grandgenett, and Grandgenett (1999) offer the beneficial advice that listening is a skill that can be taught, even though it is often ignored as a topic for teaching in our classrooms. Specifically, these authors were interested in developing strategies for teachers working with students who are disadvantaged or "at-risk." However, the suggestions they offer should be considered as important for all students regardless of status. Far too often "the primary emphasis on listening skills [in the classroom] involves the teacher asking students to be quiet so the child can take notes or attend to the day's activities" (p. 131). Additionally, these authors point to previous literature (DeVito, 1991; Hanna, 2005; Walker & Brokaw, 1998) citing general barriers to effective listening in our classrooms: a preoccupation with the self, preoccupation with external noise (distracting environments), psychological filters (e.g., preexisting personal biases), and hidden agendas or a process of hearing only what we want to hear (p. 132). Ultimately, Thompson et al. (1999) offer 12 strategies for teachers to consider using in the classrooms to help students become better listeners.*

1. Prior to the educational experience, teachers should create an environment that is conducive to listening. Teachers can use a catch phrase or hand gesture that calls children's attention to become active listeners.
2. Make learning to listen a skill that is taught within the classroom. Although teachers are often already asked to follow a taxing curriculum, it is essential that they help their students learn how to be better listeners. Parents and teachers assume that children develop these skills naturally and without direction, but in fact, listening is a skill that can be honed through educational experiences.

*From *Education, Volume 120, Fall 1999* by Franklin Thompson et al.

3. Allow time for processing of information. Teachers often will ask questions or move on to new information before full processing occurs. Silence after delivery of new information can be very useful to the learners. This time for processing may not only be useful for learners, but also essential for students who may experience learning disabilities.
4. Give structure to the message. That is, specify the important features of the information provided. Giving students numeric or bulleted information to break apart a larger message can help them better understand the information. Providing examples of the information also can offer structure and meaningfulness to the message.
5. After stating important information, restate that information. When teachers restate information, they allow students to catch parts of the message they may have missed previously. This process, in connection with the third point (i.e., allowing time for processing), will help students to make meaningful connections.
6. Identify diverse ways to communicate information. Every classroom has diversity in learners (learning style), yet many teachers use one approach to teaching. Thompson and colleagues (1999) suggest that teachers should "paint a picture of the message" through verbal illustrations or examples that bring information to life.
7. Help students keep their minds open to the content of what they hear. When receiving information, learners are encouraged to listen without preconceived notions, opinions, or ideas. True open-minded listening (easier said than done) involves listening objectively.
8. Acknowledge active listening in learners. Teachers are encouraged to be aware of students' intentional listening and then reward that behavior. This process is a beautiful example of reinforcing good behavior. Through this recognition, all students will learn the importance of actively engaged listening in the classroom.
9. Although external reinforcement for engaged listening is a great way to encourage the behavior, teachers should have a plan for helping students move to more intrinsic reinforcement. Thompson et al. note that the ultimate goal is "learning for learning's sake, not to create a generation of youth who desire a reward for what they should want to do anyway" (p. 134).
10. Be diverse in the presentation of material. In addition to presenting a verbal picture of information (see point 6 above), teachers should, where possible, integrate the use of supplemental material in their delivery of material. For example, multimedia presentations are a great way to excite and interest students in information that may be difficult, "boring," or obtuse. Remember, classrooms come with diverse learners, thus diverse presentations are beneficial.
11. Teachers should be aware and responsive to physical and emotional needs of students that can affect students' abilities to actively listen

within the classroom. If students' personal experiences interfere with their classroom performance, teachers should consider having them evaluated by a school counselor.

12. When finished presenting information, offer a summary of that information in a way that requires students to use varied listening skills. For example, students can get into small groups and describe what they've just learned. This process would not only require active listening to the teacher's lecture, but also listening skills in small groups. They need to be attentive to the accuracy of their classmates' description of the material covered. Teachers can also have students do a quick writing assignment connecting what they have just learned to previous class material. This process would require listening and connective thinking skills.

Finally, these authors point out that it is ironic that in the teaching profession, which is focused on the "spoken message," educators do not give more consideration to the process of listening and teaching of those skills.

Brent and Anderson (1993) also offer ideas for developing students' listening skills. These authors suggest that through the modeling of good listening skills by the teacher, providing specific listening instructions, and providing opportunities to practice effective listening in the classroom, students can learn to be effective listeners. Some examples for providing opportunities to practice effective listening include reading aloud to the class, providing writing workshops where the students engage in conversations and listening skills relating to the process of writing, cooperative learning groups, reader's theater (where the students turn a story into a script for reading aloud), and retelling, which includes students sharing (while other students practice listening) their favorite stories.

Figure 4.2 By reading aloud to the class, a teacher offers students an opportunity to practice effective listening.

The Classroom We Shape

Interestingly, Wilhelm (2004) suggests that to better promote dialogue and listening skills in our students, we must reconsider the physical properties of our classrooms and traditional classroom rituals. He argues that these interaction rituals set barriers to communication and encourage monologue rather than dialogue between teacher and students. For example, the arrangement of desks in rows facing the front of the classroom communicates to students that the teacher, or authority, is the only person with anything important to communicate. Rather, by putting students' desks in a large circle, groupings of smaller circles, or sets of squares (four desks together), although forcing the teacher to be creative in presentation of information to the large group, sends students the message that they are to attend to each other and value input from their peers in addition to the teacher.

Another suggestion of Wilhelm is that teachers should refrain from commenting on student responses. When the teacher comments on student responses, this author suggests that the teacher is in control of the flow of ideas and may limit the dialogue between students and teachers and students and peers. Wilhelm suggests, instead, to have students call on each other. He also suggests that teachers need to create situations where students interact with each other without the teacher being in charge (e.g., small book clubs, discussion groups, group structures, or learning center groups).

TYPES OF INEFFECTIVE LISTENING

Not only is it important to discuss the attributes of effective listening, it is also important to note the characteristics or styles of ineffective listening. Adler and Towne (1999) offer examples of ineffective listening that the teacher should avoid in his or her interactions with students, parents, colleagues, and administrators.

1. ***Pseudo listening.*** Students give the appearance of listening, but in fact they are not. Whether because of distraction (physical or mental) or lack of interest, students who pseudo listen are unengaged with the conversation.
2. ***Stage hogs-conversational.*** These students have at their basic interest a desire to turn the conversation back to them. Because of this hidden agenda, they lack attentive listening.
3. ***Selective listening.*** Both students and adults sometimes engage in a listening style whereby they pay attention only to information directly related to them and disregard other important information.
4. ***Insulated listening.*** For some students, if they do not want to discuss a topic, they will "tune out" and not listen effectively.

Pseudo listening
Giving the appearance of listening, when in fact the listener is not attending to the message

Stage hogs-conversational
Individuals whose intent is to turn attention to themselves

Selective listening
Attending to information that is only of interest or relevant to the self

Insulated listening
"Tuning out" or ineffective listening because of a desire to not discuss a topic

5. ***Defensive listening.*** Students who use defensive listening tend to take others' comments as personal attacks and thus listen defensively rather than effectively.
6. ***Ambushing.*** Students who listen for ambushing purposes listen to gather information that might be used to personally attack someone at a later point.
7. ***Insensitive listening.*** Students who listen insensitively take the speaker's comments at face value and again, listen ineffectively.

Defensive listening Taking other people's comments as personal attacks

Ambushing Listening to gather information to personally attack someone

Insensitive listening Taking the speaker's comments at face value and not considering the full message

SUMMARY

Why don't we listen better? Many reasons, stemming from internal and external forces, cause a breakdown in the listening process. Recognition of these potential distracters can assist in the listening process; however, effective listening requires continuous conscious effort. Some of the external forces that distract us from effective listening include factors such as message overload and external noise. We live in a culture that presents us with constant information, to the extent that we can become overloaded. For effective listening to occur, we must focus and filter out the constant stream of information and distraction. The listening process can also be influenced by internal forces. For example, our minds are designed such that rapid thought occurs. Specifically, according to Adler and Towne (1999), we can understand speech rates up to 600 words per minute, but the average person speaks 100–150 words per minute. Thus, with our minds working faster than the spoken word, we have time to be distracted by other internal thoughts, which can lead to distraction and a decrease in effective listening. Teachers should teach students to use the extra time to summarize what the speaker is saying. It is evident by the research presented in this chapter, effective listening is an ability that can and should be taught in our curriculums. Through direct instruction, modeling, and encouragement, effective listening is a skill to be shared inside and outside your classroom. Teachers may teach their students without ever listening to them, but teachers can never get to know their students without listening to them. The best conversationalist in the room is also the best listener.

CASE 4.A

Mike is a student in Mr. Johnson's seventh-grade science class. While Mike is generally a good student who can turn in quality work, he frustrates Mr. Johnson daily in class. When Mr. Johnson gives directions orally, Mike never seems to follow the directions. Whether it is to get back to his seat or to open his book so class can start, Mike never seems to hear Mr. Johnson. It seems to Mr. Johnson that Mike doesn't want to follow directions. One day before school, Mr. Johnson is talking to his colleague about his frustration with Mike, and she asks him where Mike sits in class. Mr. Johnson tells him that he is in the back of the room. She then wants to know if Mr. Johnson has talked to Mike about this issue.

QUESTIONS

1. What questions could Mr. Johnson ask without embarrassing the student?

a) mr. johnson needs to ask Mike questions one on one
1. asking if he enjoys class?
2. asking, does he have any problems in class?
3. having a hard time with listening?

2. Could it be that Mike has a hearing problem?

maybe

3. Where could Mr. Johnson find this information?

-first move to move him
- then have him tested if no improvement

CASE 4.B

Mrs. Burris, a veteran teacher, and Mrs. Nichols, a first-year teacher, are discussing their parent–teacher conferences from the previous night. As her mentor, Mrs. Burris asks Mrs. Nichols how the she enjoyed meeting the parents of her second-grade students. Mrs. Nichols expressed frustration that the parents of the students in class who really needed to listen to her about their child did not seem to care as much about what she told them as she would have liked. She had expressed concern at how their daughter was unable to focus in the mornings and wanted to put her head down and sleep until lunch. She told them that one of the most valuable parts of the school day was the reading block at 10:00, but their daughter did not seem to want to be learning like the rest of the students. Mrs. Nichols's frustration came from the parents not listening to her. Mrs. Burris asked if Mrs. Nichols listened to what the parents told her about their daughter and more importantly what they didn't tell her. Mrs. Nichols sat back and thought about the conference and came to the realization that she didn't give the parents much of an opportunity to speak during the conference. It was a primarily a one-sided discussion, so she never had much of an opportunity to listen to the parents.

QUESTIONS

1. What could Mrs. Nichols have done to facilitate a stronger conference with the parents?

2. What could she have done to more effectively listen to the parents?

CASE 4.C

Mr. Swanson is the principal at Mediate Middle School. He is planning and scheduling for the initial teacher in-service workshops at the beginning of the year. He reflects that many of the teachers do not listen to the presenters of the workshops and formulates the idea that he should have a session on effective listening skills and strategies. He knows that not only would that make his in-services more effective for his staff, but the strategies learned could also benefit the teachers and students in the classroom.

QUESTIONS

1. What are some important points from this chapter that Mr. Swanson should incorporate into his workshop?

2. What are the justifications for these points?

3. How could they benefit both teachers and students?

SUGGESTED ACTIVITIES

Visit the following websites to find many classroom activities for enhancing listening skills. Many of the activities are short and can be used to enhance the information in the chapter.

a. http://www.stbirinusliteracy.hostei.com/index_files/Resources/Intensive_Listening_Activities.pdf
b. http://www.healthyschoolsms.org/health_education/documents/listeningskills.pdf

The more elaborate our means of communication,
the less we communicate.
– Joseph Priestley

5

Verbal Communication

OBJECTIVES

After completing this chapter you should be able to:

- Discuss the phrase "meaning is found in people, not in the words they use."
- Explain and provide examples of how words are culturally bound.
- Describe the difference between concrete and abstract words.
- Discuss how words affect our thinking and behavior.
- Identify and provide examples of verbal villains that can destroy relationships.
- Discuss how teachers can avoid sexist, racist, or inappropriate ethnic language.
- Explain what meta-stories are and why they can help teachers effectively communicate with their students.
- Describe the three ego states used in transactional analysis theory.

KEY TERMS

Meanings
Meta-stories
Misinformation effect
Verbal villains

COMMUNICATION

Why do we communicate? We communicate to make sense out of the world we live in, and to share that sense with others. Historically, communication has been seen has having only three components: a *sender*, a *receiver*, and a *message*. Grice (1989) noted that the receiver expects the sender to be engaged in conveying a message that is appropriate to the context, that the message is relevant, true, clear, and only as informative as required. The receiver's knowledge and that these expectations are present provides the motivation to attempt to extract meaning from the message.

We now recognize communication as having two more components: *simultaneous interaction* and *mutual influence*. Simultaneous interaction means even as we talk we are interpreting and reacting to the other's response. Mutual influence means that both communication partners are affected by the interactions not just one person. Each is changed as a result of the other person's action. While you are talking and your mother is listening, you are also observing your mother's nonverbal expressions. Just because she is not speaking does not mean she is not communicating simultaneously and influencing your communication.

According to Turnbull, Turnbull, Erwin, and Soodak (2006), effective partnerships require effective communication. It is important to pay close attention to both quality and quantity of our communication. Quality means that we are positive, clear, and respectful. Quantity refers to how often we communicate and how efficient we use our and others' time.

LANGUAGE

According to Bloom (1988), language generally refers to any code employing signs, symbols, or gestures used for communicating ideas meaningfully between human beings. It is also a social tool that is used to communicate meanings, feelings, and intentions by using a symbol system specifically designed to transmit and receive social messages (Raymond, 2008).

WORDS ARE POWERFUL

Something teachers should never forget is that words are powerful. Words can heal or destroy a nation. Lincoln's Gettysburg Address is an excellent example of this. In the history of our country, no president wanted a nation to come together more than Lincoln did. It is apparent by Lincoln's words that he never thought the words he spoke would affect the generations to come.

Lincoln's Gettysburg Address

Four score and seven years ago our fathers brought forth on this continent a new nation, conceived in liberty and dedicated to the proposition that all men are created equal (Emancipation Proclamation, 11 months earlier). Now we are engaged in a great

> civil war, testing whether that nation or any nation so conceived and so dedicated can long endure. We are met on a great battle field of that war. We have come to dedicate a portion of that field as a final resting place for those who here gave their lives that that nation might live. It is altogether fitting and proper that we should do this. But in a larger sense, we cannot dedicate, we cannot consecrate, we cannot hallow this ground. The brave men, living and dead who struggled here have consecrated it far above our poor power to add or detract. The world will little note nor long remember what we say here, but it can never forget what they did here. It is for us the living rather to be dedicated here to the unfinished work which they who fought here have thus far so nobly advanced. It is rather for us to be here dedicated to the great task remaining before us—that from these honored dead we take increased devotion to the cause for which they gave the last full measure of devotion—that we here highly resolve that these dead shall not have died in vain, that this nation under God shall have a new birth of freedom, and that government of the people, by the people, for the people shall not perish from the earth.

Again, words are immensely powerful, so powerful that future teachers must constantly be on guard with their choice of words.

MEANINGS ARE IN PEOPLE

Meanings
Are in people, not in the words they use

It is important that teachers teach their students that **meanings** *are in people* and not in the words they use (Beebe et al., 2008). An old gentleman used racist words that many found intolerably offensive. Every time he used an offensive word, people would cringe. Upon many years of getting to know this person, it became obvious to many people that this person was a kind old man who was not a racist in any sense of the word. Although he regularly attended a predominantly white church, he gave his offerings to a church that was predominantly minority that needed his money more than his church did. He often taught Sunday school in the same church where he gave his money, prior to attending worship in his own church. He participated in Habitat for Humanity and generously supported scholarships for the underprivileged. Obviously, we are not encouraging or approving of offensive language; however, the message is that without knowing a person or situation, it is easy to misperceive (chapter 3) the meaning behind spoken words. This message is also one that students in future classrooms need to be taught (i.e., to look past the words that are being used in order to see the intended meaning).

The future teacher will inevitably come across the student who calls another student a "jerk" or some other not-so-nice name. The rest of the class may laugh and recognize, as will the teacher, that the "meaning" was intended to be playful between two friends. This situation will be entirely different from a student calling another student a "jerk" accompanied by no laughter and a "meaning" that is confrontational and not between friends. Notice in these two situations the same word is spoken, but the two meanings are very different. Students need to be taught to look for the meanings in people, because meanings are not found in the words people use.

WORDS ARE CULTURALLY BOUND

It should come as no surprise that words are culturally bound. A young man took the challenge of learning German as a second language. In his endeavors, he once said in German, to a German audience, that he was "hot," hoping that someone would turn down the AC or at least open a window. After a long roar of laughter, he was informed that he had stated that he was in a desperate need of a female companion. Although this cultural error is quite amusing, students may not find other cultural errors quite so funny. It is imperative that teachers model sensitivity to their students when cultural errors are made by students for whom English is their second language. This sensitivity, modeled by teachers and displayed by other students, will influence and sometimes determine if relationships (academic and social) progress or take a step backward.

WORDS CAN HAVE CONCRETE OR ABSTRACT MEANINGS

The meanings of words can be concrete. Ernest Hemingway once wrote, "The cat is black." Few would argue the vagueness of his words, clear, concise, and obvious. Nevertheless, words can also be abstract. A young man with a disability ("Tony") became very upset upon hearing that he would be separated from the woman of his dreams. When asked why he could no longer be with her, he replied, "She had burnt all of the bridges between Oklahoma and Kansas." Tony had overheard an arresting officer tell another officer that the woman had no assistance from her family and that she had "burnt all of her bridges" in Kansas. It only complicated the matter worse when someone told him, "Don't worry, Tony. There are more fish in the sea." Tony looked at him as if he had been insensitive to Tony's feeling and that all he wanted now was to go fishing. Chapter 3 contained a discussion of the importance of accurate perceptions. Using vague and abstract phrases leaves room for multiple interpretations and misperceptions. In the classroom, teachers must pattern themselves after Hemingway and not offer words left open for interpretation by their students.

ONCE CREATED, COMMUNICTION CAN'T BE UNCREATED

The judge says, "Disregard that last statement." Everyone in the courtroom, including the judge, knows that statement is not going to be disregarded. You may apologize every day of your life for something you have said, but what you said can never be unsaid, it will always be there, taking on a life of its own. Teachers should be precise and thoughtful in their use of words, because once something is said, it can never be unsaid.

WORDS GIVE INSIGHT INTO THINKING, AND THINKING IN TURN IMPACTS BEHAVIOR

Heumann (1994) reports that in Germany in the early 1980s, there was a separatist group that called itself the "*Cripple Movement*." Members of the movement stated that people treated them like cripples, so knowing how uncomfortable people felt with the term, they took it as their own and were empowered by it. The Cripple Movement was started by the fact that too much focus was on the members' deficits, looking at what people *cannot do,* instead of looking at what people *can do*. Some of the messages that this movement wanted to send include:

- I want to celebrate my difference, not hide from it.
- Our message is that disability is a normal part of life.
- We have the same basic human needs and life aspirations as everyone else.
- What to call us is often driven by people who do not live this life.

Individuals with intellectual disabilities have been called mental defectives, feeble-minded, retardates, imbeciles, village idiots, mongoloids, and so on. All of these labels were given by people who didn't live their lives with a disability. The Cripple Movement brought attention to the fact that all people should be allowed to label themselves as they see themselves, not as others see them. In allowing others their right to label themselves, we are now in a position to see the world from their eyes (this was defined in chapter 3 as being other-oriented).

Nancy Mairs (1986) writes:

> I am a cripple. I chose this word to name me. People—crippled or not—wince at the word "cripple." Perhaps I want them to wince. I want them to see me as a tough customer, one to whom the fates/gods/viruses have not been kind, but who can face the brutal truth of her existence squarely. As a cripple, I swagger.

The simple fact that many teachers have difficulty saying the word "cripple" in classes, testifies to how words can affect attitudes and behaviors. It is amazing the power words have over the interpretation of a situation. This power is illustrated by a well-known psychologist Elizabeth Loftus's research on eyewitness testimony. One element of her research found that the way a question is worded influences people's memories for an event (**misinformation effect**). For example, in one of her studies (Loftus, Miller, & Burns, 1978),

Misinformation effect
When people remember wrong information

participants viewed slides of a traffic accident. In these slides one group of participants viewed the car parked in front of a stop sign; the other group viewed the car parked in front of a yield sign. Later, participants were asked, "Did you see the green car pass in front of the red car while it was stopped at the (stop or yield) sign?" Participants who saw the stop sign and were asked the question with the words "stop sign" were 75 percent correct when asked, "Was the car in front of a stop sign?" Participants who saw the stop sign and were asked the question with the words "yield sign" were correct only 41 percent of the time. Even more surprisingly, participants who were wrong were unwavering in their belief that the car was in front of a yield sign. Again, words have a powerful effect over not only how others interpret us, but also how we interpret ourselves (e.g., our memory and confidence).

Loftus, Miller, and Burns's (1978) classic research continues to be investigated many years later. For example, Hupbach, Gomez, Hardt, and Nadell (2007) not only investigated the misinformation effect, but also examined how memories can continue to be modified as they are reactivated. Through different studies, these researchers were able to demonstrate that over a series of three days, participants' memories could be altered for lists of information. This research gives great insight into how thinking not only affects behavior, but is a malleable process that can be influenced over time and misinformation.

LANGUAGE IS USED TO NAME, EXPLAIN, AND UNDERSTAND

According to Goldstein (1948), language is more than a tool. Language is the basis of our ability to name, explain, and understand the world around us. Words offer us a tool to label the world and to identify ourselves (e.g., African Americans, Blacks, Latinos, Caucasians, Whites, Native Americans, Asian Americans, etc.). How are teachers to use this tool? How best do we, as teachers, decide on what to label our students? Simple enough: *just ask them*. Again, as our Cripple Movement, friends remind us not to impose labels on students, if labels must exist, we must allow students to label themselves because we do not live their lives. Then, more important than the label itself, is our acceptance and respect for their choices.

NEW FRONTIER

The new frontier is often described as *nonface-to-face communication over the Internet*. Many people share the opinion regarding the convenience the new frontier offers. But others point out the reduced level of nonverbal cues (facial expressions, eye contact, etc.), making It harder to accurately communicate your meaning. Many find it less satisfying than face-to-face encounters. Of particular interest, it has been noted that some students with disabilities are for the first time being treated as typical students when engaging in the new frontier.

WORDS AS VERBAL VILLAINS

Teachers should become aware of the many barriers that destroy relationships. Often these barriers come in the form of **verbal villains.** Verbal villains do not attend to the feelings or emotions of others. Instead, they keep others at arm's length and put their own interests in the spotlight (Gazda et al., 1999).

Verbal villain
Off-the-top-of-the-head responses that do not attend to the feelings or emotions of others. Instead, they keep others at arm's length and put their own interests in the spotlight.

The future teacher needs to be aware that most everyone at sometime during their lives has been all of the verbal villains mentioned above. It is certainly not the glamorous part of being a human being, but we all tend to play the part of one villain or another at various times. By becoming aware of these verbal villains, teachers can become better at defeating them when they intrude upon the efforts to create and maintain relationships with our students. Remember, verbal villains are not concerned with others; they are only concerned with themselves (the opposite of being other-oriented).

Self-Focused!

AVOID SEXIST, RACIST, OR ETHNIC LANGUAGE

Teachers should avoid and model the nonuse of sexist, racist, or ethnic language. Sexist language such as "congressman," "mailman," or "mankind" offers to students a view that the teacher is not aware of the many significant contributions women have made. Educators should not teach their students only half of history; history must be taught completely with all parties involved being presented fairly. For example, women's issues and their many contributions, women's fight for suffrage, or the remarkable lives of Dorothea Dix and Mother Teresa, should be recognized by all teachers and conveyed to their students while teaching and modeling the use of nonsexist language.

Racist or ethnic language conveys to students the insensitivity of the uniqueness of all persons and the assumption of superiority. Terms like "Indian Giver" (which is interesting in itself because the white dominant culture was the one that kept breaking promises), "I Jewed him down," and "He doesn't stand a Chinaman's chance" inform students that members of groups are all the same, and the teacher's way of life is superior to others. If a teacher agrees that the primary role of education is to produce good citizenry (as discussed in chapter 2), using racial or ethnic language is entirely contrary to this effort. Teachers who use racist or ethnic language convey two messages to their students. One message is of the lack of acceptance and tolerance for those who are seen as being different, and the second message, often in the form of modeling by the teacher, is that it is acceptable to see someone as superior to others, that is, as long as *you are not the one who is different.*

Time for Understanding

Saunders (2001) emphasizes an important point to the preservice and practicing teacher: our students live and learn in a verbal world. When students are inattentive or noncompliant, Saunders suggests it may not be because of anger; rather, it may be because they do not understand what we have said or to whom we are speaking. To combat this miscommunication, Saunders suggests that teachers take the students' perspective in the classroom. Are instructions too wordy? Too long? Too complex? Do students have enough time to process the words spoken? Saunders explains that students take 5–10 seconds or longer to process the spoken word. Now, imagine the processing time for a student with a learning disability. This time may be shorter or longer, or perhaps processing does not happen at all. Saunders states that if students do not understand or do not have time to process the information given to them in their verbal world, they may act out with behavioral problems. Thus, teachers must be intentional in their verbal communication and allow students the time to be intentional in their listening.

META-STORIES

Meta-stories
Are verbal vehicles that can be used by teachers to reach students when other strategies have been unsuccessful. They are designed to deepen students' understanding of concepts and ideas.

Meta-stories are verbal vehicles that can be used by teachers to reach students when other strategies have been unsuccessful. This technique is an underused tool that is readily available to the teacher. Meta-stories first came to the author's attention through in the work of John Bandler and Richard Grinder (1975 & 1976). Bandler and Grinder were cofounders of the field of Neuro-Linguistic Programming.

Meta-stories act as a bridge that teachers can use to deepen students' understanding of concepts and ideas. These stories are designed to tap into what students already know about the world, and to introduce larger and new concepts. They can communicate aspects of an event more vividly than can the usual request. For example, telling a student to quit running in the halls only results in the student slowing until out of sight. Meta-stories have an uncanny way of teaching the students to not run and, thus, directly affecting the behavior.

An example of a meta-story consists of teaching students to "just let things go." This meta-story is used for the students who take everything said to them too seriously. An innocent tease by a fellow student may cause a withdrawal by the student from the participation of a class exercise and delay an opportunity for learning. A teacher may approach "Johnny" and inform him to not take everything so seriously, and to just "let it go" and "don't let it bother you." However, Johnny does exactly the opposite of the teacher's suggestion.

The following meta-story, "*Two Monks*," can be instrumental in teaching the skills needed to deal with being overly sensitive to others' comments.

> Two monks in the fourth century B.C. were walking along a lane, each deeply involved in meditation. They approached a stream that was very shallow, but moving very rapidly. At the stream was

> a lady looking anxious. One of the monks asked her if he could be of service. The woman replied that she could not swim and was scared to cross the stream. The stream was known to be slippery, and she feared she would slip and fall and the fast current would take her below to a large pool of water where she would drown. She also told the monk that she worried that her expensive dress would be spoiled crossing the stream. Without saying a word, the monk picked her up and carried her across the stream and placed her gently down. The woman gratefully smiled, thanked the monk, and quickly left. The monk then turned to look back toward the second monk on the other side of the stream. The second monk had a confused look on his face. The first monk waited and finally the second monk crossed the stream, looking less confused, but more disturbed. They began walking and after about a mile and a half of traveling, the first monk stopped and asked, "What is that curious look you have on your face?" Finally, after being prodded, the second monk replied, "I cannot believe that you have broken two of our most precious vows without even a consideration of your actions. First, you helped the rich, and second, you touched a woman." The first monk replied, "I carried the woman across the stream and let her down, but you've been carrying her for the last mile and a half."

The teacher and student should share a discussion regarding the message in the story. Thereafter, the teacher, after witnessing the student get upset over something someone has said, reminds the student, "Johnny, you need to put the lady down." The other students may acquire an inquisitive look, but "Johnny," more often than not, will set the lady down and go about his business.

In the situation where a student has difficulty with diversity in the classroom, whether it is due to cultural differences or having a student with disabilities in the classroom, meta-stories are often beneficial, as seen in the next meta-story known as "The Horseman."

> An old king in the fourth century B.C. [one of your authors is partial to the fourth century] was getting ready to retire and give his kingdom over to his son, the prince. The king called in his son and made him aware of his new position and asked only one favor. The king asked the prince to retire an old monk who had served him well for so many years. The old monk had traveled the world in search of the most beautiful horses. Because of the monk's horsemanship and hard work, the king had acquired the best stable of horses in all the world. After the coronation, the young king summoned the old monk and informed him that he was going to retire and that he was to live in the castle, and never want for anything. But, said the young king, I have one last request; you are to choose your successor. Surprisingly, the old monk knew who he wanted to replace him. The old monk told

> the young king that he had heard of a young monk who had so much knowledge about horses that he could pick a horse that could walk on sand without leaving hoof prints. The young king was excited and asked to see this young wonder. The old monk summoned the young monk and brought him before the young king. The young king decided to test the young monk. He asked him to go out into the world and bring back to his kingdom the very best horse he could find. The young monk parted without a word. Months passed and the young king began to get anxious to see the young monk's skills. Finally, the young monk returned and found himself summoned in front of the young king. The young king asked where was the horse? The young monk said the horse was several weeks behind, that the sellers were taking special care to see that the horse arrived safely. The young king requested that the young monk describe the horse to him. The young monk offered a curious look, as not to understand the question. The young king finally asked, is the horse a stallion, mare, black or white? The young monk again looked confounded by the questions and quickly replied, "a black stallion," and turned and walked away. The young king waited anxiously for his black stallion to appear. Finally, the day arrived and to the young king's surprise a beautiful white mare appeared at the entrance of the castle. The young king summoned the old monk and asked if he was being made a fool of, or was it the case that the young monk had no knowledge of horses. The young king informed the old monk that the young monk didn't know the difference between a stallion and a mare, and he didn't even get the color right. The old monk at first showed concern, then his expression changed to a mild smile. The old monk turned and went out to see the mare. Upon his return he stated to the young king, "I was aware that the young monk was a good horseman, but I was, up until now, unaware of how good he really is." The old monk continued, "the young monk looked deep inside of the horse to see what the horse was made of, he examined the horse's character and stamina from within, and all along, during his examination, he forgot to look at the outside of the horse."

Students must be taught, and then often reminded, to look inside of people, to see what people are really made of and not to judge a person from outward appearances. If a reminder is needed, the teacher needs only to ask, "Johnny, I thought you wanted to be a horseman" to revisit this lesson.

In the situation where a student is having a difficult time accepting others' values or beliefs, the following, somewhat elaborate, meta-story titled "The Prince" can be used.

> There once lived a prince, who lived in the kingdom of his father, the king. The prince believed in all things except islands,

princesses, and God. Every morning in the young prince's life, he rode his favorite horse inside of his father's kingdom. The king had ordered and even pleaded to the prince to never ride outside of his kingdom because the king was unable to assure his safety. So every morning, the prince rode toward his father's borders, but always turned away before entering the adjacent kingdom. As the prince grew older, he became more and more curious about the unseen lands beyond his father's control. As his curiosity grew, the prince reached his eighteenth birthday. He awoke on this birthday and knew something was very different about this day. As he approached the neighboring kingdom, he knew that he was unable to resist the temptation and crossed into the neighboring kingdom. He quickly became excited with all the new things. He saw birds and trees he had never seen before, beautiful streams, and strange flowers. As he wandered up and down the hilly paths, he was overcome by the beauty and strangeness of the new land. As he approached the top of a hill, he observed a large body of water and in the middle of this water was an island. He quickly rode toward the water and came across a man wearing a robe. The prince asked of the man, "Is that really an island in the middle of the water?" The man replied, "Yes." The prince then asked, "What are those curious but beautiful creatures on the island?" The man replied, "Those are princesses." The prince responded by saying, "If there are islands and princesses, then there must be a God." The man replied, "Yes, I am God." The prince was so excited he mounted his horse and rode as fast as he could back to his father's kingdom. He rode his horse swiftly right up to the castle door. He ran to his father, proclaiming that he had just seen an island and princesses, and even met God. As he was describing these to his father, the king interrupted his son and asked, "What did this man claiming to be God look like?" The prince excitedly described the man as wearing a robe with long sleeves, and with a long beard. The king stopped his son and proclaimed that he had not met God but was talking to a lowly magician and that this magician had cast a spell on him which made him see these things, "things that really weren't there." As the king turned to walk away, he pleaded with his son once again, "Please do not leave my kingdom without my permission, and never again talk to that lowly magician." The prince had a sleepless night, being very aware that he had disappointed his father and that he would once again disappoint his father and confront the magician. The next day found the prince standing next to the man wearing the robe in front of water with the island and princesses. The prince began by saying that he was aware that the man was not God but only a lowly magician and that he had cast a spell on the prince, making him see things that did not exist and that he would never again believe anything the magician said. The magician responded by

> saying, "Yes, I am only a magician, but it is not me who has cast a spell on you, but it is your own father, who is also a magician, who has cast a spell and not allowed you to see islands, princesses, and even signs of God in your own kingdom." The prince got on his horse and slowly made his way back to his father's kingdom. The prince approached his father in a sulking way, and after apologizing for disobeying him for a second time, asked him to deny the magician's claims. The father was unable to deny the charge, "Yes, I am also a magician." The prince was startled with the admission and wished he could dismiss the entire claim. The prince, wanting to clear up the matter, asked, "Father, what is the truth beyond magic? I just need to know, are the islands, princesses, and God real?" The father replied, "I love you very much, but there is no truth beyond magic." The prince again attempted to persuade his father, "Father I must know the truth beyond all of this magic stuff." The father, with a sincere heart, informed his son that he would grant him any desire he had, but that there is no truth beyond magic. After further attempts to get his father to explain, and further refusals, the prince told his father that he no longer wished to live in a world where he could not tell if islands, princesses, and God existed. The father raised his hand and the prince found himself in the middle of a field, with death charging him. As death approached riding a white steed and carrying a long lance, getting louder and louder, the prince turned his head toward his father and nodded, signaling that he did indeed wish to live. The king summoned away death and approached his son. The king asked his son why he had changed his mind. The prince said, "While standing there thinking I was going to die, all I could remember was how beautiful the island and princesses were." The father replied, "Ahhh, now you too are a magician."

A dissection of the story is now useful. The prince represents the student raised in a home (kingdom) protected by his or her parents (the king). As long as the student stays close to the home, he or she can be protected, but when the student ventures outside of the home, the parents cannot always protect him or her. The island, princesses, and God are values that parents or others have instilled (represented as spells). In some kingdoms, families do not believe in islands or abortion, princesses or the death penalty, gay rights, NRA, or God, whereas in other kingdoms families do believe in islands, choices, princesses, the death penalty, gay rights, NRA, or God. At a certain age, the student becomes a young adult and moves from his or her protected kingdom into a new and strange neighboring kingdom (e.g., a college campus). Here in this new kingdom, the young adult meets other people who were raised in different kingdoms and have had different spells cast on them (taught and borrowed different values). The trick for students to become magicians is for them to hold dearly to their own values taught by loving and caring people, while learning to be accepting and tolerant of others who hold different values taught to them by loving and caring people. If the teacher finds him/herself observing the student not accepting someone else's values, a reminder might consist of the phrase, "Johnny, didn't you tell me that you wanted to be a magician when you grow up?"

Meta-stories are everywhere; you just need to look for them. All future teachers should read J. D. Salinger's *The Catcher in the Rye* while examining why they wish to become teachers.

Salinger wrote:

"I keep picturing all these little kids playing some game in this big field of rye and all. Thousands of little kids, and nobody's around—nobody big, I mean—except me. And I'm standing on the edge of some crazy cliff. What I have to do, I have to catch everybody if they start to go over the cliff—I mean if they're running and they don't look where they're going I have to come out from somewhere and catch them. That's all I'd do all day. I'd just be the catcher in the rye and all. I know it's crazy, but that's the only thing I'd really liked to be. I know it's crazy" (p. 173).

Are you, the future teacher, a catcher in the rye? Is this why you are going into teaching? How best to assure your students will not fall off the cliff? Refer to our discussion on the exchange theory (chapter 11) and always give your student the *greatest compliment* a student can get, your *full attention*.

It should be noted that meta-stories need not be all that sophisticated. *"Life is not about waiting for the storm to pass, it's about learning to dance in the rain"*[1] The power of these verbal communications is truly amazing. Just as Abraham Lincoln's words left a lasting impact, so too can the messages that are sent in the context of the meta-story. Every preservice teacher might find it beneficial to develop a meta-story to use in the future classroom. They should *find a message that is important to them and to their future students and then hide the message in an environment of their choosing* (e.g., the fourth century B.C., in a space ship, with magicians, with talkative animals, etc.).

[1]In remembrance of a "special" special educator, Cathy Posey.

Name: ______________________________

Meta-Story

Meta-stories are underused tools that are readily available to teachers. These stories are verbal vehicles that can be used by teachers to reach students when other strategies have been unsuccessful. Meta-stories act as a bridge that teachers can use to deepen students' understanding of concepts and ideas. These stories are designed to tap into what students already know about the world and introduce new concepts. They can communicate aspects of an event more vividly than can the usual request.

Offer your meta-story. Include the meta-message and title below.

____

____

____

____

____

____

____

____

____

____

____

____

Message/Title

Courtesy of Brenda Lussier.

KEEPING A CONVERSATION GOING AND POWER STRUGGLES

There are times when a teacher chooses to continue a ongoing conversation with a student and other times when the teacher chooses to remove him- or herself from an impending power struggle. For these discussions, we introduce *transactional analysis* (TA), the work of **Eric Berne** (1910–1970).

According to Berne (1961), TA is the analysis of the interaction between two people. It provides insight into self-awareness and personal growth. Berne used TA to help his clients understand themselves and change their lives. Transactional analysis consists of three ego states: the child, the parent, and the adult. These three ego states *reside in each of us and each ego state emerges from within us from time to time.*

The Child:

Innocent, spontaneous, fun-loving, evading responsibility, full of energy, self-indulgent, creative, and rebellious (e.g., clown, student, patient in the doctor's office).

The Parent:

The weakest ego, critical, superior to whom he or she is interacting with, feels a need to take care of others, imposes his or her values on others, restricts others, determines how things are done or should be done, makes decisions for others (e.g., judge, principal, clergy).

The Adult:

Mature, practical, realistic, relates to others as peers, problem solver, planner, achiever of goals, organized, adaptable, without prejudice, and intelligent (e.g., scientist, accountant, lawyer).

Each of the above ego states resides in all of us and at any time a particular ego state may emerge. The goals of TA are to become aware of each ego state, to encourage the freedom of change, and to use our adult ego state in the decision-making process. As discussed previously (chapter 2), TA has also offered an understanding of how teachers' values, and those values of their students are developed and how they can be reexamined through the use of the adult ego (Hanna, 2003).

When teachers tell their students what they should believe, it is their *parent ego* talking. When teachers hold onto their values and *allow others to believe as they choose*, this shows their *adult ego* in practice.

Name: ______________________________

Transactional Analysis

Transactional analysis (TA), developed by Eric Berne (1961), is the analysis of the interaction between two people. Berne used TA to help people understand themselves and change their lives. TA consists of three ego states: the child, the parent, and the adult. These three ego states *reside in each of us and each ego state emerges from within us from time to time.*

Describe the situation and your conversation where you played each ego:

Child

____

____

____

Parent

____

____

____

Adult

____

____

____

Courtesy of Brenda Lussier.

The teacher needs to be cognitive of the power of TA. As one of many uses of TA, through practice, a teacher can use TA to prolong a conversation (e.g., with a student who does not wish to continue a discussion) or end a conversation (e.g., with a student who wishes to engage in a power struggle). By staying at the same ego state as the student, the teacher will see how easy it is to continue the conversation, and by moving to a different ego state, the teacher will see the ease in ending a conversation. This, like many strategies, needs practice to become effective.

Berne's 1964 book, *Games People Play: The Psychology of Human Relationships,* provides a deeper understanding of social interactions as well as their motives in these transactions. The first game that Berne introduces is "If It Weren't for You . . ." Berne tells the story of a woman who complains about her husband being too restrictive and domineering. But there is a payoff for both. The man is domineering and enjoys the power he has over his wife. The woman gets to tell her friends, "If it weren't for him I could accomplish so many things in my life" (gathering sympathy from her friends), and she does not have to risk failure as she would if she were given permission to do the things she wanted to do. Berne draws attention to the fact that both are game players.

Teachers are going to be confronted by students who are game players. One type of game player is students who know that if they can get the teacher occupied in a power struggle, they always win. Picture a nine-year-old arguing back and forth with an adult; *the adult has already lost this argument and may not even know it.* Power struggles are about control (as discussed in detail in chapter 10), but the objective of a power struggle by a game player is to detract from the lesson plan. If the game players are successful in distracting the class from the lesson plan, they have won. They have accomplished what they have set out to do.

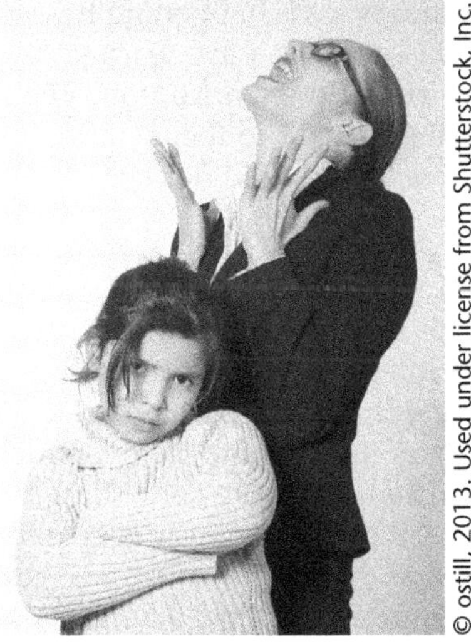

Figure 5.1 When an adult argues back and forth with a nine-year-old, the adult has already lost the argument.

Another form of game player is the student who creates something to complain about. For this type of game player, the amount of homework received is always going to be too much and too tough. The assignment, regardless of the amount or difficulty, is something the student can complain about to peers, parents, and anyone else who will listen. The game player is attempting to take all attention off the task at hand (homework), and, once attention is diverted away from the homework and onto a discussion regarding the amount or difficulty, the game player has won. Becoming aware that a game is being played is the first step in combating the game player. Once teachers recognize they are involved in a game, they can stop the game and return to the subject at hand (homework, lesson plans, etc.). In chapter 10, the discussion on combating power struggles in the classroom will be revisited, but here, by simply changing the ego state to one that is different from the game player will suffice in removing the distraction. Again, this technique is not always obvious and needs some dedicated practice.

COMMUNICATION APPREHENSION (STAGE FRIGHT)

Where does stage fright come from? We learn to fear public speaking. The first thing to understand is that fear is a *natural* and *normal* human emotion. The purpose of fear is to tell us that something isn't quite right. Learned fear is an important survival mechanism, but occasionally the wires get crossed and we learn a fear for something where it doesn't belong—where there isn't a significant danger.

For some of us, stage fright may be caused by a *single traumatic incident*—a highly stressful or frightening event at which, instantaneously, fear of public speaking is created. But for most of us it is a *slow build*. This occurs when a mild case of fear of public speaking escalates over time to become a severe one. What is happening here is that the individual is accumulating fearful events. We have learned, by watching others who exhibit fear, that we should be fearful, too. The following suggestions are designed to get the speaker to focus on the presentation versus the nonconstructive fear of speaking in public.

HOW TO COMBAT STAGE FRIGHT

- Admit to yourself and to your audience that you're nervous. This projects honesty, integrity, and gathers sympathy for your condition. (Most people are thinking, "Yeah, I'm glad I'm not up there," and when things go bad, they tend to forgive much easier.)
- Remind yourself that you have something valuable to say, or you wouldn't be there. When the anxiety is the worst, concentrate on the message not the audience. Remember that you are not as important as the message you are sending. The audience may be looking at your hair, clothes, or tattoos, but these items are not as important as the message you are sending.

- Think about and prepare what you're going to say. The mental preparation will calm you down and take your mind off of the fear. In your preparation, ask yourself if these ideas or the information presented is organized and clear, and if it will make sense to your audience. Also, being well prepared allows you to go on "autopilot."
- Act confident even though you are nervous. If you project confidence, the audience will react positively, and this will increase your confidence even more.
- When nervous, start with humor; tell a joke about yourself (not about others). Use humor to gain the audience's attention and keep them attentive.
- Start strong and end strong. A strong and creative introduction will propel you through the rest of your presentation and wipe out any fear you begin with. Ending strong will also counteract a shaky beginning due to nervousness.

Keep in mind that stage fright isn't a sickness that needs to be cured. You're not going to erase this fear from your life. Chances are you'll always be a little bit afraid before you get up in front of a crowd. We all are. The key is to learn to *deal* with your fear and *control* it so it doesn't control you. Remember, people are sympathetic. They have a lot of the same fears as you do, and they know what you're doing is hard.

SUMMARY

Words have long-lasting power, even when that is not their intention. Lincoln's Gettysburg Address is an enduring example. Teachers must first think about what they wish to communicate before choosing their words, because the words they choose have lasting power. Students should be taught to look for the meanings in people and not in the words people use. True meanings reside only in people and, without an accurate understanding of these meanings, we open ourselves up to the opportunity for misperceptions. Teachers will encounter students who struggle with the English language. These students have the right to expect sensitivity by teachers and the use of concrete, clear, concise, and obvious words, versus abstract and vague terms, which offer multiple interpretations and often misperceptions. Often, words give insight into how people think and behave as they do. For example, the members of a separatist group used the term "cripple" as a vehicle to get their messages out and draw attention to their abilities.

Teachers should become aware of and avoid the many types of word barriers (e.g., hangman, drill sergeant, guru, etc.) that damage relationships between themselves and their students. Verbal villains do not attend to the feelings or emotions of others; instead, they put their own interests first. Teachers must play an active part in removing these barriers in the classroom. Teachers should model the nonuse of sexist and racist comments. By using terms like "mankind" (versus "humankind") teachers are not recognizing the contributions by everyone. Many significant contributions by women and minorities have historically been downplayed or not acknowledged. Teachers must educate their students on the complete history, not just the half that dominates our textbooks. Racist language conveys an insensitivity of the uniqueness of all persons and highlights the teacher's assumption of superiority. The practice of using racial language offers a lack of acceptance and tolerance to differences, which overlooks the fact that in these differences strengths are found.

Transactional analysis (Berne, 1961) is a difficult technique to master and requires a dedicated focus, but with practice, many teachers become effective in continuing or ending conversations and disengaging in intended power struggles. Once the teacher is able to identify the various ego states (the child, parent, and adult), he or she can manipulate the structure of the communication to meet his/her purposes. Through practice, meta-stories can be valuable in assisting a student who has been unable to learn a concept or idea. They deepen students' understanding of what they already know, while introducing new and more complex concepts. For most students, developing meta-stories is fun and engaging, and is seen as an additional instructional strategy.

Lastly, teachers should not be surprised if something they say, with no significant or intentional meaning, becomes a significant focal point in a student's life; after all, words are powerful.

CASE 5.A

Examine the eloquence of the healing words of our former President Abraham Lincoln's Gettysburg Address.

> Four score and seven years ago, our fathers brought forth on this continent, a new nation, conceived in Liberty, and dedicated to the proposition that all men are created equal. Now we are engaged in a great civil war, testing whether that nation, or any nation so conceived and so dedicated, can long endure. We are met on a great battle-field of that war. We have come to dedicate a portion of that field, as a final resting place for those who here gave their lives that that nation might live. It is altogether fitting and proper that we should do this. But, in a larger sense, we cannot dedicate—we cannot consecrate—we cannot hallow—this ground. The brave men, living and dead, who struggled here, have consecrated it, far above our poor power to add or detract. The world will little note, nor long remember what we say here, but it can never forget what they did here. It is for us the living, rather, to be dedicated here to the unfinished work which they who fought here have thus far so nobly advanced. It is rather for us to be here dedicated to the great task remaining before us—that from these honored dead we take increased devotion to that cause for which they gave the last full measure of devotion—that we here highly resolve that these dead shall not have died in vain—that this nation, under God, shall have a new birth of freedom—and that government of the people, by the people, for the people, shall not perish from the earth.

Source: Collected Works of Abraham Lincoln, edited by Roy P. Basler.

QUESTIONS

1. How did Lincoln hope that his words would heal the nation?

   Lots of turmoil, he wanted an end to the war

2. What specific passages are most effective?

   a.

3. How do his words, written then, affect us today?

   We are able to give honor to past soldiers and the hurt of war.

4. What can future teachers learn from the words in this passage?

   Even though it was short, Lincoln focused on main points. He repeated points. He had words that lasted

SUGGESTED ACTIVITIES

1. Write a meta-story using the meta-story workbook earlier in the chapter.
2. Play "The Detective Game" to stress the importance of strong verbal communication (http://www.edteck.com/rigor/lessons/detective/Index.htm)
3. Play "Origins," a word game for teaching tolerance (http://www.tolerance.org/activity/word-origins)

The most important thing in communication is hearing what isn't said.
—Peter F. Drucker

6 Nonverbal Communication

OBJECTIVES

After completing this chapter you should be able to:

- Define nonverbal communication.
- Discuss the various elements that make nonverbal communication distinctly different from verbal communication.
- Explain the different characteristics of nonverbal communication.
- Discuss how the study of proxemics explains the four zones of spatial distance.
- Describe how touch is used in nonverbal communication, and the controversy of touch in education.
- Explain kinesics, and provide examples of body movements used in nonverbal communication.
- Identify the five basic emotions that are recognized cross-culturally.
- Describe gestures that can be grouped into perceptual categories.
- Explain the function of eye contact in nonverbal communication.
- Describe the role of paralanguage and silence in nonverbal communication.
- Discuss helpful hints given to teachers for reading nonverbal communication.

KEY TERMS

Adaptors
Affect displays
Coding
Culture
Emblems
Haptics
Illustrators
Intimate space
Kinesics
Multichanneled
Nonverbal communication
Oculesics
Origin
Personal space
Proxemics
Public space
Regulators
Social space
Territory
Usage
Vocal cues and paralanguage

Nonverbal communication Communication that does not involve spoken or written content

Nonverbal communication is a very powerful element of human relations. In fact, many researchers believe that nonverbal communication often provides more information in the communication process than the spoken word (verbal communication). Nonverbal communication is defined as communication that does not involve spoken or written content; rather, it is the combination of facial expression, eye contact, body movement and posture, paralanguage, use of personal space, and other elements that give insight to that which is being communicated. It is important to understand that these elements of nonverbal communication do not occur in isolation. On the contrary, it is the multiple and diverse combinations of these cues that give us the understanding, and often misperceptions, behind human interaction.

What does the following mean? "*It's impossible not to communicate.*" You may not be talking to someone in the elevator, snuggled up against the corner, looking at your feet, but you are still communicating to others your desire not to engage in dialogue. Teachers soon recognize that everyone in their class is communicating simultaneously. Some are delighted to be in the class and ready to go, others are "not so delighted" and are struggling to stay on task; nevertheless, everyone is communicating.

VERBAL VERSUS NONVERBAL COMMUNICATION

While making comparisons of nonverbal versus verbal communication, we quickly discover that inherent in nonverbal communication lies great complexity. The following information is an attempt to identify these complexities.

- ***Ambiguity.*** Nonverbal communication presents greater ambiguity than the spoken word. Even if we are very familiar with a person, including attitudes and beliefs, predicting and understanding the meaning behind behaviors can be difficult. Even the person displaying the nonverbal communication may not fully understand the behavior. In fact, much nonverbal communication is unconscious. Sometimes people will send a message through nonverbal communication without intending to. The following is an amusing story intended to make this point:

  Birdwhistell (1952, Ch.8) illustrated this unintentional nonverbal communication by telling a story of the visit of one of his brother's girlfriends to his family home. First, the fact that a boy brings a girl home to visit his parents suggests that the relationship between the boy and the girl is one that may well blossom into marriage. That is, "bringing-home" behavior is a gesture that communicates something. Birdwhistell was not at home at the time of the visit, so he wrote his mother asking her how the visit had gone. His mother answered with a letter that was devoted to various other topics but which contained the following description of the visit: "You ask about the visit of Miss Withers. I think some people would think she is very pretty. . . . She spent the entire time blowing smoke in your father's face and flushing the toilet." In a family in which smoking is not an approved activity for women and water is viewed as a precious commodity not to be wasted, Miss Withers had communicated nonverbally and unintentionally, through her behavior, that she was not acceptable as a daughter-in-law to the Birdwhistell family.

In contrast to nonverbal communication, literal words can be deciphered without ambiguity, and the person speaking the words is fully conscious of the message he or she is sending. However, it is when the receiver interprets the verbal message in conjunction with the nonverbal signals that ambiguity can arise. Educators have to read the cues of many different individuals (students, colleagues, administrators, parents, etc.) and decipher their relevance to the educational setting. It is important to be careful in the interpretation of these cues, however, because of the ambiguity of nonverbal messages. The meaning during the communication process does not lie within the words being spoken but rather in the person who speaks those words (as discussed in chapter 5), and the manner in which the words are spoken give meaning to the communication process.

- ***Continuity.*** Unlike verbal communication, nonverbal communication is a continuous process, often with no clear beginning and ending. Some elements of nonverbal communication have a definite start and end in time (e.g., thumbs up, smile, and clapping). However, even these elements must be considered in the context of a nonstop (continuous) presentation of messages. Students and teachers are always communicating to each other nonverbally. In fact, it is impossible to *not* communicate. For example, a smile could be genuine or sarcastic when put into the context of other nonverbal messages (e.g., body posture). Taking a snapshot of nonverbal communication may or may not inform the receiver of the meaning behind a person's behavior.
- ***Multichanneled.*** Nonverbal communication, like the multichanneled TV, presents a variety of sources for information. Just as one chooses which channels to view on TV, one must also make decisions and choices about what information he or he wants to attend to when reading a variety of (perhaps conflicting) nonverbal messages. Additionally, several potentially conflicting nonverbal messages are coupled with verbal communication, and the receiver must make perceptual decisions concerning what may be conflicting information. Interestingly,

Multichanneled
Because nonverbal messages are often coupled with verbal communication, you must decide which information you will attend to.

some research (Beebe et al., 2008) has suggested people give more attention to negative nonverbal messages (e.g., frowns, grimaces, lack of eye contact, etc.) than positive nonverbal messages when the two forms of nonverbal communication compete. Also, in some instances when nonverbal communication contradicts verbal, we may lack the ability to clearly decipher either message. However, the old adage, "actions speak louder than words" definitely holds some value!

Culture
A group of people with shared beliefs, values, symbols, and interpretations

- ***Culture.*** To be immersed in another culture (briefly defined as consisting of a group of people with shared beliefs, values, symbols, and interpretations), one would expect some differences in the language spoken and the communication process. The same is true for nonverbal communication. Often nonverbal communication cues are read very differently in different cultures. For example, the peace or victory sign (displayed by holding up your first two fingers, palm forward) is often used in the United States. However, change that gesture slightly (palm backward) and it becomes a strong insult in some cultures (Morris, 1994). Nevertheless, there is some universality in the expression and reading of facial expressions and emotion. For a more detailed discussion of this, refer to Beebe and colleagues (2008).

CHARACTERISTICS AND TYPES OF NONVERBAL COMMUNICATION

Usage
Conditions that exist at the time of the nonverbal communication

Notable researchers within the area of nonverbal communication, Paul Ekman and Wallace Friesen (1969), distinguish among three characteristics of nonverbal communication: *usage*, *origin*, and *coding*. The term **usage** refers to the conditions that exist at the time of the nonverbal behavior. For example, one must consider the external conditions (e.g., physical setting of the display), role relationship (e.g., teacher/student, teacher/parent, teacher/teacher, teacher/administrator, etc.), emotional tone (e.g., formal/informal, stressed/relaxed, friendly/hostile, etc.), and the type of information that is being communicated (e.g., informational or communicative).

Origin
Beginning location of the nonverbal communication (e.g., nervous system versus environment)

With regard to **origin**, some nonverbal communication is rooted in the nervous system, whereas other nonverbals are learned from and used in specific environments. For example, if a man hits his thumb with a hammer, the automatic, instinctual, and involuntary response is to grab the finger, twinge the face, and perhaps couple that with some not-so-pleasant words. However, when examining the learned nonverbal responses, an example found in the context of education is the raising of an arm when a child has something to say. Not all children know on the first day of school that they must raise their hands to talk, but they all learn quickly that this nonverbal communication means they have something to say and would like to be recognized to do so. In fact, the intensity of children's hand raising is an indication of how excited they are to speak.

Figure 6.1 In the school setting, children learn the nonverbal response of raising their arm when they have something to say.

Coding refers to the underlying meaning of a nonverbal action. There are two levels of meaning to which Ekman and Friesen refer: intrinsic and extrinsic. Intrinsically coded behaviors are what they signify. For example, two children "rough housing" and play punching each other are exhibiting a form of aggression. Although the action may be harmless, the behavior can be coded as a form of aggression. Extrinsically coded behaviors convey meaning of something else and may be coded arbitrarily or through iconic use. An example of arbitrary extrinsic nonverbal communication would be giving someone a "thumbs up" sign. The sign itself has no meaning; rather, its meaning is learned. Iconic nonverbal communication conveys its meaning quite clearly. For example, if a mother pinches her thumb and first finger and then pulls those two fingers across her lips, she is telling someone to "zip your lips." The gesture can be taken quite literally.

Coding
The underlying meaning of a nonverbal action

TYPES OF NONVERBAL COMMUNICATION/BEHAVIOR

Proxemics is the study of distance and arrangement of personal space used in nonverbal communication. The amount of space between communicators can be defined in four categories called *zones of spatial distance* (Hall, 1959, 1966). Beginning with the most distant space, **public space** refers to 12 feet and beyond. Typically this type of space is used for classroom lectures and observation of behavior (e.g., recess observation). With distance at great lengths, communication is typically unidirectional, meaning, one person communicates, and the other(s) watches/listens. The next distance, **social space**, is between 4 and 12 feet. This type of distance is used for impersonal communications. Typically this distance would be seen in situations of more formal social gatherings. Interestingly, this space is often accompanied by a more formal and louder speech tone, with an increase in eye contact.

Proxemics
The study of distance and arrangement of personal space used in nonverbal communication

Public space
Twelve feet and beyond; distant space often used for observation of behavior

Social space
Between 4 and 12 feet; space used for impersonal conversations

Personal space
One and a half to four feet; distance reserved for conversations between close friends and acquaintances

Intimate space
Zero to one and a half feet, space held for our most personal relationships

Personal space refers to 1½ to 4 feet of distance. This space is typical of conversations between close friends and acquaintances. With this amount of distance, touch is a possibility. We are quite aware of a person in our personal space. Many times, children, once they get to know a teacher better, feel very comfortable entering the personal space zone or the next level, **intimate space**, 0 to 1½ feet. This is reserved for our most personal relationships. It is important for the teacher to know students' spatial comfort levels. One student may desire a very close (and perhaps inappropriate) contact with the teacher, whereas another student may be very uncomfortable with entering personal space. Thus, it is important for the teacher to watch for other nonverbal cues expressed by the student as to his or her level (and the teacher's for that matter) of comfort with regard to personal space. The proximity of distance we are willing to allow others is often dependent on how well we know them and how much power or status they have over us. The specific spatial distance that one chooses depends on several variables:

- How well the person is liked.
- The status of the person interacting. Specifically, individuals with higher status are typically given more space than individuals with lower status. For example, principals are given their own office, whereas teachers often share a common workspace.
- The size of the person. Larger people are given more space than smaller people.
- The gender of the person. Women allow for closer space proximity than men.
- The size of the space for the interaction. People tend to stand in closer proximity in a large room than in a small room.

Territory
The space we claim as our own

A related topic to proximity in nonverbal communication is **territory**. Claiming of territory is generally thought of as an animalistic behavior. However, humans also proclaim ownership of space with territorial markers. For example, when students are in a library type setting, they may use things like books, notebooks, or pencils to signify their claiming of that spot. Similarly, many teachers before the school year starts decorate their classroom in a manner to make it their own. What might be more effective is to allow the students, in some way, to help in the designating of the classroom as their territory. This might include something as small as hanging pictures they have drawn, or as large as letting them set themes for the classroom décor and assist in the actual decoration.

Haptics
The study of how touch is used in nonverbal communication

Haptics is the study of how touch is used in nonverbal communication. Why do we respond so quickly with a verbal apology when we accidentally bump into someone? The answer likely has something to do with inadvertently invading a person's intimate space. In fact, touch is often used to express intimacy. Think of the last time you purposely touched someone. If you were to brush up against someone accidentally, verbal communication of "I'm sorry" or "excuse me" quickly remedies the possible misperception of an expression of intimacy. Our level of comfort with using and receiving touch in nonverbal communication is influenced by many factors, including our own family's use of touch. Why would we use touch in nonverbal communication? According to Henley (1977), reasons include but are not limited to the following:

- Getting someone's attention.
- Asking someone to do something for us.
- Sharing rather than receiving information.
- Persuading another to do something.
- Discussing intimate topics.
- Being excited to share information.
- Listening to someone share troubling information.

Additionally, Hertenstein, Keltner, App, Bulleit, and Jaskolka (2006) note that touch is a powerful communicator of emotion. These authors suggest that touch can communicate both positive (warmth) and negative (discomfort) emotion, and intensify emotional related communication. Through a series of studies, Hertenstein et al. (2006) were able to demonstrate that participants in the United States and Spain could identify touch communication of six primary emotions at better than chance level: anger, fear, disgust, love, gratitude, and sympathy.

THE TOUCHING CONTROVERSY

The use of touch in the educational setting creates much controversy. Touch is vital to human development and well-being. In fact, a recent study found a direct link between infants' not receiving adequate touch and lack of brain development (Honig, 2005). There also has been correlational research (remember, correlation does not mean causation) linking the lack of touching in childhood with violence in adulthood. However, two very important factors to consider with regard to touching another in the educational setting are (1) level of trust between the two individuals and (2) whether the touch is perceived as sexual in nature by the other person. Many researchers and administrators in the educational setting caution teachers to be keenly aware of their motives and the ethical implications of touching their students.

REASONS TO NOT TOUCH STUDENTS

Although evidence exists that supports the need for children to be touched, the teacher must consider the following.

1. There are some students who do not wish to be touched.
2. There are some parents who do not want the teacher touching their kids. Teachers often assume that parents want their children to be hugged by their teachers, which is not always the case.
3. Teachers must concern themselves with an unfortunate truth: An allegation of inappropriate touching, even if later found to have no merit and be dismissed, can have a *lasting perception* with colleagues and parents.

The Power of Touch

Honig's (2005) research suggests that infants who are not touched can suffer detrimental effects. Interestingly, this finding is not exactly new. Researchers Skeels and Dye (1939) investigated the reversibility of the effects of nonstimulating orphanage environments on children. The purpose of the study was to offer 13 children (average IQ = 64) living in an orphanage the care, nurturance, and stimulation of a child raised by loving, attentive, natural parents. This was done through the use of trained adolescent care providers. Of the 13 children in the experimental group, all but 2 were considered by state law to be unsuitable for adoption at the onset of the study because of mental retardation. For the control group (children receiving no care, nurturance, and stimulation), only 2 of the 12 children were classified as having mental retardation and, thus, unsuitable for adoption.

In 1965, more than 25 years after the original study had begun, Skeels (1966) again located the participants. His follow-up study reported that 11 of the 13 children in the experimental group had married, and all but one of the marriages were still intact. The adults' mean level of education was 12th grade; four had completed one or more years of college. All were either self-supporting or functioning as homemakers. Their occupations ranged from professional work and business to domestic service (the two who had not been adopted), and their income was consistent with state and national averages.

Conversely, the control participants showed an initial drop in mean IQ of 26 points, and as a result were generally not eligible for adoption. When Skeels located them in 1965, he found that these 11 subjects (one had died) had a mean educational level of third to fourth grade. Four of the participants in the control group were institutionalized, unemployed, and costing the state approximately $200 per month each. Findings such as these led Skeels (1966) to conclude that practitioners and policymakers now had evidence in favor of the importance of early intervention and its ability to overcome the limitations of environmental deprivation.

From this glimpse into Honig's recent research and that of Skeels and Dye, it is evident the predicament teachers are in with regard to touching their students. Touching is vital to the development and well-being of children. Touching confirms that they are valued and loved. Most people not only welcome, but need, the strong bond touch communicates. Touching conveys affection and trust. Although there are clear benefits to children being touched, it is often inappropriate for teachers to fulfill that need.

4. There are a multitude of other ways to show students that a teacher cares about them without touching them. For example, teachers can show they care about their students by noticing if they are properly dressed for the current weather, verifying they have lunch money, noticing if they acquire bruises more often than your typical students or show other signs of abuse, having an intentional interest in their educational progress, being concerned with their

health issues, giving them full attention, and always encouraging every student. When students who are dressed appropriately for the weather see the teacher being concerned about a student who is not, the message to the class is that the teacher cares about all students. When students who are not struggling with the curriculum see the teacher working with a student who is struggling, the message to the class is that the teacher cares about everyone's educational progress. When the teacher encourages a discouraged student, other students see that the teacher cares about everyone being successful. Noticing and showing concern that a student is consistently waiting long hours for someone to pick him or her up after school sends the message that the teacher cares about all students.

5. It's the parent's role to touch their children. Often teachers remind the authors that there are those parents who do not offer this vital support that touching provides. We again remind teachers, there is a multitude of ways to show kids you care about them without the need for touching.

The amount of touching we need from others, we tolerate from others, receive from others, and initiate to others depends on many factors. The amount you receive in your family is one important factor. If you are a touchy person, your family is most likely touchy, also. It is important for the teacher to remember that not all families show affection by touching.

KINESICS

Kinesics is the study of bodily movements, including nonverbal communication such as gestures and facial expressions. Examples of body movements study include **illustrators, emblems, affect displays, regulators,** and **adaptors.**

Kinesics
The study of bodily movements, including nonverbal communication

Illustrators. Illustrators typically are used to accent or complement the verbal message; however, it is important to understand that illustrators can also contradict verbal communication. For example, teachers pointing to the board as they are lecturing is meant to draw students' attention to the point. A teacher reading a book to students will often close the book while saying "the end" to emphasize the fact that the story is done.

Illustrators
Typically used to accent or complement the verbal message

Emblems. Emblems are nonverbal cues that have specific meaning in a given culture. Often emblems are used in place of verbal communication (a word or phrase). Examples of emblems include placing the pointer finger to the closed mouth or a mouth forming the "shhhh" sound. This situation clearly communicates the phrase "be quiet." Raising an open palm can be read as "stop." Sticking a pointer finger out and then brushing the other pointer finger across often symbolizes "Shame, shame" or "no, no." Emblems are culturally bound, and they may not mean the same thing in all cultures.

Emblems
Nonverbal cues that have specific meaning in a given culture

Affect displays
Nonverbal gestures that communicate emotional content

Affect Displays. Affect displays are nonverbal gestures (including facial expression, movement, and posture) that communicate emotional content. Nonverbal displays are the main mode of communication of affect. Interestingly, affect displays are considered both instinctual and learned in that one may have an initial emotional reaction (without much thought) but also may not show that reaction nonverbally because of the learned appropriate display rules. For example, boys and men in many cultures are given the message (either directly or indirectly) that it is not okay to show their sadness with open expression of tears; however, this display rule obviously does not mean boys and men cannot be and feel sad. Cross-cultural research by Ekman and Friesen (1969) indicates there are basic emotions (i.e., happiness, anger, surprise, fear, disgust, and sadness) that are displayed and read similarly across cultures. According to Ekman and Freisen, the following descriptions provide insight into facial expression of emotions:

- *Happiness* is often demonstrated by a smile (mouth open or closed), cheeks raised, and wrinkling around the lower eyelids.
- *Anger* involves a tensing of the lower eyelid, tight lips or open mouth, a furrowed brow, and glaring eyes.
- *Surprise* consists of very wide and open eyes, raised and wrinkled brow, and the mouth in an open position.
- *Fear* includes an open mouth, tension of the skin under the eyes, and wrinkling of the forehead.
- *Disgust* involves a curled upper lip, wrinkling of the nose, raised cheeks, lowered brow and upper lid.
- *Sadness* can be shown when a person's lip trembles, the corners of the mouth turn in a downward direction, and corners of the upper eyelid are raised.

Although there are a very small number of "basic emotions," some researchers have estimated that humans are capable of over 250,000 different facial expressions (Beebe et al., 2008).

Regulators
Nonverbals used to regulate the flow of conversation between individuals

Regulators. Regulators are used to regulate the flow of conversation between individuals. Examples of common regulators include head nods, body posture change, and eye contact. In your classroom, you may see other examples of regulators in your students. Students who are eager to respond to a question or add additional input initiate eye contact, raise eyebrows, open their mouths ready to respond, raise a finger or hand, and lean forward. On the contrary, students who want to avoid being called on avoid eye contact, close their mouths, lean back in their seats or away from the teacher, and cross their arms.

Adaptors
Self-manipulators that are ways of satisfying bodily needs or are habit formed

Adaptors. Adaptors are also known as self-manipulations. Adaptors appear in childhood as ways to satisfy bodily needs (e.g., scratch an itchy spot, rubbing the eyes). In adulthood, adaptors not only satisfy bodily needs but also become habitual and fall into one of three categories: *self-adaptors,* which continue from childhood (e.g., scratching), *alter* *adaptors* (e.g., arm-folding as a means to protect yourself from attack or intimacy), and *object adaptors* (e.g., manipulating objects with a purpose, smoking, tapping a pencil).

PERCEPTUAL CATEGORIES

Research by Lester Sielski (1979) reports that grouping gestures into perceptual categories helps one to better understand the nonverbal meaning behind the communication. Although Sielski offers close to 20 categories of gestures, we will focus on only the ones most relevant to the educator. It is important to note that often children are not as capable or as refined in their masking (i.e., attempting to hide feelings in their gestures), thus some of these examples may be more obvious in a child than in a teenager or an adult.

- *Openness*. Men and women who display open gestures appear more comfortable, and, in fact, may adjust their clothing or demeanor to reflect so. For example, individuals who are open keep their hands down to their sides (rather than crossed in front of them).
- *Defensiveness*. Children (and adults) often display defensiveness by crossing their arms in response to unwelcomed direction or when they are trying to make a point. Crossing of the arms also may indicate a sign of desired isolation or self-protection.
- *Evaluation*. This type of gesture is often seen when a person is giving thought to an idea or situation. Individuals using this type of gesture often put a hand to the chin or cheek and cock the head slightly to one side.
- *Rejection*. Sielski notes the most obvious form of rejection is when a person crosses his or her arms and moves away from the person or situation. A less obvious form of potential rejection is when a person (sitting) crosses his or her legs and leans backward. Additionally, the person may peer over his or her glasses or squint as a sign of careful consideration or skepticism.
- *Doubt, suspicion, puzzlement*. Gestures indicating a person's doubt or suspicion often involve rubbing or touching the face (including something like a scratch of the head or rubbing the nose). A person sitting who exhibits these gestures may squirm or physically withdrawal. It is vital for teachers to be perceptive of these types of gestures in the classroom as a means to make sure their students stay focused and grasp the information being presented.
- *Readiness*. People ready for a situation or event to occur will often place their hands on their hips and stand with their feet apart. Imagine a child standing on the sideline waiting to get back in the game.
- *Reassurance*. Children who need reassurance may exhibit regressive behaviors (e.g., sucking their thumbs, biting their nails) as a sign of their lacking confidence.
- *Cooperation*. When people are ready to cooperate, they may sit more attentively at the edge of their chairs with their feet on the tiptoes, and tilt their heads slightly.

- *Mouth covering*. When people exhibit this gesture, they may be acknowledging others telling them to be quiet or showing embarrassment for something they have done or said. A student just told to be quiet by a teacher in front of his or her peers may cover his or her mouth out of recognition of the direction to be quiet, but also out of embarrassment for being told to do so.
- *Confidence*. People exhibiting confidence tend to have more frequent and longer eye contact than those unsure of themselves. A confident student will often stand more erectly.
- *Nervousness*. Nervousness often is exhibited by fidgety behavior. A student who must stand and speak in front of the class may be very fidgety at his or her desk prior to speaking.
- *Boredom*. Boredom is often exhibited by doodling, finger drumming, or foot tapping. The teacher should be aware when students in the classroom have lost interest by their display of boredom gestures.

OCULESICS

Oculesics
The study of eye contact and use of gazes to communicate

Oculesics is the study of eye contact and use of gazes to communicate. D. G. Leathers (1986) in his book *Successful Nonverbal Communication: Principles and Application* notes that eye contact serves six essential functions:

1. To transmit a degree of attentiveness, interest, and arousal.
2. To persuade or attempt to change attitude.
3. To regulate interactions.
4. To communicate emotion.
5. To define power and status in relationships.
6. To regulate impression management.

It is important to remember that eye contact usage differs among cultures. In the United States, eye contact is desired. However, in many Asian cultures, direct eye contact can be seen as an insult to authority.

VOCAL CUES AND PARALANGUAGE

Vocal cues and paralanguage
Use of pitch, tone, tempo or rate of speech, and volume to give shades of meaning to our spoken word.

Vocal cues and paralanguage give a greater understanding of the spoken word (verbal communication) by focusing on not what people say but how they say it. Through examination of pitch, tone, tempo or rate of speech, and volume we can better understand the different shades of meaning behind a person's verbal communication. Research has offered evidence that some emotions are easier to detect through vocal cues (Laukka, Juslin, & Bresin, 2005). For example, sadness and anger are more clearly communicated through tone of voice (Pittam & Scherer, 1993) than shame and love. The manner in which we speak also provides insight into our level of knowledge and confidence about a subject manner. When a person stumbles on words, frequently uses "um" or "uh," or consistently mispronounces words, it quickly becomes clear to the receiver that the person either knows very little about what is presented, is very uncomfortable with the material or the presentation, or does not believe strongly in the information being presented. Obviously, if a person falls into any of these categories and uses these vocal cues, the person is less likely to effectively persuade someone rather than the person who speaks clearly and fluently, at an appropriate pace.

Educators who work with children may also note that it is common for young children not to be able to "get out" what they are trying to say. Different from stuttering, young children who are excited often repeat the beginning of their sentences and may use more frequent "ums" than older children may. This stumbling is very natural and should decrease with age; however, it is important to understand that the experience can be frustrating for both the student and the teacher. The best advice for the teacher is to be patient with those children and give them an appropriate time to finish what they are saying. If teachers too quickly correct or finish students' sentences, they may instill in the students a sense of inferiority or inadequacy.

Another powerful part of vocal cues and paralanguage is the use of silence. "*Silence* speaks volumes." This statement clearly says it all. There are many reasons why a person remains silent. Alerby and Elidottir (2003) explored the power of silence as it relates to teaching and learning. These authors first note there are *multiple meanings* of silence:

- Exploration of the inner self.
- As a means to "work things out" in our head.
- Making sense of thoughts, emotions, actions, and the context in which these are embedded. (p. 42)

Alerby and Elidottir (2003) also note that silence can be something good and bad that is used for various reasons, including:

- Timidity or caution.
- Fear to expose one's self by speaking openly.
- Self-protection.
- As a means to shut oneself off from the outside world.
- As a way to show understanding.
- As a wordless agreement, when people understand each others' thoughts and no words are necessary (also called mutual silence). (p. 43)

Lastly, in the context of education silence must be used in a reflective manner. For example, Alerby and Elidottir (2003) mention that in the classroom setting a teacher may at first struggle to "get the pupils to be silent" and then in the next moment use a topic that requests or requires the breaking of that silence. What happens when one of the students remains silent? How does the teacher react? How do the other students react? Does silence reflect an unwillingness to participate, a lack of understanding, a lack of attention, or the inability or courage to speak his or her voice? Although difficult, it is the teacher's responsibility to decipher the meaning behind the student's silence. Also within the classroom, teachers must use silence to allow students time to process information, thus giving students time to take information in, think it over, and develop a response. Even though this silent time may be uncomfortable for the teacher and the students, with practice, the allotted time will become part of the teacher's classroom style. If the teacher quickly interrupts that silence with new information or directions, the teacher may leave some students behind and not allow them to resolve their thinking on the previous matter.

READING NONVERBAL CUES: SOME HELPFUL HINTS

Obviously, nonverbal communication is a powerful and complex process. How, then, can teachers better their abilities to read such cues? The following are a few helpful hints:

- *Analyze the Context*. Nonverbal communication does not happen in a vacuum. Thus, it is important to not only read the nonverbal messages that are being sent but also to examine the context in which those cues are being sent. For example, an adolescent in the middle of class is sitting with his arms crossed and his head down. The teacher could read these signals in several different ways: he's sleeping, he's ignoring the teacher, he's upset, or he's possibly daydreaming. However, when the teacher puts these nonverbal cues in context, it is entirely possible that the room he is sitting in is cold, his arms are crossed to keep himself warm, and his head is down blowing warm air into his shirt. Is context important? Absolutely!
- *Nonverbal Grouping*. Just as it is important to read the context when interpreting nonverbal communication, it is also important to look for a series of responses or multiple cues to truly understand what a person is communicating through his or her nonverbal actions. For example, it is important to examine body posture, eye contact, personal distance, silence, and so on all together to really understand a person's nonverbal message.
- *Nonverbal History*. Frankly put, the more familiar the teacher is with a student, the better the teacher is at reading the student's nonverbal messages. For example, a student walks into the classroom, throws her book bag down and makes a very angry facial expression. If the teacher knows this student well, the teacher is in a better position to determine whether this behavior is unusual or consistent with her attitude and pattern of behavior. If the teacher knows her well and the behavior is unusual, the teacher may respond much more quickly than if the teacher is unfamiliar with the student.
- *Collaborative Perception*. If the teacher is unsure of a student's nonverbal messages, it never hurts to check his perceptions with others who are also witnesses to the nonverbal communication. Another important way to check his perception is to ask for

confirmation of the message by the student sending the message. In doing so, the teacher has a more direct verification of his reading of that student's nonverbal message.

Throughout this chapter various elements, types, and purposes of nonverbal communication have been discussed. The following activities are designed for preservice teachers and practitioners taking courses in human relations as well as and, when appropriate, for future students of future teachers and current practitioners.

NONVERBAL ACTIVITIES

Label Reading. This activity gives the student practice at portraying and reading nonverbal communication. First, the instructor gives every student a Post-it note. Next, each student writes on the Post-it note a label for a type of person (e.g., sword-swallowing nun, garbage collector wearing a business suit, ex-boxer wearing a tutu, red-headed sumo wrestler, astronaut, etc.). Place the Post-it notes on the backs of the students without the students knowing what is on the label. The students then walk around the room viewing the labels on their classmates' backs. Students are instructed to give only *nonverbal clues* regarding the labels on their peers' backs. After a period of time, the instructor asks if anyone knows what is on their label. After several attempts, have the students remove the labels from their backs and discuss the effectiveness of the nonverbal communication given to them by the other students.

Signals. Have four students stand in a circle and discuss their summer break or the current semester. The instructor is to make sure each student participates in the discussion. The rest of the class is to note the nonverbal signals given when one of the students interjects a comment. After a period of time in which each student has offered comments, the instructor will have all four students turn their backs to each other and continue the conversation. The rest of the class should note the lack of obvious nonverbal cues for the interjecting of comments. Often what occurs is uncomfortable silence; then two students will start talking at the same time, both stop, and then, again, an uncomfortable silence, until someone else risks conversation. It becomes obvious to everyone how much we depend on nonverbal cues during the communication process.

Eye Movement. Bandler and Grinder (1979), in their fascinating book on neuron-linguistic programming, discuss eye movements. They report that most people look up and to their left when remembering images and up and to their right for constructing visual images. One could work off the assumption that a lie is a constructed visual image. In class, one of your authors asks for three volunteers and then asks them to leave the room. Instructions are given to the remaining students to draw an arrow showing which direction each of the volunteers' eyes move when the volunteer is asked a question. The class is to draw these arrows, signifying direction of eye movements, *without the volunteers being aware what is being done.*

The instructor brings the volunteers back into the classroom one at a time. The instructor takes a seat in the middle of the students (so the class can best observe the eye movements of the volunteer). The instructor asks two sets of questions. The instructor asks the volunteer not to answer any of the questions verbally but to acknowledge nonverbally (usually a nod) once an answer is formulated. The first set consists of six questions requiring the volunteer to remember an experience. For example, is the red or green light at the top of a traffic light? Or, what color are your mother's eyes? Or, what is the letter in the alphabet just before R? Students, hopefully, now have an idea which way the volunteer's eyes move when they remember an experience. The second set also consists of six questions requiring the volunteer to construct an image. For example, can you hear your mother's voice saying "Stay out of trouble"? Or, do you know what you would look like with flaming red hair? Or, can you picture an elephant with very tiny ears? After the class has had the opportunity to draw arrows diagramming eye movements to questions designed to remember an experience or construct an image, the instructor asks the volunteer to verbally answer the following question and explains that the volunteer can tell the truth (remember an experience) or choose to lie (construct an image). The instructor asks the volunteer what he or she did on a family member's birthday last year. This experience, a total of 13 questions, is repeated for each of the three volunteers. Afterward, a class discussion is directed at the accuracy of our initial assumption. Is this a tool a teacher might use? What are the consequences of this tool?

Name: ______________________________

Eye Movement Exercise

The odd numbered questions (1, 3, 5, 7, 9, and 11) are designed for the volunteer to draw upon things he or she remembers (R). The volunteer is to offer only nonverbal recognition. Students are to notice and draw the direction of the eyes (*without the volunteer being aware*) when the volunteer is remembering images. The even numbered questions (2, 4, 6, 8, and 10) are designed to draw upon things the volunteer must construct (C). Again, the volunteer is instructed to offer only nonverbal recognition. Students should be aware that when people lie, they are constructing images versus remembering images. The students are to draw the direction of eye movements when the volunteer is constructing images. For the last question (12), the volunteer will be given an opportunity to tell the truth (requiring the act of remembering) or lie (requiring the act of constructing).

Answer NONVERBALLY (nod when you have an answer).

1. In the United States, there is an interesting phenomenon called traffic lights. Is the red or green at the top of the traffic light? (R) _____
2. Picture an elephant with very tiny ears in your dorm room. (C)_____
3. On your way to this class, how many buildings on campus did you pass? (R) _____
4. Picture yourself with flaming red hair. (C) _____
5. What color are your mother's eyes? (R) _____
6. Picture yourself on a sandy beach. (C) _____
7. How many different colored carpets are in your parent's home? (R) _____
8. See yourself wing-walking on an old airplane. (C) _____
9. What is your favorite piece of music? (R) _____
10. See yourself with a snake wrapped around your neck. (C) _____
11. What is the letter in the alphabet just before "R?" (R) _____

Last Question: Answer VERBALLY with an option to LIE.

12. (*Think about the question / decided to tell the truth or lie / verbally respond*) Describe what was your most favorite Christmas present ever.

Did the volunteers "remember" or "construct" their last answers?

Courtesy of Brenda Lussier.

Statues. In this activity, a team of students designs a scenario using nonverbal messages. A possible scenario could be a student being ostracized by his/her peers. One team member acts as a sculptor and puts the other team members in poses as if they were statues showing one student being ostracized. The remaining class must decipher the message being sent by the group of statues.

OTHER ITEMS FOR DISCUSSION

- Freud believed that women who played with their wedding rings were having an affair.
- In the Arabian culture, intermediaries arranging a marriage will sometimes ask to smell the prospective bride, rejecting her if she does not smell nice.
- One researcher reported that he worked with a psychiatrist who was able to smell anger in a patient at a distance of more than 6 feet.
- What annual event, with an audience of millions, depends on participants lying about their feelings? (Miss America Pageant; runner-ups act like they are delighted.)
- What is the nonverbal message when students wear blue hair, tattoos, nose rings, tongue rings, and underwear showing? Teachers must remember that every generation attempts to separate themselves from the previous generation. When students do "outrageous" things, ask yourself, are they just trying to find their own generational identity? Most often there is no need to overreact. Remember, *differences don't separate us; it's our reaction to differences that separate us.*

SUMMARY

The nonverbal communication process is complex. The multitude of variables, working in conjunction with each other (e.g., facial expressions, eye contact, body movements, posture, personal space, etc.) offers evidence that these variables do not work in isolation. It is not enough for the teacher to focus and act on one nonverbal behavior; the teacher must go in search for additional signs and cues to confirm his or her suspicion regarding the meaning of any particular behavior.

To illuminate the complexity of nonverbal behaviors, the ambiguity of this process which makes the predicting and understanding of the meaning that much more difficult was examined. It was also noted that nonverbals are continuous, and in this continued flow of information, the sender may be giving off conflicting messages. For example, one minute the student is concentrating on the lesson, the next minute he or she is concerned with the upcoming weekend, and the next minute the student is back focusing on the lesson, offering conflicting messages in a short amount of time. It is impossible not to communicate. People are always sending messages to others whether they intend to or not.

This is something teachers and students alike should be concerned with and focus on. Teachers must take into consideration the culture in which they are trying to interpret nonverbal communication. Different cultures read nonverbals very differently.

The chapter then continued with the characteristics of nonverbal communication. Ekman and Friesen (1969) lead this discussion by distinguishing between the *usage*, referring to the conditions that exist at the time; the *origin*, whether the nonverbals are rooted in the nervous system or learned; and *coding*, the underlying meaning which is offered in two levels (intrinsic and extrinsic). Next, the discussion of proxemics (study of distance of personal space) was examined by distinguishing the different zones of spatial distance (public, social, personal, and intimate). Related to these zones is territory, the space we claim as our own.

The examination of haptics (the study of touch in nonverbal communication) leads to the discussion of the "*touching controversy*." It is a vital need for students to be touched. Touching is seen as being instrumental in human development and well-being; however, teachers should not be touching students for a variety of reasons. (1) Some students don't want to be touched, (2) some parents do not want teachers to touch their children, (3) the concern for allegations of inappropriate touching (even when dismissed, the allegations are long lasting), and finally, (4) there are a multitude of ways to show students teachers care about them without the need for touching. Ultimately, it is the parents' role to touch their children, not the teachers. There is a multitude of ways for teachers to show students they care for them without touching them.

The touching controversy was followed by the examination of kinesics (the study of body movements). The field of kinesics includes illustrators (to accent or complement a verbal message), emblems (cues that have a specific meaning in a given culture), affect displays (gestures that communicate emotions). Ekman and Friesen offered descriptions of basic emotions that provide insight into facial expressions (happiness, anger, surprise, fear, etc.).

The next section was devoted to gestures, eye contact, and paralanguage. Sielski (1979) grouped gestures into over 20 categories in an attempt to better understand the meanings behind nonverbal communication. These categories included openness, defensiveness, evaluation, rejection, doubt, readiness, and more. Oculesics is the study of eye contact and the use of gazes to communicate. The work of Leathers (1986) noted six essential functions of eye contact: degree of attentiveness, interest, and arousal; attitude change and persuasion; regulating interactions; communication of emotions; defining power and status; and to regulate impression management. The next section discussed paralanguage, the use of pitch, tone, rate of speech and volume to offer insight into the meaning of our spoken word. A powerful part of paralanguage is the use of silence and its multiple meanings, including the exploration of the inner self, as a means to work things out in our head, and allowing time to make sense of thoughts, emotions, and actions, and the content in which these are embedded.

CASE 6.A

Jonathan lined up at the back of the line behind his classmates as they got ready to come in from afternoon recess. The teacher on recess duty, Mr. Parks, looked at Jonathan; his head was down, his shoulders were slouched and he looked as though he were ready to cry. He knew something was wrong with the boy, who was generally joking with him as he waited to go in from recess. "You okay, bud?" Mr. Parks gently probed. "Yea, I'm fine," Jonathan said with a sigh. Mr. Parks knew Jonathan was less than fine. He now pondered how he should approach Jonathan.

QUESTIONS

1. What should Jonathan's body language tell Mr. Parks?

2. Why would Jonathan tell Mr. Parks that he was fine when clearly he wasn't?

3. How should Mr. Parks address Jonathan, knowing that Jonathan does not want to talk about his problems?

CASE 6.B

Principal Michaels called for a Monday faculty meeting before school started. Although this wasn't completely unusual, the teachers all knew something was not right when she walked into the room and they saw her. Her eyes were red and swollen, her appearance was not as "put together" as she normally was, and she did not meet their eyes for a few minutes before she started speaking.

QUESTIONS

1. What can the faculty assume about Ms. Michaels from her nonverbal communication?

2. In this instance, how can interpreting nonverbal communication be both helpful and detrimental?

3. What impact can Ms. Michael's nonverbal communication have on the faculty before and as she speaks to her staff?

If we manage conflict constructively, we harness its energy for creativity and development.
–Kenneth Kaye

7

Conflict Management

OBJECTIVES

After completing this chapter you should be able to:

- Describe how conflict can be an opportunity rather than an obstacle in a relationship.
- Identify differences between individualistic versus collectivist cultures.
- Describe different types of conflict and provide examples of each.
- Discuss techniques for managing conflict.
- Explain Saul Alinsky's rules of power to combat social injustice.
- Describe the balcony view as a conflict resolution technique.
- Discuss how empathy training can decrease aggression and conflict in children.
- Explain how peer mediation can be used as a useful tool for conflict resolution.
- Describe the steps used in a collaborative style approach to conflict resolution.
- Discuss the advice Carl Rogers gives for acceptance of others for who they are in the context of disciplining children.

KEY TERMS

Balcony view
Brainstorming
Collaborative style
Collectivist
Conflict
Empathy training
Ethnocentrism
Individualistic
Lack of understanding
Moral dilemma
Peer mediation
Personal conflict
Rules of power

Conflict
Occurs because of different desires, needs, and goals

One important thing to remember about relationships is that *all relationships experience* **conflict**. Conflict, in itself, is not at issue; rather, how teachers choose to manage conflict is integral to maintaining a positive relationship with students, parents, and colleagues. This chapter will offer concepts and strategies that assist the future teacher in managing conflict, not in preventing it.

Conflict should not be seen as something to be avoided. Professional and personal growth can, and often does, come from conflict. Exposure to different perspectives found in conflicts can enlighten individuals and offer vehicles for establishing and maintaining productive relationships. After effectively managing conflicts, teachers can become closer and enjoy more satisfying relationships with their students and parents of students, while also acquiring more professional respect from colleagues and supervisors. Johnson and Johnson (1990) agree—they see conflict as an "opportunity not obstacle" that does the following:

- Enables a person to become aware of problems in a relationship.
- Serves as a catalyst for positive change.
- Energizes and motivates individuals to deal with immediate problems.
- Stimulates interest and curiosity.
- Relieves minor tensions.
- Causes decisions to be made more carefully.
- Promotes self-knowledge.
- Clears the air of unexpressed resentments.

Often conflicts occur in the classroom because students have different desires, needs, and goals than the teacher or other students. Imagine the classroom where all of the students have a desire to obtain a quality education, where everyone's needs are being met (e.g., to belong to a group, to be recognized as a unique individual, to feel physically and emotionally safe, etc.), and where everyone's ultimate goal is to obtain a diploma and further their education. Managing conflict in this type of classroom would be very different from a classroom where only a few students desired an education, felt their needs were being met, were recognized as individuals, felt physically and emotionally safe, or saw the value of an education. The reality is that each class the teacher encounters will have students with goals different from the teacher's and different means for accomplishing those goals. These student-driven desires, needs, and goals can be encouraging and supportive, or detrimental to the educational process. It is the teacher's responsibility to become familiar with each student's desires, needs, and goals. This is the first step in making conflict management manageable.

CULTURE: INDIVIDUALISTIC VERSUS COLLECTIVE

Each student's desires, needs, and goals are frequently culturally driven. Culture influences how we look and dress, what music we listen to, and even who our heroes are; basically, every aspect of our lives revolves around culture (as discussed in more detail in chapter 8). At the most fundamental level, culture can be conceptualized on a dichotomy: **individualistic** versus **collectivist**. According to Triandis (1994), individualistic cultures, like our own, focus on the achievements and accomplishments of the individuals within the society, creating winners and losers. However, collectivist cultures, such as those found in Asia, focus on the efforts and successes of the group. Conflict may escalate when both parties come from a culture that reinforces the win/lose attitude, whereas collectivist cultures attempt to find ways for everyone to get something from the conflict (referred to as the win/win approach).

Individualistic
Cultures focus on the achievements and accomplishments of the individuals

Collectivist
Cultures focus on the efforts and successes of the group

Often our Western culture (and our classrooms are a reflection of that culture) rewards only the winner, and we tend to forget the efforts of the person in second place. An individualistic stance (where one wins and one loses) does not emphasize the importance of teaching students how to listen to others' views or to develop solutions that are acceptable to all parties. Rather, an individualistic approach teaches students that our culture (along with our beliefs and attitudes) is superior to others (referred to as **ethnocentrism**), and people who think and act differently should be feared. Often, a person using the individualistic approach believes that "my way is the right way, and the only way." *Perhaps this is why conflict is inevitable.*

Ethnocentrism
The belief that your culture is superior to others

In an attempt to manage conflicts, teachers should consider the type of culture they wish to establish in their classrooms (e.g., individualistic, win/lose; or collectivist, win/win). They should emphasize the need for students to learn to understand and appreciate differences in cultures, along with the different beliefs and attitudes of the people the students will come in contact.

Figure 7.1 It is the teacher's responsibility to become familiar with each student's desires, needs, and goals.

TYPES OF CONFLICT

When attempting to manage conflict, it is best to first understand the type of conflict with which you are dealing. The three basic types of conflict are **lack of understanding, moral dilemmas,** and **personal conflicts.**

Lack of understanding
Conflict that results from a simple misunderstanding.

Moral dilemma
Conflict that arises when there are opposing points of view on a controversial issue that cannot be resolved

Personal conflict
Type of conflict whereby individuals involved begin to attack the character of each other.

LACK OF UNDERSTANDING

This type of conflict is easily corrected as long as the parties recognize there has been a simple misunderstanding. For example, a student misunderstood a professor's expectations for his class. Not meeting these expectations and the impending consequences caused severe conflict between the student and her professor. Neither the student nor professor recognized that the conflict was simply a misunderstanding, and this misunderstanding escalated into a much bigger personal conflict. Once the misunderstanding was clarified, the situation was quickly resolved. In managing this type of conflict, it is vital that the individuals involved are allowed an opportunity to express their understanding of the situation in a nonthreatening environment. Once each side of the conflict is presented, the simple misunderstanding likely will resolve itself. If not resolved, the teacher and student, at the very least, will have a clearer understanding of where each person is coming from and, thus, can attempt to address each person's needs, desires, and goals.

MORAL DILEMMA

A moral dilemma is an issue that cannot be resolved. Whether it be a stance on abortion, gay rights, the death penalty, assisted suicide, the American Civil Liberties Union, or the National Rifle Association, there will always be others who feel as strongly as you do on the other side of the issue.

The world is rarely a convenient place. Protestants, Catholics, Buddhists, Hindus, or Muslims, none of them, are likely to change their beliefs for anyone else's benefit. Nor is it likely that the Democrats, Republicans, or Independents are going to change their beliefs for another's peace of mind. When a moral dilemma becomes a conflict, often resolution consists of agreeing to disagree, specifically disagreeing in a manner that is respectful of the rights of others to believe as they wish.

PERSONAL CONFLICT

Personal conflicts are often more covert in nature and, thus, not as easily detected. However, for those individuals experiencing this type of conflict, the tension is easily felt. A simple misunderstanding or moral dilemma that could be easily managed by clarifying the issues or agreeing to disagree can, unfortunately, escalate to name calling and personal attacks. When a conflict becomes a personal attack, the issue that started the conflict becomes "*hidden*" and the personalities of those involved in the conflict become the central issue. Often in personal conflicts, people become defensive and stop listening to the other's view. It is very important that once teachers recognize they are witnessing or participating in a personal conflict, they need to take a step back and return to the issue that started the conflict (e.g., a simple misunderstanding or moral dilemma). For effective resolution in the classroom, the teacher must separate the people participating in the conflict from the issue of concern. The focus of the conflict must return to the task of solving the issue in question versus the continuation of personal attacks. It is imperative that in conflicts, teachers take responsibility for their own emotions, and encourage their students to do so as well. When teachers model control of their emotions (via the absence of personal attacks), students can begin to recognize their responsibilities and actions in escalating conflicts.

MANAGING THE CONFLICT

The management of the conflict begins when one party actively seeks to understand the perspective of the other. If neither party is willing to do this, then the conflict will potentially escalate without resolution. When seeking to understand, the teacher should offer students the *greatest compliment* that a teacher can give students: *the teacher's full attention.* The teacher should actively listen to the student's view, ask questions for clarity and to assure the student of the teacher's interest, and follow the student's logic, whether the teacher shares that view or not. Once students have communicated their position, the teacher is now in a position to convey his or her view, or an alternative view (e.g., another student's view) as needed, in an effort to get the complete picture of the issue at hand.

If we are successful in the first step of managing the conflict—by understanding each other's views—we are now in a position to take the next step and see the *conflict as a problem to be solved.* The following story is designed to illustrate how conflict can be resolved by seeing it as a problem to be solved:

> There is a well-known story of a man who had three sons. He stipulated in his will that the eldest son would inherit half of his camels, the middle son would get one third of the camels, and the youngest son would be the owner of one ninth of his camels. By the time the old man died, he owned 17 camels. The sons could not agree on how to divide the camels in accordance with their father's will. Villagers began taking sides and turning on each other. Months and months of bitter conflict went by. Finally, the three brothers sought the advice of a wise old woman in the village. She heard their complaints and observed their bitterness and felt sorry for the brothers who were fighting and putting so many families into turmoil. The wise old woman gave the brothers one of her favorite camels. The estate, now totaling 18 camels, was divided easily according to the father's wishes. The eldest

> son took nine camels, the second son put six camels beside his tent, and the youngest son took home two camels (totaling 17 camels). The brothers were happy, the village was peaceful, the father's last wishes were honored, and the *wise old woman took her favorite camel and led it home.*

Fortunately for these brothers, there was a wise old woman who was attentive to the brothers' needs, desires, and goals, and looked on the conflict as a simple problem to be solved and not as a personal conflict engulfed in turmoil.

BRAINSTORMING

Brainstorming
A conflict resolution tool whereby several individuals come together to create multiple solutions to a problem

Once we begin to see conflict as a problem to be solved, many teachers choose to practice **brainstorming.** Brainstorming is a technique in which a group of people generate as many solutions to the problem as possible. To be best utilized, a timeline for creation of possible solutions should be set, and as these solutions are generated, they should be written down. Often others will use a previous idea mentioned to create an alternative or different option (referred to as "piggybacking"). After the time limit is expired, the group reviews the possible solutions, omitting unacceptable ones, and expounding or revising others that may be acceptable.

CONFLICT RESOLUTION STRATEGIES

Once we have determined the type of conflict (simple misunderstanding, moral dilemma, or personal) and managed the conflict by seeking to understand another's perspective and recognize the conflict as a problem to be solved, we can now focus on resolution strategies.

Educators must develop the capacity to do and say those things that will help students feel they have control over their lives, that they are not powerless, and that choices exist even when it appears there are none. On occasion (hopefully a rare occasion), a teacher or student may become aware of a social injustice and feel powerless to correct the situation.

One of the most effective, if not *most controversial*, strategies for conflict resolution was developed by **Saul (Sal) Alinsky** (1909–1972). According to Alinsky (*Rules for Radicals*, 1971), the following "rules" are designed to eliminate social injustice in an effort to obtain a better quality of life. The focus of Alinsky's strategy is to take power from the *haves* and give power to the *have-nots* through community organizations.

Alinsky accomplished a great deal by empowering the "have-nots" and making his opponents live up to their own set of rules. As Alinsky reminds us, students do not have to feel the sting of helplessness in their attempt to right a wrong. Although Alinsky may be seen as controversial in his use of words like "enemy," "tactics," "ridicule," and "radicals," he is most often seen as being inspirational, stimulating many to right encountered social injustices.

Alinsky's Rules of Power

- Power is not only what you have but what the enemy thinks you have. (The enemy is the person or persons responsible for the social injustice.)
- Never go outside the experience of your people; this causes confusion, fear, retreat, and collapse of communication.
- Whenever possible, go outside of the experience of the enemy. This creates confusion, fear, retreat, and collapse of communication.
- Make the enemy live up to their own book of rules.
- Ridicule is man's most potent weapon. (Your authors recommend caution in the use of ridicule; this may destroy any future opportunities to develop productive relationships.)
- A good tactic is one that your people enjoy.
- A tactic that drags on too long becomes a drag.
- Maintain a constant pressure on the enemy.
- The threat is usually more terrifying than the thing itself.
- The major premise for tactics is the development of operations that will maintain a constant pressure upon the opposition.
- If you push a negative hard and deep enough it will break through into its counter side (positive).
- The price of a successful attack is a constructive alternative (we must be able to offer an alternative solution, or we will have no more credibility than our enemy).
- Pick the target, freeze it, personalize it, and polarize it. (According to Alinsky, it should be obvious that the target is always trying to shift responsibility to get out of being the target, 1971, p. 126.)

Rules of power
Rules developed by Saul Alinsky to help individuals who do not feel they have the power to fight social injustice.

BALCONY VIEW

Another strategy (much less controversial) for resolving conflicts is to use the **balcony view.** The balcony view examines the conflict from three distinct vantage points: your view; other's view; and society's view.

In a college class, a professor asks a volunteer to come to the front of the class and describe a recent altercation he or she had with another person. The volunteer stands facing an adjacent wall (turned sideways to the class or the audience) and role-plays his or her view of the altercation. The volunteer is then asked to face the opposite wall (again, turned sideways to the class or audience) and role-plays the other's view of the altercation. Lastly, the volunteer is asked to stand in a chair (representing looking over the balcony), facing the audience, and role-play society's view. Society's view might best be described as what a stranger on the street, *an emotionally detached person knowing neither party*, would think about the altercation being witnessed. After three volunteers have described their recent altercations, a class discussion occurs. Most times, a class consensus can be reached, including the volunteers, that when looking at the conflict from the balcony view (a detached, outside view), most incidents were not worth getting upset over. Many volunteers have noted how silly the conflict in question is now, but how serious it was at the time.

Balcony view
A conflict resolution technique that involves distancing yourself from the problem in order to take a more objective look at the situation

Using the balcony view as a conflict resolution strategy provides learning opportunity that illustrates how conflicts can often be resolved by stepping outside of the situation (going to the balcony), distancing emotionally from the action, stepping back and looking at the problem objectively. Imagine climbing to the balcony overlooking the stage where the action drama is taking place. Calmly look at the situation with a detached or third-party perspective. Remove the natural impulses and emotions. By doing so, we often realize that many conflicts are not worth getting upset over.

The balcony view offers many benefits to students. After the teacher has demonstrated and modeled how the process works (direct instruction and role-playing are very effective in this demonstration), the balcony view allows students to observe and participate in how adults appropriately manage conflicts. The balcony view also teaches students the benefits of seeing the world from others' perspectives (referred to as being other-oriented) and the advantages of looking at problems from a detached, unemotional, and objective view (as did the old wise woman). It is also important to note that the balcony view lessens the possibility of misperceptions, as discussed in chapter 3.

EMPATHY TRAINING

Kahn and Lawhorne (2003) note that empathy is the "critical factor in maintaining peace, respect and civility in our schools" (p. 2). Generally defined in the literature, empathy involves taking the perspective of another. This perspective can be cognitive (i.e., understanding another person's feelings) or affective (i.e., sharing an emotional experience or reaction with someone). Arguably, having the ability to take the perspective of another would decrease conflict. In fact, Eisenberg, Fabes, Shepard, Murphy, Jones, and Guthrie (1998) found that children who could cognitively take the perspective of another also had an increase in emotional and empathic responding.

Empathy training
Process by which students are taught to take the perspective of others both cognitively and emotionally as a way to decrease aggression and conflict

Beland (1996) described an additional **empathy training** program called Second Step that was developed for the school setting. This program was designed to teach students skills in empathy, impulse control, problem solving, and anger management. When the program was evaluated (as compared to a school without this empathy training program), researchers found that students who had received the training showed a greater improvement in prosocial behavior (e.g., cooperation and helping).

Peer mediation
Process in which students are taught to assist others in peacefully negotiating solutions to interpersonal conflicts.

Peer Mediation and Conflict Resolution. Schools across the country are implementing conflict resolution (CR) strategies through the process of **peer mediation** (PM). Shepherd (1994) notes that CR-PM was one of the fastest-growing school responses to violence. Theberge and Karan (2004) define peer mediation as a "process in which students that have been taught a structured, step-by-step model assist others to peacefully negotiate solutions to their interpersonal conflicts" (p. 284). Smith, Daunic, Miller, and Robinson (2002) describe CR-PM programs as designed to teach students to "manage their own conflicts, [and] represent a move away from programs that depend on punitive, seclusionary methods of behavior control" (p. 568). These programs aim to increase safety in the school setting. In an examination of the effectiveness of CR-PM programs at three middle schools, Daunic, Smith, Robinson, Miller, and Landry (2000) find that these programs can be effective and have a positive impact on the students, teachers, and administrators involved *if* there are committed administrators, an implementation team "invested in the program's success," and appropriate scheduling that allows for the mediation process and supervision. Interestingly, although there has not been a substantial amount of research outlining the effectiveness of CR-PM programs, Smith et al. (2002) note that "(a) approximately 85 to 95 percent of the mediated student conflicts resulted in lasting agreements and (b) that referrals to administrative personnel for inappropriate student behavior decreased" (p. 568).

Empathy Training

Much of the literature on empathy training focuses on empathy being linked to prosocial (e.g., helping and sharing) rather than antisocial (e.g., conflict oriented) behavior. To highlight this connection, we would like you to consider the research by Iannotti (1985). Iannotti examines the relationships among different categories of prosocial behavior (i.e., sharing, cooperation, and helping), using different assessment procedures (i.e., naturalistic observations, teacher ratings, and structured measures with children and their peers), as well as the role of empathy and perspective taking as mediators of prosocial responding. Iannotti found that children's spontaneity of helping was associated with their ability to recognize the needs of others. Iannotti argues that the process of prosocial responding in children often consists of (a) a recognition of the other's need, (b) an empathic response (i.e., a vicarious experiencing of the needy other's feelings), and then (c) a helping response if an appropriate empathic response motivates the child to act prosocially. Using empathy training, children can learn to recognize the needs of others, thus appropriately responding in a prosocial manner and reducing conflict in the classroom.

Salmon (2003) offers guidance for empathy training in children through the use of what she calls P.E.A.C.E. curriculum (**P**arent Empowerment, **E**mpathy Training, **A**nger Management, **C**haracter **E**ducation, **E**ssential Social Skills). In her curriculum, she describes the promotion of empathy through helping students learn to be compassionate toward others. Teachers can promote empathy and compassion through having students: "hold the correct body posture, [give] eye contact, assess the person's feelings correctly, respond appropriately with your face, [and] say the person's feelings in your own words" (Salmon, 2003, p. 168). Salmon also notes that her curriculum involved having students develop "space empathy." That is, "students were given activities explaining personal boundaries and appropriate gestures while getting in touch with others'

(Continued)

rhythm and various spatial issues" (p. 168). Teachers should develop activities to allow students to practice the skills recommended by Salmon to create empathy in their students. By creating an empathic student, teachers will see an increase in prosocial behavior and decrease in antisocial behaviors.

Theberge and Karan (2004) conducted research in a junior high school and found that although 95 percent of the enrolled students were aware of the PM program, fewer than nine percent had personal experience using it. The researchers conclude that peer mediation is more likely to be used actively by students if the following occur:

- There is commitment from all levels within the school to use PM for CR.
- There is adequate financial resources and support for mediation programs.
- PM is taught in elementary schools around the grades of fourth and fifth for adequate understanding (preferably with the assistance of mediators from upper grades).
- Community volunteers are available for modeling and assistance.
- The school is of an appropriate size to allow for adequate numbers of positive contacts between students and adults.
- Peer mediators reflect the diversity of school community.
- Peer mediation programs attend to power imbalance, fair discipline procedures, and opportunities for high-quality relationships between students and adults.

COLLABORATIVE STYLE

Collaborative style Conflict resolution designed to be a team or joint effort.

Collaborative style, described by Johnson and Johnson (1990), addresses conflict resolution as a team or joint effort. These authors offer useful steps to "constructive conflict resolution" using a collaborative style:

1. *Define the conflict together*. Once the conflict is aired, the parties involved need to define the conflict in such a way that is objective and avoids defensiveness. In this process, it is vital that those involved are as clear and specific as possible.
2. *Communicate personal positions and feelings*. This step is where the lines of communication need to be most open. It is not enough to speak during this process; the parties involved need to be open in the listening process as well. Through this process, an uncovering of differences and a common ground can be established. It is also at this stage that a discussion of what each person must do to solve the problem occurs.
3. *Express cooperative intentions*. As discussed earlier in this chapter, conflict can actually strengthen a relationship, and it is during this stage that each person must state a desire not to undermine the relationship and find ways that they can work together to successfully bring the conflict to an agreeable solution.

4. *Understand the conflict from the other party's viewpoint.* As discussed during the empathy training section of this chapter, taking the perspective of another can give great insight into the conflict and help to decrease conflict. This suggestion also leads us back to the balcony view as well.
5. *Be motivated to negotiate in good faith.* Successful resolution of conflict will occur only if all parties have good intentions. If there is resistance to resolution, the conflict will ultimately continue and resolution will be undermined.
6. *Reach an agreement.* Once having worked through the previous steps, the authors note that a win-win situation means everyone is satisfied with the results. Even though this may be easier said than done, it is important to the successful resolution of conflict.

Jones (2004) discussed the successful elements of conflict resolution education (CRE) that has been adopted by many schools to manage conflict within their schools and communities. Jones notes, "Conflict resolution education programs provide students with a basic understanding of the nature of conflict, the dynamics of power and influence that operate in conflict, and the role of culture in how we see and respond to conflict" (p. 234). To compliment the information presented by Johnson and Johnson (1990) and Jones (2007), it is important to remember when engaged in a conflict, fight fairly. By fighting fairly the parties involved in conflict retain the opportunity to engage in productive relationships in the future. When in disagreement with another, note the following:

- Be specific when introducing a complaint.
- Do not just complain; ask for a change that will make the situation better.
- Make sure to understand the others' view.
- Make sure they understand our view.
- Try tolerance. Be open to our own feelings and equally open to theirs.
- Consider compromises if appropriate.
- Deal with one issue at a time.
- Do not assume to tell partner what he or she knows or feels.
- Attack the issue, not each other.
- Do not call each other names or use sarcasm.
- Do not burden partner with too many issues.
- Think about thoughts and feelings before speaking.

It is obvious that modeling conflict management to resolution is paramount in teaching students how to appropriately deal with conflicts. A strategy that should be implemented when modeling is showing students that the teacher has *taken responsibility for his or her part of the conflict or misunderstanding.* Modeling the teacher's focus on his or her part of the conflict and not focusing on others' parts in the conflict (e.g., blaming others) sends the message that the teacher is self-reflecting, taking ownership of his or her part of the disagreement, and dealing with the issue in a professional and mature manner.

DISCIPLINING STUDENTS

Those times exist when conflict resolution may involve disciplining students. This discussion on disciplining begins by noting the work of **Carl Rogers** (1902–1987). Rogers suggests that teachers should instruct and discipline students without making them ashamed of themselves. He believed that teachers should criticize inappropriate action but not the student. When disciplining, the teacher must remember to send two messages to the student. The first message must be of acceptance of who the student is (that the student is fine the way he or she is). The second message is of showing disapproval of the behavior. The first message should be of compassion and understanding; the second message should be stern and blatantly clear. Teachers should actively look for ways to increase self-esteem in all students (the intent of the first message), not destroy self-esteem by criticizing the student. The preservice teacher often finds separating these two messages is awkward at first, but through practice and role-play, the preservice teacher will be more comfortable using it in the classroom.

As noted above in the first message, the teacher must show acceptance of who the student is. Rogers assumed that basic human nature is positive and that there is nothing inherently negative or evil about humans. Specifically, if we are *accepted for who we are*, we will live in ways that enhance both society and ourselves.

Rogers offers insight into this process of accepting others through his own self-examination and reflection. Rogers (1956) presented a paper to the Illinois Guidance and Personnel Association Annual Conference, in which he discussed what understanding and acceptance mean to him. His message is one that should be given serious consideration by future teachers. Rogers spoke in terms of the lessons he learned through being a therapist and a *teacher*. These lessons speak for themselves and give much to think about:

1. In my relationships with persons I have found that it does not help, in the long run, to act as though I were something that I am not.
2. I have found it effective, in my dealings with people, to be acceptant of myself.
3. I have found it of enormous value when I can permit myself to understand another person.
4. I have found it highly rewarding when I can accept another person.
5. I have found it of value to be open to the realities of life as they are revealed in me and in other people.
6. The more I am able to understand myself and others, the more I accept myself and others, the more that I am open to the realities of life, the less do I find myself wishing to rush in . . . become less inclined to hurry in to fix things.
7. It has been my experience that persons have a basically positive direction.

Chapter 2 examined the need for future teachers to know who they are. Rogers has offered to the reader an excellent example of a lifelong examination of self. The more teachers know about themselves and learn to accept themselves (as Rogers did), the easier it becomes to accept their students for who they are. If the classroom offers this acceptance and tolerance to all students, the need for conflict management will be minimal.

SUMMARY

Conflict is often an unavoidable part of life, and rather than trying to avoid conflict, conflict should be approached as an opportunity to establish and grow relationships with others, learn the perspective of others, and mature both professionally and personally. Not only can conflicts not be avoided, but not all conflicts can be resolved (in the case of a moral dilemma). Teachers must remember that good can, and often does, come from conflicts. The answer is not in avoiding conflict but in how we choose to manage conflict. Managing conflict entails (1) recognizing that conflict occurs when we get between (often unintentionally) a student and his or her needs, desires, and goals, (2) recognizing that often culture plays a part in conflict, (3) recognizing the type of conflict (a simple lack of understanding, moral dilemma, personal conflict) we are involved in, and (4) seeing conflict as a problem to be solved. Several conflict resolution strategies are offered for the reader's examination. Once we find ourselves in a conflict, it is important that we fight fairly. The unfair fighter has little or no opportunity to establish productive relationships with students, parents, colleagues, or supervisors. Fighting fairly also requires the teacher to model taking ownership of his/her part of the conflict.

This chapter ends with a discussion on disciplining students as a result of conflict. Rogers notes the importance of sending two messages while in the act of disciplining, one of acceptance and self-worth and one of disapproval of the undesirable behavior; both messages must be received by the student. Lastly, Rogers offers an excellent example of lifelong self-examination and reflection. The message we wish to offer the reader is that if teachers get to know themselves (as discussed in chapter 2) and learn to accept themselves for who they are (following Rogers's example), it becomes easier to accept their students for who they are. The outcome of this process of acceptance is to have a classroom with less conflict.

CASE 7.A

While Mr. Jones was on lunch duty, he noticed two students had gotten up from their tables and taken their trays to the appropriate spot, the whole time staring at each other. They were clearly in disagreement over something. He started to make his way over to the boys, who were now drawing attention to themselves and swearing at each other. Before he could get to the boys, a group of students started circling around the two boys, taunting them to hit each other. As Mr. Jones makes his way through the crowd, he sees one boy punch the other in the face.

QUESTIONS

1. What should Mr. Jones do in this situation?

2. How can this conflict be resolved between the two boys?

3. What is the impact of the group on the conflict in the situation?

CASE 7.B

In her high school speech class, Jamie was required to research and write a speech on a controversial topic in the area where she lived, the Northwest United States. Jamie decided to research the need for tighter gun control in the area. She enthusiastically researched and prepared her persuasive speech. As she was delivering her speech in class, a classmate started laughing and called her a "no-good tree hugger." Jamie was clearly devastated and affected by the rude comment her classmate made during her presentation.

QUESTION

- What should Mrs. Claussen, the speech teacher, do in this situation?

CASE 7.C

During a parent–teacher conference, Mrs. Barker meets with Mr. and Mrs. Smithson, the parents of Shellie, a student in her second-grade class. The conference starts well, with Mrs. Barker telling the parents that Shellie is a wonderful student to have in class; she is very kind and thoughtful of the other students in class. As the conference moves to academic issues, Mrs. Barker tells them that she has noticed Shellie struggles with reading proficiency. Immediately, both parents become defensive. Mrs. Barker realizes that they may be in denial of their daughter's low proficiency, but she realizes that it is going to take the parents coming together with the school to get Shellie the added help she needs to read at a more proficient level.

QUESTIONS

1. What can Mrs. Barker do at this point in the conference to help ease the tension that is now evident in the room?

2. How can she help resolve this conflict so that Shellie will have success in reading?

SUGGESTED ACTIVITIES

Complete any of the following exercises:

a. Lost on the Moon (http://www.unionstation.org/pdf/Lost_on_the_Moon.pdf)

b. Nuclear Holocaust (http://www.monarchknights.com/teacherwebpages/moss/documents/SurvivalGroupActivities.pdf)

c. Lost at Sea (http://dsa.csupomona.edu/osl/studentmanual/files/Lost_at_Sea_327.pdf)

We all live with the objective of being happy; our lives are all different and yet the same.
—Anne Frank

8 Student Diversity

OBJECTIVES

After completing this chapter you should be able to:

- Identify and discuss the different types of diversity that teachers and students experience in the classroom.
- Define the fluidity of culture and how students can learn *from* culture, not *about* culture.
- Define ethnocentrism, and discuss how teachers can overcome their own ethnocentrism.
- Discuss how teachers can create a classroom that cultivates the strengths of student diversity.
- Explain how students might experience culture shock entering a new classroom, and what teachers can do to alleviate that shock.

KEY TERMS

Collaboration
Cultural journey
Culture
Culture shock
Student diversity

Student diversity The existence of dissimilar students contributing to the unique experiences found in the classroom

For many teachers, student diversity is an uncomfortable, difficult, even frightening topic. **Student diversity** is the existence of dissimilar students contributing to the unique experiences found in the classroom. Student diversity may include differences in culture, ethnic groups, religious beliefs, sexual orientation, socioeconomic status, and disability, along with many other differences. Once teachers recognize and begin to understand that *strengths are found in diversity,* they begin to learn to accept, tolerate, and more importantly, appreciate the differences that make each student unique. Dettmer, Dyck, and Thurston (1999) noted that accepting and tolerating differences are not enough. According to these authors, the teacher must *value* individual differences, which means accepting the fact that people are different and that the world is better for the diversity. The key in learning to value individual differences begins by alleviating fears and cultivating those strengths found in diversity. We begin this process of alleviating fears and cultivating strengths by first understanding that *student diversity is not the problem*; the problem exists in *how we react to the diversity*.

How can it be that some teachers are tolerant, accepting, and appreciative of differences while other teachers are not? The reason for this broad range of reactions to differences is that the level of comfort with dissimilar students *has nothing to do with the students themselves* but only with the individual *reaction* to these students. If teachers choose to be self-reflective, they can recognize that it is their own *reaction* to student differences that causes problems. Teachers who are respectful of, and display a lack of reaction to, student differences allow their classrooms to be a welcoming place for all students.

Encouraging teachers (chapter 2) put aside their potential adverse reactions to differences, along with their fears, and see all students as unique individuals who have something to contribute to the classroom. In this view, that every student has something to contribute, both the teacher and students learn that strength is found in these contributions and differences.

Vast differences abound in classrooms, much more than the preservice teacher can imagine. It is through these differences that variety gives life its mystery and most of its challenges. Life would be boring and stale if everyone were the same.

THE MANY FACES OF STUDENT DIVERSITY

Student differences are not going to go away. Wishing they would disappear is wasting valuable classroom time. Differences are here to stay, and this should be seen as a good thing.

STUDENTS FROM DIFFERENT CULTURES

The face of our nation continues to change. The American landscape has been called a kaleidoscope. Two thirds of all of the world's immigrants come to the United States (Beebe et al., 2008). Teachers should develop an understanding of why this is such a popular country to migrate to.

The majority of the entire world's wealth belongs to only a select few; a large majority of these select few live in the United States. Teachers must become aware and educate those around them to the facts that the majority of the world lives in substandard housing, is illiterate, and suffers from malnutrition. Teachers will have a notable portion of their students coming from diverse cultures, and they must attempt to understand student diversity by recognizing why these students are coming to America. Raymond (2008) reminds the teacher that students who find that their own culture is devalued in the school, frequently fail to develop the ability to adapt in different settings.

RACE

Only one race exists on the planet: the human race. If everyone in the world were to be lined up shoulder to shoulder from the darkest complexion to the lightest complexion, no one would be able to distinguish where one race begins or another race ends. In this abstract scenario, the distinction between races is removed, as it should be. Although there is only one race, the human race, it is important to note that diversity in cultures can create differences in student relations and student performance in the classroom. The boxed feature on page 193 addresses the power of stereotype threat as it relates to race recognition and performance in the classroom. Teachers need to look well beyond the color of your students' skin (the metastory of "The Horseman"); but that should not be misinterpreted as minimizing students' heritages. Students should be allowed to openly express their beliefs and practices associated with their heritage. Teachers should affirm students' knowledge and pride in their cultural identity.

STUDENTS WITH DISABILITIES

Students with disabilities *will* be in general education classrooms; this issue is not up for debate. All students have a right to an appropriate education, alongside their peers, regardless of their abilities. As soon as the teacher sees students with disabilities as unique individuals with something to contribute to the classroom, differences become strengths. If appropriate supports are available, as they should be, everyone (typical students, students with disabilities, and general educators) will benefit from having students with disabilities in their classrooms. Typical students learn how to appropriately interact with a person with a disability, making them better citizens. Evidence has been offered that, when appropriate supports are made available, typical students do not suffer academically when students with disabilities are in the general classes (Rex, 2000; Smith, Polloway, Patton, & Dowdy, 2001). Students with disabilities, when included in general classes, learn to appropriately interact with people without disabilities, making them better citizens. Additionally, the general educator is exposed to different strategies and differential methodologies for teaching all students. One of the teacher's primary responsibilities is to help facilitate appropriate supports for *all* students.

STUDENTS WITH DIVERSE SEXUAL ORIENTATIONS

Having students with different sexual orientations may be uncomfortable at first, but recognizing that the *reaction* to these differences may be the problem (as discussed previously) will be beneficial in making this relationship more productive. This process starts by noting that gay students, like all other students, bring unique perspectives to the educational experience and always have something to contribute in the classroom. For example, "Although gay people are gaining legal rights and protections, they are still subject to discriminatory laws and social intolerance" (Beebe et al., 1999, p. 105).

HOMELESS

Children and youth are identified as being homeless when they sleep in shelters (e.g., family shelters, runaway shelters, domestic violence shelters, etc.), routinely stay at homes of friends or relatives because of inadequate shelter, are awaiting institutionalization or other placements, or sleep in cars, tents, abandoned buildings, or other places not ordinarily used as sleeping accommodations for human beings (Stewart B. McKinney Homeless Assistance Act, 1987). The number of children and youth who find themselves in these precarious situations continues to grow at an alarming rate. Homeless children and youth, other than being homeless, have only one thing in common: they share unsafe, emotionally insecure, and uncertain living environments. Homelessness is often the accumulation of several factors, for example, unemployed parents; substance abuse; unexpected pregnancies; physical, mental, and/or sexual abuse; refusal to follow rules; youth not getting along with stepparents or parent's significant other, and so on. Awareness is the first step to providing appropriate educational services. Awareness can be accomplished through nonthreatening strategies: have children draw pictures of their living environments or have conversations that are intended to show that we are concerned about their well-being. The McKinney Homeless Assistance Act is designed to ensure that students in homeless situations are not excluded from educational opportunities. When making a determination regarding the eligibility status of a youth, it is always better to be inclusive rather than exclusive.

Our educational system was never designed to meet the needs of homeless students. Since the living situations of homeless students cannot change in order to make it easier to manage schools, educators must be attentive to the needs of all students.

AT-RISK STUDENTS

At-risk students are students who are not in need of special or related services now, but who are at risk of becoming in need of services. Students who find themselves at-risk include students who "have fallen through the cracks" (they are in need of supports but do not qualify for services), are gay or lesbian, come from migrant families, live in poor inner city or rural areas, are homeless, have health-related issues, are victims of abuse, live in violent environments, are unsupervised, use drugs, and are in danger of an unexpected pregnancy. The list is seemingly endless, including much more than is provided here. Teachers must keep in mind two points when working with at-risk students. First, all students are at risk at one time or another in their lives. For example, unexpected (and some expected) deaths of those close to students can have a devastating impact. The second point is that collaboration is the most effective way of dealing with at-risk students. **Collaboration** consists of coordinated actions by teachers to create solutions and reach their common goal (Thomas, Correa, & Morsink, 1995). Two or more teachers with diverse expertise come together in a mutual effort to plan, implement, share responsibilities, and evaluate a program for a given student. Because so many students experience so many difficulties, and because their difficulties are so complex, teachers working in isolation are challenged to provide these students with appropriate educational programs. When it comes to working with at-risk students, two heads will almost always produce a better outcome than one.

Collaboration
Consists of coordinated actions by teachers to create solutions and reach common goals

IN SUMMARY OF THE MANY FACES OF STUDENT DIVERSITY

It will not be the differences in cultures, physical characteristics, sexual orientation, intelligence, or religious views of students that will cause problems; instead, it will be the teacher's *reaction* to these differences that will be detrimental to the development of productive relationships with students. There is no pragmatic way to include all of the student differences the teacher will encounter. The examples offered in this section were designed to cut across the wide range of differences and hopefully encourage and stimulate discussion points. What is important to remember is that the teacher's reaction and modeling of acceptance, tolerance, and appreciation of differences, have a tremendous impact on the relationships developed with students.

CULTURE

Culture is defined by Kottak (1982) as traditions that govern the thought and behavior of individuals exposed to them. For the purpose of this text, we define culture as a group of people with shared beliefs, values, symbols, and interpretations. Cultures are distinguished by the artifacts being used and the shared experiences among its members.

Culture
A group of people with shared beliefs, values, symbols, and interpretations.

An enlightening analogy is that culture is like air. We can't see culture (or air), but it constantly surrounds us, and we find that we cannot live without it. Culture plays an important part in the choices we make. Stated differently, the choices we make come from our culture. A student's decision to wear long hair or short hair, have a shaved head, nose rings, tongue piercing, tattoos, and blue or pink hair demonstrates choices found in our culture. In themselves, these choices are not a problem; the problem resides in the *reaction* teachers have to these choices. Teachers must learn to accept, tolerate, and then appreciate the differences they find in their students. With practice, a teacher can learn to see inside students (the message found in the meta-story "The Horseman," presented in chapter 5), versus judging them by the color of their hair.

Every generation wishes to separate itself from its parents' generation. We look to our culture for ways to make this separation. A previous generation wore long hair to distinguish its generation from the one before it. The present generation wears pants low enough to see their underwear. Long hair and the presence of underwear or tattoos in itself is not a problem, but the *reaction* (often the overreaction) signifies to the generation that they have indeed separated themselves from their parents. This is all the younger generation is seeking—the acknowledgement that they are different. What will the next generation do to separate themselves from their parents' generation? When this separation occurs, teachers (and parents) must recognize this for what it is and learn to tolerate (hopefully even appreciate it), without overreacting.

Teachers should make their students aware that cultures are not static. Cultures continue to change, often abruptly. For example, the ability of medical science to detect birth defects prior to the birth of the child has had more of an impact on the rate of abortions in this country than all of the previous and ongoing heated debates. Email and text messaging connect everyone instantly. Students should be reminded that this high-speed and instant communication was not always available. Seemingly overnight, the Internet has changed the way people think and behave. Increasingly, customers shop online. eBay is reported to be the fastest growing company in America. And unfortunately, there is no denying that September 11, 2001, had and continues to have a great impact on our culture; we as a people have changed to meet the changing times. In summary, we as a society continue to change, and this change has an influence on our culture. In return, our culture continues to change, and this change constantly (and at times abruptly) influences our thoughts and our behaviors. Students should recognize cultures as living, breathing, and always-changing entities.

It is vital that the teacher refrain from making negative judgments about another culture. When students hear teachers putting another culture down, this creates suspicion and mistrust. Instead of making judgments about another culture, teachers should simply acknowledge the differences and view them as an interesting challenge rather than an obstacle to be eradicated or feared (Beebe et al., 2008). *Every culture has strengths and weaknesses.* Too often, students are presented with only the unfamiliar and uncomfortable parts of particular cultures, while not being given the opportunity to learn the strengths and exciting uniqueness that makes those cultures different from the students' own cultures. The old saying has merit: students should not be learning *about* other cultures; instead, students should be learning *from* other cultures.

There is a special problem for students and teachers alike when *cultures clash*. The dominant culture expects students to act in a conforming way.

However, some students, due to their cultural heritage, refuse to conform to the school's expectations, and this refusal can, and often does, interfere with their educational progress. Their culture demands from them prescribed behaviors, which are often at odds with the dominant culture. For example, a student from a culture that devalues education, preferring to emphasize family relationships and cohesiveness, may choose to disidentify with the educational process. This student may find him- or herself getting mixed messages, one message from home (without concerns of grades, attendance, and homework) and another message from the school (being concerned with grades, attendance, and homework). Additionally, a student who was raised in a culture that focuses more on the collective efforts of the group rather than individualistic performances may struggle in school. The student, trying to hang on to his or her culture, often finds that he or she has a hard time keeping up with the competitive nature of education and our society in general.

The most disturbing and anxiety-producing part of a culture clash is when students from a different culture feel they are denying their heritage by submitting to the expectations of the dominant culture. This student's prospect of succeeding in the dominant culture is not always good. Students who comply with the dominant culture's expectations may feel they have turned their backs on their own people and that they must leave their own people behind in order to gain a better opportunity to succeed. Students finding themselves in this uncomfortable position may describe themselves as living in two distinctly different worlds, while being looked at with suspicion from both worlds. The perceptive teacher who finds students in this difficult situation will teach these students the benefits of an education and assimilation in the dominant culture, while instilling pride and showing interest in the students' heritage.

ETHNOCENTRISM

Teachers must be vigilant in combating ethnocentrism in the classroom. Ethnocentrism comes from the perception that our culture is superior to other cultures. Where does this attitude of superiority come from? We are taught this attitude early in our lives. Residents of the North American continent make up only a small portion of the people on this planet (approximately 5.3%). However, we often act as if our culture is the only culture fit to live in, and that all the other cultures of the world need to change their way of life because our way of life is superior to theirs. The teacher must fight this temptation by recognizing that there are no "good" or "bad" cultures, just different cultures, and in learning *from* (as opposed to "about") these differences we find strengths.

CULTURAL JOURNEY

Because students often don't see their culture (remembering the analogy that culture is like air), many students believe they do not have a culture—that it just belongs to others. The teacher is charged with changing this perception. One way of doing this is for students to take a **cultural journey.**

Cultural journey
A lifelong examination and experiences of a group of people with shared beliefs, values, symbols, and interpretation

This journey begins with *students first becoming aware of their own culture.* Self-awareness of one's heritage, traditions, and customs is often the first step in understanding and learning to appreciate his or her own culture. This journey is a process whereby students learn about themselves, while learning about others. Students begin by discussing their family origins, sharing stories that were told about their ancestors, reporting on traditional foods that were brought from the "old country," unique celebrations, traditions, or ceremonies in their families, languages other than English used in their families, advice handed down from one generation to another, and so on. This first part of the cultural journey is designed for students to learn to value and appreciate their own culture and to see for themselves how important their culture is to them. Once this is done, it then becomes easier for students to see how important others' cultures are to them. *In essence, students learn to value and appreciate others' cultures through learning to value and appreciate their own.*

The second part of the cultural journey focuses on values, beliefs, biases, attitudes, and behaviors students may have. This may include negative comments students have heard about their country of origin, differences between their family and their neighbors, experiences with individuals from different cultures, experiences with others from different cultures that shocked the students, any behaviors students displayed that was inappropriate while in another culture, and so on.

The third and last part of the cultural journey focuses on the students' imagination. For example, what culture would students choose to become a part of, what attracts students to other cultures, what concerns or frightens students about other cultures, how would their lives be different if they were from a different culture, and if from another culture, would they believe their culture was superior?

After the cultural journey has been completed, it is important that the teacher *creates a classroom that cultivates the strengths found in*

Figure 8.1 Students learn to value and appreciate others' cultures through learning to value and appreciate their own.

student diversity. To create such a classroom teachers must adhere to the following:

- Affirm and foster children's knowledge and pride, not superiority, in their cultural identity.
- Foster children's curiosity and enjoyment of cultural differences and similarities.
- Expand children's concept of fairness and feeling of empathy for others.
- Help children change uncomfortable and inappropriate responses to differences into respectful and comfortable interactions.
- Help children think critically about stereotyping.
- Help children develop the skills and self-confidence to stand up for themselves and others against prejudice and discriminatory behavior.

Although this is a seemingly long and challenging list, in making these efforts teachers will guide their students on a *lifelong* cultural journey that will facilitate a better understanding of themselves and others.

STEREOTYPING

Although there are cognitive benefits to stereotyping (e.g., organizing the unfamiliar with the familiar) and stereotyping occurs very naturally in people, the process of stereotyping can be very harmful in that information about the individual being stereotyped can be lost. Stereotyping, again, is when a person is placed into an inflexible category (chapter 3). It is the *act* of placing this unique individual in an inflexible category that makes stereotyping wrong. Everyone on this planet is a unique person; no two human beings are exactly alike. To put a unique human being into an inflexible category is not to recognize that we are all different. For every stereotype offered, there are those who defy the category.

All students will have something about them that separates them from everyone else the teacher knows. Instead of stereotyping the student based on similarities of other students (e.g., class clown, troublemaker, delinquent, etc.), the teacher should recognize and learn to appreciate the things that make them unique. It is important for the teacher to remember that students often meet expectations (referred to as the self-fulfilling prophecy, chapter 1) because teachers have failed to find the unique student underneath the stereotype.

Stereotyping is often detrimental to student diversity. Johnny is a new student. He has an IQ of 64. Panic sets in for his teacher. The natural ability to stereotype tells the teacher that he or she is in for a long semester. But IQ scores offer limited information for the teacher. The teacher has no information about how well Johnny can read and write, about his social skills, about how excited he is to learn, if he stays on task, if he does his homework, if he will be pleasant to be around, or what kinds of support he has at home. It would not be surprising if Johnny becomes one of the best students in the class. Teachers must resist the natural desire to stereotype and find ways to learn about and appreciate the uniqueness of each of their students.

Name: ______________________________

Stereotyping

Stereotyping is placing a unique person into an inflexible category. We place the same judgments on anyone placed into a given category. Stereotyping focuses on similarities among people of one group when, in fact, not all people within that group are the same.

Offer a stereotype (e.g., a student athlete) and then offer a description of a unique person that is being stereotyped.

A Stereotype

____

____

____

A Unique Person Being Stereotyped

____

____

____

____

____

____

____

Stereotype Threat

A problem that is closely associated with student diversity that individuals in the minority or associated with a particular group experience is a *stereotype threat*. Stereotype threat, a phrase coined by Claude Steele (1999), explains why students of a minority, specifically Black students, perform at a lower level in academia. Steele defines a stereotype threat as the "threat of being viewed through the lens of a negative stereotype, or the fear of doing something that would inadvertently confirm that stereotype" (p. 46). Steele and others have consistently offered evidence that has demonstrated this effect. How does the teacher reduce stereotype threat in the classroom? The two suggestions Steele and others have made are to reduce the presence of the stereotype and increase students' confidence in their personal performance.

Rydell, McConnell, and Beilock (2009) help teachers understand how to eliminate stereotype threat in their classroom. These authors suggest the presence of a positive stereotype (e.g., college students versus noncollege students are good at math) can counteract the presence of a negative stereotype (e.g., women are bad at math) to help students recognize their multiple-group identities and reduce the effect of the negative stereotype. Teachers need to make the greatest efforts to decrease the presences of stereotypes in their classrooms; however, when stereotypes cannot be decreased or eliminated, students should be assisted in the understanding they have multiple-group identities that may have negative and positive attributes.

CULTURE SHOCK

Many students of diversity face **culture shock** after leaving familiar surroundings and upon entering the new teacher's classroom. They may experience confusion, anxiety, stress, and the feeling of loss (Beebe et al., 2008). The teacher can alleviate these feelings by practicing tolerance for differences and accepting students for who they are (referring to the work of Carl Rogers). Once students learn that their teacher appreciates them for who they genuinely are, students begin to feel welcome and comfortable being who they are in the new environment, and the effects of culture shock is greatly lessened.

Culture shock
Upon entering a new environment, the experience of confusion, anxiety, stress, and the feeling of loss

WHAT IS THE PURPOSE FOR EVERYONE BEING DIFFERENT?

There is an enormous amount of differences found in our classrooms—way more than you can imagine. Every student and colleague is different from everyone you have ever met. In this difference you find variety that gives life its mystery and its most challenges. But this variety is what *we all have in common, which makes us all the same*. What is the purpose for everyone being so different? The purpose for everyone being different is so that *we can help each other*.

SUMMARY

Tolerance, acceptance, and an appreciation of differences are the teachers' most important assets in developing productive relationships with students from diverse backgrounds. The teacher must recognize that student differences in themselves are not the problem, but *our reactions* to these differences can create problems. There is no inherent problem with a person practicing the Buddhist religion; the problem lies in *our reaction* to this choice. The teacher's job is to put aside his or her reactions to differences, along with fears, and see everyone as having something to contribute to the educational experiences in the classroom. Built on the contributions of all students we find great strengths. It should be obvious to the reader how divergent thought can generate insight to problem solving. Without differences life would be boring and stale–without mystery or the needed challenges.

There are a multitude of differences that will be found in the classroom. Each classroom will have students from different cultures, socioeconomic backgrounds, with disabilities, with different sexual orientations, homeless students, and those students who are at risk. As noted throughout this text, modeling tolerance, accepting students for who they are, and learning to appreciate differences will guide teachers to their desired outcomes.

Cultures are not static; they change often and abruptly. As events in society (e.g., September 11, 2001) influences changes in our culture (e.g., taking off shoes in airport terminals), our culture in turn influences how we think and behave (we now pay attention and react to security levels: yellow, orange, etc.). Students must learn that cultures are living, breathing, and always-changing entities. In the classroom, the most notable change in culture may come from students trying to separate themselves from their parents' generation. These attempts to separate themselves should not be viewed as threatening or something to be feared, but recognized for what they are. Teachers must model tolerance and learn to appreciate differences without overreacting (which is often the purpose behind students' actions).

Teachers should be especially aware of the possibilities of culture clashes. The dominant culture with its expectations and prescribed behaviors can clash with a student's cultural heritage. Students may feel that in order to succeed in the dominant culture, they may have to turn their backs on their own people. Obviously this would produce anxiety and suspicion. The teacher must teach the benefits of succeeding in the dominant culture while instilling pride in the students' heritage.

Culture shock often accompanies students from diverse backgrounds. Students experiencing culture shock may feel confused, anxiety, stress, and loss. However, once students believe that the teacher is accepting of who the students are, the students become comfortable in the classroom and the effects of culture shock greatly lessen.

The use of ethnocentrism (thinking one's culture is superior to others) should be discouraged in the classroom, and teachers should encourage the view of other cultures as being an interesting challenge rather than an obstacle to be eradicated or feared. Teachers should focus on the strengths and the exciting uniqueness of other cultures. Students should not be learning *about* other cultures, but instead, learning *from* other cultures.

Life is a long cultural journey. The first part of the journey involves getting to know one's own culture. The end result of a better appreciation of one's culture is a better appreciation of others' cultures; students learn about themselves, while learning about others. The journey then focuses on values, beliefs, and attitudes associated with cultures. The last part of the cultural journey allows students to use their imagination in envisioning themselves as part of a culture different from their own.

After the cultural journey has been completed, it is important for the teacher to create a classroom that cultivates the strengths found in student diversity.

CASE 8.A

Mr. Roth has a student teacher in his high school history classroom second semester. The student teacher commented to Mr. Roth that she is surprised at the diversity in the classes that she will be teaching. Mr. Roth responded by chuckling a little, "You know, I don't really see these kids that way; I just see them as kids." However, because the student teacher obviously sees the students as diverse, Mr. Roth knows that he must help her see the students as "just kids."

QUESTIONS

1. What can Mr. Roth do to help his student teacher get to this reality?

2. What advice can he give her?

SUGGESTED ACTIVITIES

1. Take the multicultural education quiz (http://www.mhhe.com/socscience/education/multi_new/activities/awareness.quiz.html)
2. Play Diversity Bingo (http://www2.mercer.edu/nr/rdonlyres/27732149-e7fb-4a17-9704-8a76a28b7877/0/diversitybingo.pdf)

"Individual commitment to a group effort—
that is what makes a teamwork."
—Vince Lombardi

9

Relationships with Supervisors, Colleagues, Paraprofessionals, and Parents

OBJECTIVES

After completing this chapter you should be able to:

- Explain the concept of teamwork and describe techniques for structuring and nurturing teams.
- Describe the types of sexual harassment and provide examples of how it can occur within educational setting.
- Discuss the relationship between teacher and paraprofessional and the use of consultation.
- Discuss how teachers can have quality communication with parents and care providers.
- Describe how collaboration and successful outcomes contribute to good relationships with colleagues.

KEY TERMS

Best practices
Collaboration
Consultation
Family
Quality communication
Teamwork

Most of the professional relationships teachers have with others center on accomplishing goals that focus on the best interests of a student or students. Progress on these goals often requires relationship-building skills that facilitate interactions with supervisors, colleagues, paraprofessionals, and parents. This chapter will examine various models and concepts that can be used to facilitate the intended student progress.

TEACHER AND THE SUPERVISOR

Teamwork
Process by which individuals bring forth unique knowledge, skills, and experiences that, when accumulated, provides a more complete and complex understanding of a situation

Working with a supervisor requires two specific elements: **teamwork** and knowledge of the supervisor's goals. Teamwork is essential in accomplishing goals because too many complex and demanding issues face educators. When working as a team with the same goals in mind, individuals bring forth knowledge, skills, and experiences that when summed together are greater than any one person's knowledge, skills, and experiences working alone. "It is unlikely that any one person possesses enough knowledge and ability for every circumstance" (Dettmer, Dyck, & Thurston, 1999, p. 1). Through teamwork, better strategies, interventions, and solutions can be developed and decisions that are more thoughtful can be made. Simply stated, the outcome of teamwork often is a product more beneficial to students than efforts produced by the teacher alone. Katzenbach and Smith (1993) similarly note that in comparison to individual work, teamwork creates more than the sum of its parts (a reference to Gestalt psychology).

Johnson and Johnson (2000, pp. 553–555) offer suggestions for structuring and nurturing teams once they have been formed.

1. *Once the team is formed, develop or present a mission for the team.* Structure the team in such a way that allows for productive interdependence among members and allow the team to redefine or restate the mission in such a way that will allow for concrete goals and action to be taken.
2. *Incorporate frequent and regular meetings.* Face-to-face interaction is a means by which team members can encourage each other and reflect on successes.
3. *First meetings are especially important.* Early meetings help to discover the team dynamics, objectives, and leadership styles of members of the team. Having this knowledge will assist in group organization and practice in later meetings.
4. *Establish clear rules of conduct.* Discuss with members rules for the team to consider: (a) attendance (including interruptions by phone calls, etc.), (b) discussion guidelines, (c) confidentiality requirements, (d) analysis of the facts, (e) assignments for each team member to focus on enabling the team to get to an end product, (f) constructive confrontation, and (g) expectations for contributions to ensure all members do their work.
5. *Ensure accountability.* Accountability can be met by directly measuring the progress of the team in achieving its goals.

6. *Show progress.* Not only is it important to discuss progress, but having concrete measurement of progress allows for a better understanding of the team's effectiveness.
7. *Redefinition and understanding of its mission.* At times, it is important to redefine the purpose of the team.
8. *Provide training.* In some instances, external or internal training is necessary to help the team members accomplish the goals they set.
9. *Team celebrations and recognition.* Often when teams have a task in front of them, they become focused on the minute details and forget to celebrate the achievements that occur along the way. Celebration of achievements and recognition for a job well done will strengthen the team as a whole.
10. *Ensure team-processing sessions.* Throughout the entire teamwork process, it is important for open dialogue and the processing of what is happening to make certain the team accomplishes the goals set before them.

Having knowledge of the supervisor's goals and assisting him or her in accomplishing these goals allow for the opportunity for advancement for both the supervisor and the teacher. The best time to become knowledgeable and assess a supervisor's goals is during the teacher's job interview. During the interview, the supervisor will ask questions regarding the teacher's expertise, knowledge, skills, and interests. After fully answering all of the questions, the interviewing teacher should counter by asking the goals the supervisor wishes to accomplish. This teacher has not only suggested to the supervisor that he or she is a team player, but that he or she may be willing to assist in accomplishing these goals.

Teachers should take notice that not only does teamwork aid in the accomplishments of the supervisor's goals, but teamwork acts as a training ground for future leaders. Teachers can learn how to become effective leaders by first learning how to follow a supervisor's lead. By learning to support another's vision and recognizing what works and what does not work in this process, the teacher will be in a better position to assist others in supporting the vision. The teacher, in the role of a team player, assists in accomplishing goals by researching the intended goal, getting acquainted with relevant background information, providing input and suggestions on the process of goal attainment, asking questions for clarity, and being critical and evaluative of information being used.

As is always the case, it is essential that teachers do not compromise their ethics while learning to follow. For the teacher, ethical considerations should be in the forefront of every decision made. Prior to becoming practitioners, teachers need to prepare themselves for ethical situations that might arise. Teachers must continuously be on guard, because the ethical decisions they make will impact their professional lives and, more importantly, the lives of their students. Although teamwork is essential, when dealing with ethical considerations, *what is in the best interest of the student* should drive the decision-making process.

New teachers should carefully read the school's teacher handbook to know what is professionally expected of them and to be aware when requests that go against school policies are made.

SEXUAL HARASSMENT

Sexual harassment is a topic that is sometimes confusing and difficult to understand because what one person may see as inappropriate, another may view as harmless. According to the U.S. Equal Employment Opportunity Commission (2004), over 13,000 charges are filed each year, 85% of which are made by women, with fines reaching $50 million each year to resolve the conflicts. Even attorneys are accused of sexual harassment. One noted case involved Anita Hill (1998) and her testimony against Clarence Thomas.

Sexual harassment is *any* unsolicited sexual advances, requests for sexual favors, or other inappropriate verbal or physical behavior of a sexual nature (Beebe et al., 2008). The legal system recognizes two types of sexual harassment: *quid pro quo* and *hostile environment.* Quid pro quo harassment consists of an authority (e.g., teacher, principal, school board member, etc.) suggesting or demanding an exchange of sexual advances or behavior for promotion or employment decisions. An example of quid pro quo between a teacher and student would be the teacher requesting or demanding sexual conduct in exchange for a better grade. Hostile environment harassment occurs when unsolicited or unwelcome sexual contact interferes with an individual's performance or creates a work environment that is offensive or intimidating. An example of a hostile environment in the school system might include a female student taking a machine shop class and having to enter the class by walking by a calendar with a "scantily" dressed model, accompanied by verbal comparisons being made by other students, with the shop teacher overhearing the comments and not intervening.

There are two things teachers should concern themselves with regarding sexual harassment. First, *sexual harassment is in the eye of the beholder*. It is very important for teachers to recognize that the person being accused of sexual harassment is not in a position to argue what is or is not harassment. The shop teacher with the calendar is not in a position to argue whether or not the picture is offensive or if the behavior of his students is acceptable. The person feeling victimized or offended by the conduct is the person whose feelings we, as teachers, must be sensitive to. It is also important to note that the offender must be given the opportunity to stop the behavior (remove the calendar) or it is not sexual harassment.

Second, because the accusation of sexual harassment can be as damaging to the teacher as the unethical behavior, teachers should never put themselves in a position to be questioned. It is unfortunate, but once an accusation is made, it never goes away, even if the teacher is found innocent of the charge. Although unfair, the accusation tends to linger in the minds of others (e.g., students, parents, colleagues, supervisors, board members, etc.). Even after a multitude of years pass, after being found innocent of a charge and with the accuser admitting that the incident never happened, the accusation (although unfounded) can easily resurface. Teachers must be diligent at protecting themselves prior to any accusation occurring. Rare is the situation in which a student should be in a teacher's office or classroom alone, with the door shut. If teachers are requested to transport a student, they should bring along someone else. Why hug students when there are other alternatives to showing students that a teacher cares?

Student-to-Student Sexual Harassment

Grube and Lens (2003) discuss the importance of recognizing the impact of student-to-student sexual harassment. These authors offer this discussion in light of a legal ruling in 1999 in the case of *Davis v. Monroe County Board of Education*, which sets school liability for sexual harassment at a more stringent level than that of employers. Grube and Lens suggested that this court ruling exists in contrast with a larger amount of research indicating a substantial amount of sexual harassment that goes unnoticed or ignored in the school setting. These authors acknowledge that part of the problem stems from the inconsistent or confusing definitions of sexual harassment because "the court created no standard for when schoolyard taunts become sexual harassment" (p. 180). Grube and Lens (2003) state that "typically, student-to-student harassment is more likely to include unwanted sexual comments, jokes, looks or gestures; touching, grabbing, or pinching in a sexual way; and spreading sexual rumors, than the more extreme acts of sexual coercion, assault, or rape" (p. 175). Social worker and school counselor involvement are key elements to identification and elimination of sexual harassment because there are severe social, emotional, physical, behavioral, and academic effects of this experience.

Recently, there has been much discussion and debate about teenage use of cell phones for "sexting" purposes. That is, preteens and teens have been caught sending explicit messages and pictures via cell phones. Feyerick and Steffen (2009) describe the Florida case of Phillip Alpert, an 18-year-old male convicted of sending child pornography when he texted a nude picture of his 16-year-old girlfriend to friends of his. Alpert was sentenced to five years probation and had to register as a sex offender. His attorney, Larry Walters, stated "Sexting is treated as child pornography in almost every state and it catches teens completely offguard because this is a fairly natural and normal thing for them to do. It is surprising to us as parents, but for teens it's part of their culture" (para. 6). Teachers, administrators, and counselors can work together and with parents to create a wider awareness of the potential problem of student-to-student sexual harassment. Additionally, teachers and counselors can provide a "'safe haven' for victims" (Grube & Lens, 2003, p. 183) and develop peer leader and peer mediation programs to provide support and discussion on the issue of sexual harassment among peers.

There are those students who do not wish to be touched, there are those parents who do not wish their children touched, and the teachers who think they will never find themselves in front of a judge are the ones who do. This problem can be exaggerated in special education. Teachers need to know that touching students with disabilities provides special problems. Parents, school administrators, and the courts pay heightened attention to any accusation from students, or their parents, who are seen as not being able to protect themselves.

A study by the American Association of University Women (AAUW, 1993) reported that sexual harassment is not something that just involves teachers with students or teachers with colleagues or supervisors. The study reported that sexual harassment occurs more commonly between students than one might expect. Through their research, the AAUW offered evidence of peer-to-peer sexual harassment including sexual comments, jokes, gestures, or looks; touching, grabbing, or pinching in a sexual manner; intentionally brushing against another in a sexual way; flashing or "mooning" others students; spreading sexual rumors; pulling on clothing in a sexual manner; and showing or giving sexual pictures, photographs, illustrations, messages or notes.

Stone and Couch (2004), disturbed by the findings reported by the AAUW, conducted a study examining teachers' opinions and reactions toward peer sexual harassment in high schools. These authors found that although teachers voiced intolerance of sexual harassment and confirmed that, especially when witnessing more severe forms, even though they would take action, personal factors (e.g., teacher's age, sex, and sex-role identity) and situational factors (e.g., size of school) influenced teachers' addressing of sexual harassment between students.

TEACHER AND PARAPROFESSIONAL

One of the areas that pre-professional teacher preparation programs are most lacking in is training the future teacher to work with paraprofessionals. Working with paraprofessionals requires teamwork (as discussed), consultation, and the recognition of responsibility.

Consultation
An activity whereby an expert shares specialized knowledge or skills with others about the issue being discussed

Consultation is an activity in which a person performs the role of an expert who possesses and shares more specialized knowledge or skills than other team members about the issue being discussed (Thomas, Correa, & Morsink, 1995). When working with paraprofessionals, teachers should encourage and facilitate teamwork, share their knowledge and expertise through the consultation model, but, ultimately, teachers must be cognitive that they are responsible for decisions being made and the educational progress of students.

Conflict, both overt and covert, can occur when the new, and most often younger, teacher is given responsibility for the educational progress of a student(s) with whom the paraprofessional has worked for many years. Teachers will best be served by recognizing that paraprofessionals believe that their educational views and methodologies are in the best interest of the students under their care. Often, paraprofessionals have many years' experience working in an educational system and may have worked with and known a particular student quite well. Thus, allowing the paraprofessional to serve as a consultant (an expert) on a particular issue can be in the best interest of the teacher, paraprofessional, and student.

It is important that teachers communicate a willingness to be open and accepting of the paraprofessional's view of what is in the best interest of the student(s). Teachers must devote time and energy in understanding what the paraprofessional is communicating as being in the best interest of the students. Once teachers have a complete understanding of student needs, as presented by the paraprofessional, the teachers must then seek to be understood by the paraprofessional. Often this requires teachers to consult with the paraprofessional in the role of an *expert* in the philosophy and use of **best practices.** Teachers should be advised that negotiation on methodologies is always encouraged, especially if there is the possibility of a stronger outcome. Nevertheless, teachers must always be aware that they ultimately will be held accountable by supervisors, colleagues, parents, and the community for the educational progress (or lack of) of the students.

Best practices
The linking of research evidence to classroom practices

It is only natural for a new teacher to want to be liked by everyone, especially someone as close as the paraprofessional, and, there are no rules that forbid a teacher from being well liked. However, it is unethical for a teacher to compromise what is in the best interest of a student in an effort to be well liked by the paraprofessional or others.

TEACHER AND PARENTS

Teachers face many realities both in and out of the classroom. The nuclear or traditional family is no longer typical. Single-parent families are the fastest growing type of family in the United States (Beebe et al., 2008). Families may not have the natural supports or resources of the extended family that was common to another generation. The constantly changing culture requires that we continually ask, "What is a family?" Although we may never enjoy a consensus, most agree that the **family** is a self-defined unit with an assumption of love and caring among its members. Turnbull, Turnbull, Erwin, and Soodak (2006) define the family as two or more people who regard themselves as a family and who carry out the functions that families typically perform.

Family
A self-defined unit with an assumption of love and caring among its members

Although the vagueness of this definition is critical for understanding the complexity of what the family is in our culture, it adds special problems for the teacher. It is imperative that the teacher is knowledgeable about who has *legal custody* of the student when working with the family. It is not uncommon for a biological parent *without* custody to make demands that are counter to a stepparent *with* custody. Teachers are strongly encouraged not to insert themselves in the middle of a family dispute. The professional teacher knows the importance of following legitimate mandates from the courts.

Quality communication Requires active listening, empathy, openness, honesty, trust, encouragement, and a genuine concern

Along with this train of thought, teachers are encouraged to never disregard or alter a doctor's directive (e.g., prescription dosages/times, etc.), regardless of parental directives or comments from the student. For example, "My mom tells me to only take half of the pill because if I take the whole pill it makes me sick." In this scenario, the teacher is obligated to encourage the parent to inform the prescribing doctor of the side effects and obtain new directions.

Working with parents requires consultation and **quality communication.** Through ongoing and quality communication with parents, decisions that are in the best interest of students are more likely to be made. Quality communication with parents requires active listening, empathy, an openness (unbiased) to the issue(s) of concern, honesty, trust (which must be earned), encouragement, and a genuine concern for the student.

The teacher must recognize that the parents know more about their children than the teacher does (thus, making the parents *experts* in the consultation model) and that the parents have a vested and long-term (after graduation) interest in their children's education. Once the teacher becomes cognitive of this vested and long-term interest, it becomes essential for the teacher to integrate the parents into the educational decisions best suited to their children. Parents should feel welcome and know that their contributions to the educational process are appreciated.

Not only is it important for teachers to be engaged with parents when problems occur, but teachers should also be in contact with parents when positive and productive things happen in the classroom. If teachers contact parents only when something undesirable happens, the parents will dread, and then avoid, having conversations with the teacher. "Ms. Green is on the phone. Johnny must be in trouble again. That is the only time she calls. You deal with her. I dealt with her last time." If teachers are to be agents of encouragement, they will find

Figure 9.1 Working with parents requires consultation and quality communication.

something positive to say about every student. For example, instead of Johnny being "stubborn," Johnny now becomes "persistent." The teacher may purposely contact a parent with nothing but achievements and positive comments on occasion, especially if a concern seems to be lurking around the corner.

After quality communication has been established and is ongoing, and the teacher has recognized the parents as *experts* in the knowledge of their son or daughter, the teacher is now able to perform and be accepted in the role of an *expert* who possesses and then shares specialized knowledge or skills on how students progress academically. Because of the quality communication and rapport building with the parents, the parents will recognize that the teacher's views, strategies, and methodologies are in the best interest of their children.

An essential goal for teachers is to establish relationships with parents that are productive and, whenever possible, even enjoyable for all concerned. Teachers should become sensitive to signs that indicate a failure in establishing productive relationships with parents. These signs may include defensiveness, blaming, personal attacks, insults, sarcasms, and withdrawing. The teacher must continually reach out to all parents, even when parents seem standoffish. Unfortunately, it is inevitable that conflicts between parents and teachers will occur. The conflict itself is not the issue, but rather, how the conflict is managed is vital to everyone's interest. As stated previously, good things can come from conflict is managed appropriately. The teacher must remain professional at all times, willing to offer quality communication and manage all disagreements as if they were problems to be solved.

TEACHER AND COLLEAGUES

Working with colleagues requires **collaboration** and successful outcomes. Collaboration is an interactive process whereby team members develop creative ways to solve issues students may encounter (Thomas, Correa, & Morsink, 1995). While collaborating, colleagues work together in a joint effort to meet common goals and specific outcomes. Team members take turns sharing their knowledge and expertise in a reciprocal rather than authoritarian manner. In the process of collaboration, at one point, a team member may be the consultant (*expert*), and at another point, the one being consulted these roles continually change. The person who consults possesses the necessary knowledge and expertise on a given topic at a particular time. Once this information is disseminated to the other team members, the role of consultant is released to another member, who takes on the role of consultant or expert. When teachers collaborate with colleagues, their interaction assures that each team member contributes and every contribution is valued. The whole team then acknowledges, respects, and appreciates everyone's contributions and creativity. Collaboration encourages varying opinions, and in these different opinions, teachers find strengths. Collaborative activities allow teachers to step outside of their knowledge base and experience new

Collaboration
An interactive process whereby team members develop creative ways to solve student issues

learning opportunities from colleagues. Through professional interactions in which everyone participates and their contributions are valued, team members declare ownership in the process and create or renew their commitments. This development of ownership facilitates the sharing of responsibilities, sharing of decision making, and ultimately, the successful outcomes of the issues in question.

It is only natural for a teacher to turn to a colleague for emotional support. Teachers may find themselves sought out in times of emotional stress, especially if they continue to be uplifting to everyone around them (e.g., students, colleagues, paraprofessionals, supervisors, parents, etc.). Teachers must be reminded that they cannot help anyone become healthy, unless they are healthy themselves. To help another requires a very conscious decision and commitment on the helper's part, and one must recognize not only one's ability to help, but one's qualification to help another.

As in all decisions a teacher makes, ethical considerations are always on the forefront. The teacher must be prepared to deal with unethical requests by colleagues, and ethical decisions should always be decided by what is in the best interest of the students.

SUMMARY

Teachers have the professional obligation to interact with everyone they meet in a respectful, courteous, and conscientious way. Working with supervisors requires teamwork and knowledge of their goals. Through teamwork, we are able to solve complex and demanding issues that may not be able to be dealt with by anyone person acting alone. Often the outcome of teamwork is a product more beneficial to students than efforts by a single person. Knowing supervisors' goals is beneficial to all. Upon meeting their goals, supervisors can gain the reputation as leaders from colleagues. Teachers, by supporting and facilitating goal achievements, can show their supervisors their competencies as future leaders. When all is said, students may be the biggest winners when teachers assist in meeting supervisors' goals. The best time to learn about a supervisor's goals is during the hiring process.

Sexual harassment is in the eye of the beholder. Teachers must remember that the person being accused of sexual harassment is not in the position to argue that his or her conduct is not harassment. The person feeling victimized or offended by the conduct is the person to whom we must be sensitive. There are two types of sexual harassment: *quid pro quo* (an authority suggesting or demanding an exchange of sexual advances or behavior for promotion) and *hostile environment* (unsolicited or unwelcome sexual contact interferes with an individual's performance or creates a work environment that is offensive or intimidating).

Consultation, teamwork, and the recognition of responsibility are needed when working with paraprofessionals. In essence, teachers must actively listen to their paraprofessionals, thoroughly understand their views, and recognize their input is in the best interest of their students.

Ultimately, teachers must be aware that they alone will be responsible for the educational outcome of their students.

When working with parents, teachers must consult with them (remembering that parents also play a role as an expert in the consultation model) and use quality communication. Quality communication requires active listening, empathy, openness, honesty, trust, encouragement, and a genuine concern for the student. Teachers should be constantly looking for opportunities to interact in positive situations with parents; they should not contact parents only when students act out. Once reliable and quality communication has been established, the teacher will be regarded as an expert in the educational strategies best suited for the student.

When teachers work with colleagues, collaboration and a successful outcome is essential. Through collaboration, teachers develop creative ways to solve a multitude of issues. The joint efforts to meet common goals often lead to specific and productive outcomes. Collaboration offers teachers professional growth in their knowledge and experience gained from new learning opportunities. Through participation by all team members, an appreciation of everyone's contributions, an acquired ownership of the issues, and commitment, successful outcomes are better achieved.

The concepts presented above are neatly packaged, but in truth, is much overlap. For example, while working with parents in a consultation fashion, collaboration is a very productive strategy. Second, conflict in all the above situations is inevitable. The conflict in itself is immaterial, what is relevant is how the conflict is managed. Finally, preservice teachers should prepare themselves today for the ethical decisions they will be making tomorrow.

CASE 9.A

Eric is a second grader who is struggling in Mrs. Elm's classroom. It is not that he isn't capable of doing good work in her class, but he is continually misbehaving in class, and that misbehavior impedes him from learning all that he can in class. One day he decided to take the whiteboard markers and write his name on the walls of the classroom. Another day, he crawled under his table and did not come out. On another day, he would throw his pencil at nearby classmates and then would crawl on the floor to retrieve the pencil. Every time he would do something in class, she would stop and try to get him back on task. Mrs. Elm has tried many strategies to assist Eric in staying focused and on task. Unfortunately, her attempts have not been successful.

QUESTIONS

1. What should Mrs. Elm do?

2. What has she been doing wrong with Eric?

3. Who can she turn to for help?

4. What advice should they give her?

5. What are some strategies that Mrs. Elm could employ that might help increase the positive behavior that she is looking for Eric to provide in class?

Success always comes when preparation meets opportunity.
—Henry Hartman

Give me six hours to chop down a tree and I will spend the first four sharpening the axe.
—Abraham Lincoln

10 Relationships with Students: Before They Arrive

OBJECTIVES

After completing this chapter you should be able to:

- Describe what an educationally safe environment is and provide examples.
- Explain behavior management techniques that can be used to shape behavior.
- Discuss why students can use the avoidance and escape strategy in a classroom and what a teacher can do to eliminate this behavior.
- Explain the 90/10 rule and why it should be reversed.
- Describe differentiated instruction and how students can be placed into instructional categories to meet their needs.
- Identify and provide examples of the levels of Abraham Maslow's hierarchy of needs.
- Compare role theory and the existentialist perspective.
- Discuss how teachers can effectively avoid creating dependency issues in their students.
- Describe situations when teachers should not help students.

KEY TERMS

Avoidance and escape

Dependency

Differentiated instruction

Educationally safe environments

Need for control

Role theory

90/10 rule

BEFORE THEY ARRIVE

Building productive relationships with students begins prior to the students entering the classroom. The first and most important step in this process of building relationships is creating environments in which students want to be. As obvious as this advice may be, many teachers need to be reminded of where *they,* themselves, learned the most.

Educationally safe environments Classrooms that are physically and emotionally safe, that encourage and appreciate risk taking, that offer continuous encouragement, and that promote mutual respect

We begin this first step by ensuring that the classroom is an **educationally safe environment.** Educationally safe environments (ESE) are classrooms that are physically and emotionally safe, that encourage and appreciate risk taking, that offer continuous encouragement and promote mutual respect. Numerous chapters in many books are devoted to the benefits of seating charts, kidney tables, and well-organized classrooms. While these are important points to keep in mind when planning the classroom, the teacher needs to recognize that seating charts without the benefits of an ESE do not create a classroom conducive to relationship building or learning. These ESE are at the heart of student success. Teachers need to self-reflect on the times they took risks and participated in their classes the most, where they worked the hardest and gained the most knowledge, and where relationships were established. These are the environments that teachers should create, and they are created prior to the students arriving.

If the teacher creates a physically and emotionally safe environment that students want to be in, behavioral issues are less likely to occur, and when they do occur, they are much more manageable. This point leads to the contributions of the behaviorist. Historically, behaviorists are called in only after a problem with a student has become unmanageable. Although behaviorists are effective in dealing with undesirable behaviors, the point is being missed; behaviorist's ideas should be called in prior to the students arriving in the classroom.

BEHAVIORISM

The founders of human relations had shared beliefs; they "saw human beings as being social in their basic nature and as having no existence apart from existence in relationship to other human beings" (Swensen, 1973, p. 8). There exists a dissenting vote, **John B. Watson** (1878–1958). Watson contributed to the founding of the behaviorist movement in American psychology. According to him, cognitive theory lacks verifiability because the processes take place internally, and there is no way to confirm their existence. Watson reduced human behaviors to pure overt behaviors. He harshly objected to introspection (a research methodology used by Wilhelm Wundt), which he considered unscientific. Psychology's real concern, according to Watson, is to study behavior, not consciousness. He believed that science can exist only through the recording of behavior objectively.

Watson (1913) advocated the complete abolition of any datum in psychology that did not result from direct observation. He considered such concepts as mind, instincts, thought, and emotion both useless and superfluous. Watson removed the *self* from scientific discussions and inaugurated a purely objective experimental branch of the natural sciences in which there was no place for such mentalist concepts as the self or consciousness. He thrust aside all introspective interpretations of thinking.

Today's teachers who have an expertise in behaviorism use direct observation methods for problem definition in observable and measurable terms, identification of target behaviors for change, and the use of data-based intervention and assessment methods. Teachers with a background in behaviorism also offer a positive and systematic way of managing classroom behavior and arrange/manipulate the learning environment to produce desired behavior changes. See Alberto and Troutman (2003), *Applied Behavioral Analysis for Teachers*, for a complete and comprehensive discussion of behaviorism in the classroom.

Conscious Discipline Program

Reinforcement and punishment are techniques that have been used in the classroom for many years. Behaviorist theory explains that anything that increases or strengthens a behavior is a reinforcer and anything that decreases or weakens a behavior is considered a punisher. Teachers can use praise, prizes, and various privileges as reinforcers to shape student and classroom behavior. Additionally, when a student displays an undesirable behavior, a time-out or negative consequence can be used as a punishment to manage that misbehavior. When used effectively, these techniques can have a positive impact on the classroom climate; however, Hoffman, Hutchinson, and Reiss (2009) have developed and tested a new training program for teachers that creates an emotionally intelligent classroom, decreasing the reliance on the use of rewards and punishments. Teachers from pre-kindergarten through the sixth grade participated in 8 one-day workshops from the program titled Conscious Discipline over the course of one academic year. A total of 117 teachers took part in both the preassessment and postassessment of learning and attitudes. According to these researchers, the "Conscious Discipline program is designed to help teachers enhance social and emotional skills of children and thus enhance the overall school climate" (Hoffman et al., 2009, p. 17). Teachers who completed the follow-up assessment demonstrated a better understanding of classroom management techniques including "releasing external control, embracing conflict resolution and implementing a more emotionally targeted reward structure in the classroom" (p. 13). From Hoffman and colleagues we learn that teachers should seek out training in classroom management techniques that "foster more intrinsic motivation to behavior, learn, and excel" and use emotional intelligence principles taught in programs such as Conscious Discipline.

Figure 10.1 When a teacher creates a physically and emotionally safe environment, behavioral issues are less likely to occur.

CONTRIBUTIONS OF BEHAVIORISTS

Behaviorists have made significant contributions to the field of education. Behavior-management techniques are used by teachers to ensure an environment that is conducive to rapport building and learning. Through the use of direct observations and effective strategies, behaviorists have given teachers many tools for and much better understanding of behaviors that exist in the classroom. Behaviorists have offered much evidence, and enlightened teachers regard the lack of benefits punitive measures offer.

For example, punishment:

- Provides a model of aggression.
- Produces avoidance and escape behavior.
- Only suppresses behavior.
- Fails to teach desirable behaviors.
- Gives undesired attention to behaviors

Nevertheless, a teacher's most immediate response to acting-out behavior is to punish the student. Behaviorists have offered many efficient strategies to get students to display desirable behaviors by replacing the undesirable behaviors without the use of nonbeneficial punishers.

Another example of the contributions behaviorists have given the educator is evidence that time-out procedures are often overused and found to be ineffective owing to the lack of understanding of this concept. It is important to remember that *teachers are obligated to create an environment that students want to be a part of.* The teacher may be preoccupied with using time-out as a punitive device but instead should be preoccupied with designing a classroom in which, once students are removed, they will wish to be reinstated. If teachers create a classroom in which their students wish to be included, then sending a student to time-out is a very effective strategy and needs only a short time (e.g., 5 minutes) in time-out. Much too often, a student does not wish to be included in a classroom. When the student returns from time-out, the teacher is amazed to find that time-out is ineffective, resulting in the teacher only sending the student away for longer periods of time ... *but this is not time-out.* If the environment is truly reinforcing to the student, 5 minutes in time-out is all that is necessary; *if the environment is not reinforcing, the teacher is not sending the student to time-out but just getting rid of the student for the teacher's own benefit.* Again, *teachers are obligated to create an environment that students want to be a part of.* Once this environment is created, behavior management techniques, like time-out, become much more effective.

A very powerful contribution by behaviorists that can be easily applied in the classroom is the concept of functions of behaviors. Most often the focus of undesirable behavior is on the student's behavior itself. Although this sounds logical, it misses the point. There exist reasons (known as "functions") for all behaviors. Focusing on "Johnny's kicking of the trash can" will only promote the continuation of undesirable behaviors. The teacher must analyze the function of this behavior or the *reason* for this behavior. Most undesirable behaviors in the classroom serve the function of obtaining *attention, avoiding or escaping something undesirable,* or attempting to get *control* of their lives. For example, if Johnny has an emotional need for "attention" and is unable to obtain this emotional need from his teacher in a desirable manner, kicking the trash can (or distracting a classmate) would be one immediate course of action to meet this need. If the teacher chooses to focus only on the behavior of kicking the trash can, after raising his or her voice numerous times the teacher can likely put an end to this behavior, but the emotional need for attention will persist and manifest itself in other undesirable behaviors such as dropping books off the desk, tossing pencils and paper balls in the air, and getting out of his seat without permission. However, if the teacher chooses to deal with the function or reason for the behavior rather than the behavior itself, a great deal of constructive relationship building can be accomplished. Teachers must decide, "Do I want to give my attention for doing desirable behaviors?" or "Do I want to ignore the functions of the behaviors and give my attention to undesirable behaviors?" The teacher should not make the mistake and assume the need for "attention," "avoidance and escape," and "control" will go away. These emotional needs must be addressed or undesirable behaviors will persist.

The weakest area of many school curriculums is the lack of giving students *choices* and *decision-making opportunities* that impact their lives. Nevertheless, teachers expect their graduates to go out into the world and make good choices and decisions. Many undesirable behaviors found in the classroom often stem from the students' perspective that they have no control in decisions that affect their lives. For these students, the **need for control** is the "function" (or reason) for their undesirable behaviors. Acting-out behaviors can be an attempt to maintain *some* control in their lives. Offering choices, *especially when disciplining*

Need for control
Natural desire to feel a sense of control over one's environment, Often the function or reason behind undesirable behaviors in the classroom

students, allows students the opportunity to gain back some control of their lives. The teacher can decide on three consequences for an undesirable behavior, all three consequences being fair and appropriate for the rule infraction. The teacher must remind the student that he or she is a person of worth and is responsible for the infraction, and he or she must choose the consequence, leaving the student the feeling of some control of their lives.

Interesting and worth noting is that when principals withdraw or remove control from teachers, mutiny and all-out war is often the response. Ironically, teachers will fight tirelessly over decisions that impact their positions, but then the same teachers will march into a classroom and think nothing about taking control away from their students. According to Nastasi, Clements, and Battista (1990), if students perceive they have no control over their environment, then their motivation or efforts often will decline; however, if students perceive they have some control within their environment, they are more motivated to achieve.

Teachers should recognize that power struggles are often a result of students attempting to get some control of their lives. One thing that is apparent to many seasoned teachers is that if a teacher is engaged in a power struggle with a student, the teacher has already lost. The very act of a nine-year-old to get the teacher to play the "power struggle game" means that the nine-year-old has won.

Teachers are to make clear and concise requests. When a student attempts to initiate a power struggle, the teacher should repeat the request and move away leaving the student to deal with the lack of compliance on his or her own. The teacher should move toward another student who is doing the work as requested and show appreciation for the compliant and desirable behavior. Note that the teacher is giving attention for desirable behaviors versus attention for undesirable behaviors. Although this is an effective strategy for dealing with power struggles, teachers should not forget that everyone has the right to have *some* control over their lives. When teachers offer *some* control (via choices and decisions) to students, power struggles are better managed and greatly minimized.

Avoidance and escape
A strategy used by students who struggle academically to avoid and escape the curriculum by acting out and being removed from the classroom.

A popular strategy that students who struggle both academically and socially engage in is **avoidance and escape.** It is often more desirable for a student to act out and be asked to leave the classroom than to admit to the teacher and their peers that they do not understand the subject matter. The teacher must recognize that some undesirable behaviors may have the function of avoiding or escaping the curriculum. If teachers become aware of avoidance and escape behaviors, they must work with the student to ensure academic success, thus eliminating the need to avoid or escape the curriculum.

It is important that teachers prepare before the students arrive to meet the emotional needs of all their students. This process is not as hard to do as it sounds and only requires teachers to establish some good habits. Teachers should prepare themselves to give all of their students attention. Some students will have more emotional needs for attention than others will, but all students deserve attention. The students with more emotional needs for attention *will find ways to get attention,* one way or another. The teacher's choice will be in deciding whether to give attention for desired or undesired behaviors. Teachers must also prepare to offer choices to all of their students. Some students who have emotional needs to gain a measure of control over their lives will engage in power struggles in an attempt to get this need met, but all students should be given the opportunity to practice making choices and decisions that impact their lives. How else can we prepare our students for the adult world? Finally, teachers should be preparing themselves to ensure the academic success of all of their students, thus eliminating behaviors intended to avoid and escape the curriculum. In essence, teachers should develop the habits of giving all students attention, choices and decision-making opportunities, and the means to be successful in the curriculum. The outcome of these habits will be that disruptive behaviors will be manageable and minimal and an environment conducive to beneficial relationship building.

Another contribution to education by behaviorists is the concept of the **90/10 rule.** It is important that teachers verbally acknowledge, reinforce, and draw attention to the numerous desirable behaviors that go on in their classrooms. Teachers must find ways to compliment students for the behaviors they wish students to repeat to the classroom (e.g., being on time, staying on task, participating in discussions, turning in homework on time, etc.). The 90/10 rule states that teachers spend 90% of their time looking for undesirable behaviors and only 10% of their time looking for desirable behaviors. These percentages must be reversed. Teachers must be on the look out for desirable behaviors 90% of the time and be willing to acknowledge their presence, while spending the other 10% of their time watching for and addressing the undesirable behaviors.

90/10 rule
Teachers spend 90% of their time looking for undesirable behaviors and only 10% of their time looking for desirable behaviors; this must be reversed.

Many teachers believe that classroom management begins with putting student rules on the walls. The behaviorists believe that if teachers do not create classrooms that students want to be in, *the list of rules on the walls may only serve to remind students what they need to do to be asked to leave the uninviting classroom*. Rarely does learning occur in an environment that is not emotionally safe, where risk taking is not appreciated or encouraged, where only the opinions of the teacher are examined, and where the relevance of the subject to the real world is not apparent. However, when these characteristics do exist, students not only desire to be in that setting but also excel in their efforts for academic success and productive relationship building.

RULES FOR TEACHERS

We have noted that many teachers believe classroom management begins with putting student rules on the walls. One interesting view is that teachers should post *rules for teachers* on the walls. For example: teachers will be respectful, courteous, accepting of students, encouraging, never use sarcasm or ridicule, and so forth. Maybe, students will be reminded of the behaviors being modeled to them by their teachers. One way or another, this is an interesting message being sent to the students.

Along these lines, it is always a good idea to involve students in developing **classroom rules** which provides opportunities for students to become invested in classroom behaviors and decision making that governs a group.

ACADEMIC PROGRESS PROMOTES PRODUCTIVE RELATIONSHIPS

Academic progress promotes productive relationships, and productive relationships in turn promote continued academic success. In an effort to address *all* students' academic needs we introduce the reader to the field of **differentiated instruction.** According to Mastropieri and Scruggs (2007), "differentiated instruction is based upon the idea that all learners do not necessarily learn in the same way, and refers to the practice of ensuring that each learner receive the methods and materials most suitable for that particular learner at that particular place in the curriculum" (p. 126).

Differentiated instruction
The practice of ensuring that each learner receive the methods and materials most suitable for that particular learner.

A simplistic way of addressing *all* students' academic needs is to put the students into four categories, *obviously, without drawing attention to the students*:

1. Talented students who the general curriculum is not able to challenge.
2. Typical students who are being challenged by the general curriculum.
3. Students who, for whatever reason, are not motivated to progress through the curriculum (although having demonstrated the abilities to do so).
4. Students with identified disabilities, or at-risk of being identified, who need strategies and accommodations to be successful.

Creative teachers, who are interested in the success of *all* their students, design lessons to challenge the talented students (e.g., expanding or enhancing the curriculum); continually assess whether the typical students are being challenged and progressing through the general curriculum; find lessons that are challenging, interesting, student-centered, and relevant to the real-world topics to motivate those students who find learning as uninteresting and a waste of time; and identify those students with disabilities or at risk, who are struggling and in need of support, resources, and/or accommodations in order to be successful. One strategy that is often underused by teachers is to have discussions with students regarding supports and resources that will make their learning easier. We, as educated professionals, tend to believe that because we are teachers, we should be making these decisions on our own. In truth, often students know more about how they learn than any professional will ever know.

Teachers should assess each student's needs, and placing each student in an appropriate category should be done through informal assessments developed by the teacher. Strategies for assessing students' abilities include having students write informal papers on topics (e.g., on their background, personal experiences, interests for motivational purposes, and knowledge of a subject matter, etc.), analyzing quizzes or tests (versus just adding up the number wrong), noting the amount and quality of participation in class discussions, and self-identification in areas of strengths and weaknesses.

Being an educator means being willing to teach *all* students versus only certain students. Students in all four of the categories mentioned above must be *challenged* and must *experience success* in the classroom. It may be difficult, if not impossible, to develop and maintain productive relationships with students who are not able to progress academically. Again, good relationships promote academic progress, and academic progress promotes good relationships.

HIERARCHY OF NEEDS AND SELF-TRANSCENDENCE

Relationship-building requires teachers to focus not only on the academic needs of their students, but also on their nonacademic needs. Prior to students arrival at school, teachers should develop strategies to ensure students' nonacademic needs will be met.

Abraham H. Maslow (1908–1970) is a cofounder of humanistic psychology. He credits the events of a parade soon after the bombing of Pearl Harbor, in which he cried, as the reason for the shift to a humanistic view. He often referred to humanistic psychology as the "third force in psychology" (behaviorism and psychoanalytic theory are the first and second forces). Humanistic psychology emphasizes and studies the healthy side of personality and thus offers an alternative to the pessimistic determinism of Freudian psychoanalysis and the mechanistic determinism of behaviorism (Alexander, 2000). Humanists believe that human beings have free will and contend that behavior is organized primarily around the positive motive of self-fulfillment. Maslow believed that people are inherently good, moral, and prosocial, and are capable of developing in healthy ways if given an environment in which their potential can be expressed.

Maslow saw an individual's needs as arranged in a hierarchy. The needs that are lower in hierarchy (known as deficiency needs) must be satisfied before individuals can move on to the needs that are higher in the hierarchy (known as being needs). The hierarchy, beginning with the most basic, includes the following:

1. ***Physiological Needs***. These must be satisfied if the body is to keep functioning. They include water, food, air, rest, and sleep.
2. ***Safety Needs***. After the physiological needs are met, the safety needs emerge. These include safety from physical harm or threat of harm, the need for security, and freedom from fear.
3. ***Belongingness and Love Needs***. Needs at this level include finding and maintaining relationships. Individuals desire to be part of a

Figure 10.2 Maslow's hierarchy of needs

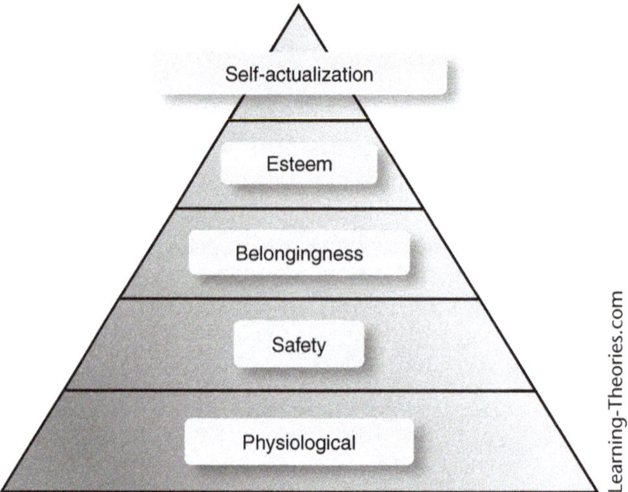

community. Often these needs are met by sustaining meaningful relationships, marrying, having a family, joining a church, or becoming members of an organization they value.

4. ***Esteem Needs***. Generally, esteem needs center on the issue of establishing a reasonable self-esteem. However, this level of needs can be broken into two levels. At the lower level, people seek to gain respect from others (e.g., fame, status, recognition, etc.), whereas at the higher level they desire self-respect (e.g., confidence, competence, sense of achievement, etc.).
5. ***Need for Self-Actualization***. At the highest level of needs is Maslow's description of the need for self-actualization. Again, to reach this point of the hierarchy, one must have filled all the other needs previously stated; thus, according to Maslow, not many people reach this level. At stage five, self-actualization, one has understanding, creativity, and aesthetic appreciation. According to Maslow, self-actualization is an ongoing process, not an end-point at which a person arrives once and for all.

Teachers must have an understanding of where their students are in the hierarchy of needs and provide those things that will help them fulfill that need. It is imperative that teachers learn to recognize their students' needs. If students are hungry, cold, or fearful, teachers will have a difficult time creating environments conducive to learning. The teacher's goal is to meet as many of these needs as possible, knowing that *each student may be on a different need level*. In a classroom, the teacher may be challenged with getting warm clothes for one student, while raising self-esteem for another; both will be necessary for either student to learn.

Viktor Frankl (1905–1997) disagreed with Maslow's perspective. Frankl, a survivor of several concentration camps during the Holocaust, proposed that the real aim of human existence cannot be found in self-actualization, but in *self-transcendence* (1978). Self-transcendence is the need to rise above the narrow absorption with the self. One achieves this by overlooking oneself and by giving of oneself to other people and good causes (Alexander, 2000). The more one forgets oneself by giving over to a cause or to serve or another person, the more human that person is. This involves transcending personal interests. According to Frankl, "Self-actualization is not an attainable aim at all, for the simple reason that the more one would strive for it, the more he would miss it. In other words, self-actualization is possible only as a side-effect of self-transcendence" (p. 115). Frankl notes that careful consideration of a situation will often lead to the conclusion that personal interests are not separate from the interest of others.

Teachers must recognize and be willing to focus outward in efforts to make a difference in the lives of their students. Much of this text has focused on the need for teachers to become other-orientated (Beebe et al., 2008) when considering the most effective ways to relate with others. As noted previously, this requires that we consider the needs, motives, desires, goals, thoughts, and feelings of our students. Your authors believe that teachers should focus on students' needs (Maslow's hierarchy) and teach students to focus on others' needs (Frankl's self-transcending).

ROLE THEORY AND EXISTENTIAL PHENOMENOLOGY

According to Bruner (1990):

> When we enter human life, it is as if we walk on a stage into a play whose enactment is already in progress—a play whose somewhat open plot determines what parts we may play and toward what denouements we may be heading. Others on the stage already have a sense of what the play is about, enough to make negotiation with a newcomer possible. (p. 34)

Prior to students arriving, teachers should examine the impact and the many influences that roles play in the development of students. According to Swensen (1973), **role theory** is an application of social interaction. In any social interaction there are roles being played out (e.g., principal-teacher, professor-student, colleague-colleague, etc.). Whether overt or covert, every role has prescriptions that specify what behaviors are *expected* from the person who occupies the role (Biddle & Thomas, 1966, p. 14). A teacher, for example, must interact in a *prescriptive fashion* with people occupying several other roles (e.g., students, principal, faculty, and parents).

Role theory
Every role has prescriptions that specify what behaviors are expected from the person who occupies the role.

It is important to note that we are not born with the knowledge necessary for acting out the many roles we will play; rather, we learn the appropriate scripts through *socialization by others* (Goffman, 1959).This goes back to the discussion on Cooley and Mead (chapter 1). Mead (1934) sees the development of the self and the ability to take on roles occurring simultaneously. According to Cooley (1902), whether significant others give approval or disapproval, their attitudes guide in learning to play the roles, either assigned or assumed. **Role theory** assumes that personality (the self) depends on the demands of the role one plays (e.g., class clown, troublemaker, scholar, athlete, etc.) rather than on fixed and long-term characteristics of the person.

Role definitions are associated with particular positions and refer to behavior that is *expected* of an individual, not to the actual behavior (Cardwell, 1971). According to role theory, if a student with a mild learning disability were to be put into a special education classroom designed for students with intellectual disabilities, the student with a learning disability would learn the role of a student with intellectual disability. According to Jane Mercer (1973), mental retardation exists only as a "category of thought." She notes that society locates all these persons who hold this status and those who are playing this role and then classify them as such. Urie Bronfenbrenner (1990) agrees with Mercer's view. He offers evidence that persons with typical intelligence who were institutionalized would soon take on the role of a person with an intellectual disability and, after being placed back into the community, revert back to being "typical." Teachers might choose to infer from role theory that there are no *"bright kids" or "slow kids," only kids who have taken on these roles.*

Teachers must decide on which roles they want their students to learn and be able to perform. Students should learn and take on the roles of being self-determined, self-disciplined, with high self-esteem and self-worth, and having the confidence to challenge themselves and the world they live in.

Tied closely with role theory is the existentialist perspective. The existentialists see much of our modern torment as rooted in our alienation from ourselves and from our fellow beings. They seek to put us back into contact with that from which we are alienated—particularly with our own experiences. The existentialist sees impersonal communication occurring when we treat people as objects, or when we respond to their roles rather than who they are as unique people.

According to **Ronald David Laing** (1964), we have been cut off from others by being trained to perform certain functions and fill certain roles so that we do not interact with our fellow beings as one person relating to another person but as one role relating to another role: as teacher to student, as clerk to customer, or as doctor to patient. The interaction with the person has been lost. The most important element of the relationship of one person to another person has been repressed (Swensen, 1973). Instead, the person has become "doctor," acting out that role to the patient who is not a person, but rather the "pneumonia case in room 188" (the message in the movie *Patch Adams*).

Role theory and the existentialist perspective offer an interesting dilemma for teachers. On the one hand, the teacher must recognize the importance of instructing a person in the role of becoming a productive student (e.g., good students develop good study habits, are self-disciplined, attend class, and participate in discussions, etc.). On the other hand, in the instruction of the role of students, the teacher must never interact with students as roles. Once teachers see students as roles and not as unique individuals, they have cut themselves off from the opportunity to establish healthy, productive, and quality relationships.

DEPENDENCY ISSUES

Prior to students arriving at school, teachers must become aware of their part in creating **dependency** issues. Humans want to be liked; it is an important part of human nature. New teachers work especially hard to be liked by their class. In an attempt to be liked, we often run into dependency issues. Being unaware that this is a dependency issue and wanting students to like us, we find ourselves intervening on behalf of the student(s).

Dependency
An undesirable situation in which a student becomes overreliant on a teacher for assistance, reassurance, or confidence building.

Several issues accompany dependency. Interestingly, dependency is most often caused by *fear*. The fear of failure is commonplace with a dependent student. Once a teacher rescues a student by removing the fear, the student becomes dependent on the teacher when the fear returns.

Caraway, Tucker, Reinke, and Hall (2003) examined personal characteristics of high school students including self-efficacy, goal orientation, and fear of failure as predicting student school engagement. In their research, Caraway and colleagues note that a high fear of failure is often associated with a low self-efficacy or confidence in performance that leads to students avoiding failure at all costs for fear of shame or embarrassment. These authors also found that students who have a fear of failure show less engagement with school. It is not difficult to imagine a student who lacks school engagement and has a fear of failure seeking help from anyone who is willing to offer it. Thus, when a teacher intervenes and rescues the student once, the teacher will likely find the same student asking for more intervention to remove another fear in the future.

Another issue of dependency to consider is that once the teacher recognizes a student-dependency relationship and decides to stop the dependency, the teacher now becomes open to attack from the student. In this situation, the student often turns on the teacher because the student now realizes that the teacher, who was there previously to rescue the student, is no longer willing to save the student. This absence of perceived support causes additional anxiety and *fear* within the student and is then manifested in anger toward the previous rescuer. In the worst situation, this anger may manifest itself into a verbal or physical altercation or an accusation of some type of wrongdoing.

A third issue that the teacher should consider when a student has become dependent is that dependence often results in a student regressing. This unnecessary reliance on others impedes the growth of self-esteem, self-worth, self-determination, and academic confidence.

How do teachers go about combating dependency? If a teacher becomes aware of the above issues regarding dependency, the teacher is in a position to support and encourage the student to deal with fears in an appropriate manner. The teacher can offer suggestions to the student on how to go about discussing this issue with another teacher. In some situations, the teacher may offer role-playing or a type of rehearsal as strategies to increase the confidence of the student to face his or her fears. During role-play, the teacher can ask questions and require assurances from the student that this behavior will not happen again. The teacher is also in the position to let the student know that this issue, which is presently very serious to the student, is not as serious as the student believes. (Colleges and parents do not deny or evict students because of one test score.) The teacher may offer personal experiences, explaining that this will one day be not nearly as serious as the student is envisioning. A meta-story (chapter 5) titled "The Stuff Heroes Are Made Of," sends the message that personal growth, independence, confidence, self-worth, and self-esteem are acquired through facing one's fears.

When students learn to confront and conquer their personal fears, they grow in self-esteem, self-worth, self-determination, and academic confidence. Lastly, interestingly, by encouraging and supporting the student to confront his or her fears, the teacher is often in a more favorable position to be liked by the student.

KNOWING WHEN NOT TO HELP STUDENTS

Prior to students arriving, teachers must become aware that there are those times when teachers should not be helping their students. As strange as this may seem, if a teacher cannot be *open* and *accepting* to the student and the situation, the teacher should rely on someone else to help the student. If teachers find themselves in a situation in which they cannot be objective, they have a professional obligation to refer the student to someone else who is not emotionally involved. Teachers, as members of the human race, feel strongly about many issues (e.g., abortion, gay rights, assisted suicide, gun control, death penalty, etc.). Professional teachers recognize their convictions (also known as "hot buttons"). Bringing in these biased views into the student's situation removes the teacher's openness. If a teacher feels strongly about an issue, it is difficult (if not impossible) to be open to the student's situation and accepting of the student's views.

Another time that a teacher should not attempt to assist a student is when the *teacher believes that the student is unable to solve a problem on his or her own*. If teachers do not feel confident that the student, *with guidance*, can solve the problem, they are professionally obligated to find someone who *does* believe the student can solve the problem. Having the belief that a student is incapable of solving problems is being discouraging and disrespectful to the student. By owning the belief that the student is not capable, the teacher is creating the *dependency problems* warned about earlier in this chapter. Often teachers, because they are in a position of authority, think that they must solve all problems that come their way. It is crucial to understand that referring a student to someone else is not a sign of weakness or inability, rather an awareness that the teacher is working in the best interest of the student.

As awkward as this may sound, it is also important for the teacher not to attempt to help a student if the teacher is not as *emotionally healthy* as he or she would like to be. We hope that the teacher can recognize that it takes two healthy people to have a healthy relationship. If a student approaches you distraught over an important issue (e.g., an eating disorder), and you are not emotionally healthy (e.g., have an eating disorder yourself), the student and you together are likely to arrive at a conclusion that is not desirable for the student. Conversely, if you are emotionally healthy, you are better able to guide the student in finding his or her own solution.

Lastly, teachers should not attempt to assist a student when they are being *pressured, are hassled, or tired.* The practitioner in the field often chuckles at this, noting that if teachers were to follow this suggestion, no student would ever be helped. Nevertheless, if the teacher is being pressured to make a decision, especially one that is obviously an ethical decision, making the decision while being pressured rarely is in the best interest of the teacher or student. Teachers should attempt to hold off making important decisions until the next morning; the assumption is that they are not as tired as they would be at the end of the day. As far as being hassled, if teachers find themselves feeling frustrated or angered by a situation, decisions are best put off until emotions are calmed. In summary, there really are those times when it is not advisable to attempt to help students.

SUMMARY

There are two purposes for developing this chapter and titling it "Before They Get Here." The first purpose is to give to future teachers the opportunity to think about what kind of classrooms they wish to create and to spend time reflecting on how to go about achieving this desired environment. The type of environment a teacher creates is strongly correlated with relationship building. The second purpose of this chapter is to start a dialogue with teachers regarding the skills they need before they enter the classroom. As teachers grow in skills their students progress academically, and as students succeed the opportunity for relationship building is increased which, in turn, produces continued academic success.

It is important for relationship building and academic success that students are in educationally safe environments (ESEs). These are the classrooms that students want to be in, are physically and emotionally safe, where risk taking is encouraged and then appreciated, and mutual respect is promoted and modeled by the teacher. In ESE, undesirable behaviors are less likely and when they occur are much more manageable.

It is very difficult to develop relationships with students if their nonacademic needs are not being addressed. Maslow's hierarchy of needs furthers this discussion. The issues surrounding students' needs are in the identification of these needs and in the recognition that each student is going to be on a specific need level. Some students will have "deficiency needs" (e.g., need for warm clothes, lunch money, etc.) while others will have "being needs" (e.g., needs for increased self-esteem, self-worth, self-determination, etc.). A dissenting view of Maslow's perspective is the work of Frankl. Frankl notes that we should learn to transcend our own personal interest, which is the true aim of human existence. Teachers should focus on students' needs (Maslow's hierarchy of needs) and teach their students to transcend their own interest to that of others (Frankl).

What skills do teachers need before entering the classroom? The behaviorists offer a great deal of insight into behaviors found in classrooms. A teacher trained in the principles of behaviorism will use direct observation methods to identify problems in observable and measurable terms, develop and implement interventions for desired change, and then monitor the change.

One of the contributions offered by behaviorists is the need and obligation for teachers to create classrooms that students want to be in. In doing so, time-out strategies become very effective. If students do not wish to be in teachers' classrooms, teachers are not sending students to time-out, teachers are only sending students away for their benefit.

Teachers need to focus on the function of behaviors; the reasons behind the undesirable behaviors. Most of the functions of undesirable behaviors found in classrooms have to do with students having emotional needs for attention, control of their lives, and a perceived need to avoid and escape impending academic failure. Teachers need to focus on and reinforce the positive things going on in their classrooms. By complimenting desirable behavior teachers are much more likely to see these behaviors return. By ignoring the desired behaviors and focusing on the undesirable behaviors, teachers reinforce the undesirable behaviors for the students with the emotional need for attention; they learn that if they want attention, they need only to act out, versus learning to obtain attention for desirable behaviors.

CASE 10.A

Johnny, a first-grader, has been moved repeatedly to different seating assignments in Mr. Waller's class. Inevitably, a situation arises in which Johnny needs to be moved again. Mr. Waller has decided the best place for Johnny is right next to him. A detail Mr. Waller didn't expect by seating Johnny next to him is that Johnny is now in a position to kick the trash can. Mr. Waller doesn't want Johnny to think he is in control of the situation by having to move his trash can, so he has decided to focus on repeatedly telling Johnny to "Stop doing that; it is distracting."

QUESTIONS

1. What has Mr. Waller done correctly to help Johnny find success in his classroom?

2. What else could Mr. Waller do with Johnny?

3. What needs might be contributing to Johnny's behavior? (See Maslow's hierarchy of needs.)

4. How can Mr. Waller address Johnny's need for control?

It is time for us all to stand and cheer for the doer, the achiever—the one who recognizes the challenge and does something about it.
—Vincent Lombardi

11 Relationships with Students: After They Have Arrived

OBJECTIVES

After completing this chapter you should be able to:

- Define idiosyncratic credit as it relates to education.
- Discuss how self-disclosure, trust, and intimacy affect relationship building.
- Describe how exchange theory may lead teachers to pay more attention to some students than other.
- Explain how by actively listening and giving students their full attention, teachers and students benefit.
- Discuss social comparison theory and how it relates to the classroom.

KEY TERMS

Encouragement
Exchange theory
Idiosyncratic credit
Intimacy
Self-disclose
Social comparison theory
Strengths
Trust
Your full attention

Idiosyncratic credit
Exists when a person grants privileges to others because of who the person is or the position the person holds

IDIOSYNCRATIC CREDIT

It is interesting that for some teachers the beginning of the semester starts so well, and then things begin to change. By midterm teachers may believe they have a totally different class. Idiosyncratic credit may offer some insight into this phenomenon.

When relating the concept of idiosyncratic credit to education, the works of Gazda and colleagues (1999) are in the forefront. According to these authors, idiosyncratic credit means that people grant *privileges* to others because of who the person is or the position the person holds.

Drivers comply with a police officer's request to see their driver's license whether they know the officer or not. Few would comply with a request from a complete stranger to remove their clothes. But, when people go to a new doctor, they often do just that. In doing so, they have granted the police officer and the new doctor *privileges* because of the degree, assumed knowledge, and an association with the profession. If the doctor does not cure the patient's illness but sends a large bill, the patient may choose not to return for further treatment.

The important thing for a new teacher to understand is that idiosyncratic credit, although given to the teacher in the beginning, must eventually be earned. At first the teacher is given certain privileges (the same privileges given to a police officer or a new doctor) because of the title (teacher), but in order to continue receiving these privileges in the future, these privileges must be earned. If a teacher chooses to not take teaching seriously, chooses to come to class unprepared, chooses not to treat students with respect, the teacher will find these privileges once given by the students are now gone.

Of interest, **trust** is related to idiosyncratic credit. Often, we give people the privilege of our trust. Then we sit back and watch to see if our trust is earned.

Once teachers become aware of and understand the need to continue to earn privileges students offer, they can start the actual process of relationship building. Relationship building starts with **self-disclosure,** trust, and **intimacy.**

Self-disclosure
The sharing of information about oneself that others would not know if the information wasn't offered

SELF-DISCLOSURE

Self-disclose
Sharing of information about him- or herself that others would not know if the information wasn't given.

If the teacher is not willing to **self-disclose** (share information about him- or herself that others would not know if the information wasn't given) relationship building will not occur. In truth, without self-disclosure there would be no relationship. When teachers continually ask questions of their students without self-disclosing, this questioning will be perceived by the students as interrogation. Teachers must decide prior to entering the classroom what information they are willing to self-disclose. The decision of what information to share and what information not to share must be decided with the utmost professionalism, ethical considerations, sensitivity, age-appropriateness, and sincerity in mind. Generally, the more information disclosed by teachers, the more disclosures will be given by the students.

Once information is disclosed, the person disclosing the information no longer owns the information and may become vulnerable to the person now sharing the information. Relationship building requires teachers diligently to show students that they are not vulnerable, that their disclosures are safe with teachers, and that teachers are indeed trustworthy. The teacher must be aware of what information is required to be shared with supervisors or authorities. For example, any threat (perceived as real or not) of harm to self or others, or indications of abuse (physical, emotional, or sexual) are required to be reported. As mentioned previously, teachers are strongly encouraged to become familiar with this area in their teacher handbook.

Goldstein and Benassi (1994) offer a good illustration of the impact of self-disclosure. Their research offered evidence that the more the teacher self-disclosed, the more the students participated in class activities. These authors attributed this effect to the social exchange model (developed by Archer, 1979), which notes that students feel inclined to respond with self-disclosure because of the rewarding nature of the teacher's self-disclosure. Interestingly, Mazer, Murphy, and Simonds (2009) investigated the impact of teacher self-disclosure on Facebook. When participants viewed a teacher's Facebook page that was high in self-disclosure, they rated the teacher as more credible than when they viewed a teacher page with low self-disclosure. Mazer and colleagues' research supports previous research on self-disclosure benefits for teachers. Although self-disclosure can be a very effective tool in gaining students' trust and, in-turn, gaining a sense of credibility, preservice and current teachers must carefully censor their self-disclosure so as not to put themselves in professionally awkward situations (i.e., sharing too much or inappropriate information with students).

Blogging

An interesting and worthwhile article by Harper (2005) takes a unique look at what he calls a "new student-teacher channel" for self-disclosure. The author suggests that teachers should integrate the technology of blogging to allow for teacher-students' self-disclosure. Blogging as described by Harper consists of "an unfiltered perspective on countless topics . . . consisting largely of personal commentary . . . [and] once posted online, practically anyone is free to 'post' a response to the 'blogger'" (p. 30). Through focus groups with students and instructors who had blogged, Harper found that many students felt more comfortable expressing themselves via the blog than they did in class. Obviously, blogging can be done only in a classroom that has sufficient technology and sufficient student (as well as instructor) competence to do so, but definitely is something for future teachers to consider!

Trust
Having confidence in someone else's reliability, judgment, word, and action to care for and not harm the entrusted person

TRUST

It quickly becomes obvious that there are no shortcuts in building relationships. Relationship building takes time and trust. Turnbull et al., (2006) define trust as having confidence in someone else's reliability, judgment, word, and action to care for and not harm the entrusted person. It exists when people believe that the trusted person will act in the best interest of the person extending the trust and will make good-faith efforts to keep their word.

The teacher builds trust when the exchange of information is open and honest and students are treated with dignity. Students must believe that they can trust their teacher and that the personal information disclosed to the teacher will remain confidential. Interestingly, a study with 7-, 10-, and 13-year-olds implemented by Belle and Burr (1991) asked students specifically why they *do* and *do not* confide in others. Some reasons reported by students for not confiding in others consisted of nervousness, overwhelmed with emotions, self-reliance (i.e., "I don't want any help"), embarrassment, fear of being teased, and fear of unlikely consequences. More important are the reasons Bell and Burr found that students would confide in others: emotional support, understanding, recognition, for the benefit of others, practical help, and feedback or advice.

Teachers should be aware of an interesting phenomenon that occurs in the classroom. Those teachers who are perceived to jump to conclusions without all of the information are the ones less likely to be trusted by their students. It is imperative that before teachers act, all the information is gathered, and teachers are confident of their findings.

For students to develop trust in their teachers, it is essential that teachers keep their word and always follow through on their promises. Never say one thing to one person and something different to another. This "double-talk" is often apparent to students, and the teacher is in danger of not being seen as genuine in future endeavors with students.

Of interest, Goddard, Tschannen-Moran, and Hoy (2001) conducted a study looking at faculty trust of parents and students and offered evidence that this trust by faculty had a positive effect on student achievement. They reported that faculty trust makes schools better places for students to learn.

Intimacy
The ability to see another person as the person sees him- or herself.

INTIMACY

Intimacy occurs when one person is able to see another person as he or she sees him- or herself. Often teachers misperceive students and see them as someone they are not. Only through relationship building do we learn about the actual person (as the person sees him- or herself) and not as some label, reputation, or stereotype. It is important that teachers develop relationships that allow them to see the genuine student. In order to develop intimacy with students, teachers must self-disclose, establish and earn trust, and be willing to accept students for who they are. In fact, if one were to measure intimacy, it would be the ability of one person to accept another person for who he or she is. How can people claim to be intimate and genuinely know other people without accepting them for who they are? The acceptance of a person for who he or she is leads to the discovery of the real person.

Teachers will have contact with students who have different sexual orientations, religions, customs, and languages, most having different beliefs, values, and attitudes from themselves. A teacher who has no real interest in relationship building may choose to argue these differences. The teacher who wishes to develop a genuine relationship with students will display acceptance for who the students are and tolerance to those things that are different from the way the teacher may see the world. The teacher wishing to establish a beneficial relationship with students seeks to understand others' views and perspectives and grow from the strengths found in these differences.

After realizing the need to maintain privileges that students offer, and beginning relationship building by self-disclosing, establishing trust, and getting to know and accept students for who they are (intimacy), teachers must concern themselves with the largest crevasse in relationship building—the **exchange theory**. According to Thibaut and Kelley (1959), our interactions can be predicted on the basis of the exchange of benefits. The exchange theory describes the interaction between two people as a function of what each person gets out of the relationship: if there is no payoff in the relationship, there is no relationship. If a person behaves toward another person in a certain way, it is because he or she expects to gain from the other person some profit from the transaction (Swensen, 1973).

Exchange theory
The relationship between two people is a function of what each person gets out of the relationship. If there is no payoff in the relationship, there is no relationship.

According to Hanna (2003), relationships can be assessed by what the participants are receiving compared to what they are giving. Relationships can end because one or both are no longer receiving enough from the other; the costs of the relationship have exceeded the benefits.

Every individual voluntarily enters and stays in a relationship only as long as it is adequately satisfactory in terms of the rewards and costs. Economically stated, relationships are motivated by profit. According to the theory, when the profit in a relationship drops to or near zero, a person will begin looking for another relationship that promises more profit. There is nothing to be gained from an unprofitable relationship. Interestingly, often individuals build up a "savings account" and a relationship may continue until the savings account is depleted and the other person is convinced that there will be no further return.

The open secret of human exchange is to give other people behavior that is more valuable to them than it is costly to you and to get from them behavior that is more valuable to you than it is costly to them.

We tend to choose to relate to others who agree with our attitudes and opinions. People who agree with us provide us with rewards by validating our opinions, and they do not exact from us the heavy cost of a disagreement. Unfortunately, long-distance relationships often suffer or end because the cost of maintaining the relationship at a distance is more than the reward for keeping it alive.

According to the exchange theory, teachers will gravitate to only those students who offer something back for their efforts. Those students who are prepared for class, who wish to participate, who show interest in the subject are the students that teachers will reward with attention. According to the theory, teachers are apt to give to those students who give back and *stop giving* to those students who offer no rewards for our efforts. Teachers must make a pledge to resist the exchange theory, not to fall victim to its negativity, recognize its pitfalls, and be prepared to give attention and show concern to *all* students, those interested and those displaying a lack of interest.

ENCOURAGEMENT

Encouragement
A form of support that can be given to anyone at any time. This is in contrast to praise.

There are no doubts that **encouragement** is a major component of relationship building efforts. A significant portion of chapter 2 was devoted to this message. Remember that encouragement can be given at any time and to anyone. Conversely, praise can be given only to those students who excel, and is often given to students who don't need it and already have high self-esteem. Those students needing encouragement the most often get it the least. Encouragement (along with choices) can be given and is highly recommended even when disciplining a student. Teachers must encourage not only their students but their colleagues, supervisors, paraprofessionals, parents, school board members, and everyone else they encounter. The secret to becoming the best teacher in the school system is to be the teacher who uses encouragement the most. Students relate to and hear "genuine" encouragement; however, they do not relate to discouragement.

ACTIVE LISTENING

Another important component of relationship building is active listening (as discussed in chapter 4). Parents want professionals to listen carefully, nonjudgmentally, and without predetermined idea. Listening takes diligence and practice, but it clearly conveys our level of interest, commitment, and understanding (Turnbull et al., 2006).

Teachers must first seek to understand. The trick to understanding another's view is in being an active listener. It is essential for teachers to recognize that they *learn nothing by talking*. Only when teachers listen do they gain knowledge. Teachers must recognize the great benefits of being silent and gaining insight, after which teachers are in a position to seek to be understood. Without actively listening to students, the teachers will see that the quality of the relationships is severely impaired. Through active listening, teachers place themselves in positions to establish long-lasting relationships.

Your full attention
The greatest compliment you can give a student.

A truth that should never be forgotten by the teacher is that the *greatest compliment* one can give students is a teacher's **full attention.** If relationship building is a priority, teachers must find ways to let their students know they are interested in them. Giving full attention is one very powerful way of doing so.

An interesting phenomenon in relationship building occurs when teachers listen to what students have to say about what the teachers want them to know. After teachers have informed the students about what they want them to know, students are then given an option to give input about the information presented to them. This process has many benefits for the teacher, such as the following:

- The teacher is better able to assess how much and to what quality the students understand the material presented. For example, a student cannot offer an informed opinion on the importance of the subject matter being taught unless there is a full understanding of the material in the first place.
- The input presented by students may offer the teacher information for self-reflection on teaching methodologies.
- The discussion offers students the feeling of ownership (or possibly perceived "control") of the material being presented. This perception by students of ownership in materials being presented promotes an environment conducive to relationship building. Students should not determine what subjects should be taught; however, offering students input on materials presented creates an environment that promotes rapport building.

The teacher should become an expert in looking for **strengths** in students. It is ludicrous to think that a student does not have strengths. Teachers must find the strengths, encourage the use of them, and then, not keep them secret. Let students know what their strengths are; many students may be unaware of them. Once identified, strengths should be built upon. Building upon strengths (versus deficits) increases the likelihood of academic success. Academic success promotes relationship building.

Strengths
Abilities, talents, or areas in which individuals excel

A relevant theorist to this discussion is **Howard Gardner.** Gardner is well known for his contemporary theory of intelligence. Historically, intelligence has been thought of as a person's ability to excel in conventional areas (e.g., math, verbal, spatial, etc.). However, Gardner developed a theory (introduced in *Frames of Mind*, 1983) that suggests not only should we view intelligence as a multifaceted construct, but also, individuals can excel in areas that are seen as less traditional. Since 1983, Gardner has refined and expanded his theory to include nine different types of intelligences. One significant message of Gardner's theory is that we all have strengths and abilities, and if we play to those abilities, we can achieve and succeed.

WE NO LONGER BLAME STUDENTS FOR EDUCATIONAL FAILURES

Building relationships with students requires teachers to recognize that *we no longer blame students for educational failures*. Blaming students for academic failures does not increase the opportunity to establish productive relationships. Nothing good comes from blaming. Even when it is obvious that the student is at fault, blaming does not change the grade or promote beneficial relationships.

When teachers lay blame on students for academic failures, they are engaging in *finding excuses*. Finding excuses for students' academic failures is much easier than taking responsibility for finding new and creative ways of reaching students who are not being successful in the classroom. For example, Sally is failing because of her situation at home. This excuse allows the teacher to "wash his or her hands" of any responsibility for Sandy to receive an appropriate education. "After all, it not my fault she has a terrible home life."

Unfortunately, it does not end there. Once one excuse is found, it becomes easier, thus more likely, to find excuses for other students. If the teacher continues to look for excuses, he or she is certain to find them. Not only is Sally's home life terrible, but Johnny's father is in prison, and Jimmy is just lazy; now we have a total of three students where the teacher no longer needs to accept responsibility for their educational progress.

Of relevance, when teachers' computers decide to stop working, it does absolutely no good to start yelling at them, threatening them, or even bribing them (although these occurrences happen more often than we wish to admit). For whatever the reason, when students stop progressing, that is precisely what teachers do; they yell, threaten, and bribe. Interestingly, the end results are the same; yelling, threatening, or bribing does not work with either computers or students. It is important that teachers stop blaming computers (or students) for being broken and get the computers fixed. If we sit around waiting for the computer (or student) to fix itself, it won't. The teacher has to be the one to change. We, as teachers, have a professional obligation to change our behaviors and methods by trying something new and creative to get students to progress in their education. If we don't change our behaviors in the classroom, then we will find ourselves *looking for excuses* for why students don't progress. Once we find excuses, we are no longer responsible, and can blame the students for their academic failures. The exceptional teachers take the perspective that they no longer blame students for failures and avoid all inclinations to find excuses for those students not being successful in their classrooms.

RULES FOR NOT BLAMING STUDENTS FOR ACADEMIC FAILURES

1. Take the perspective that we no longer blame students for failures.
2. Avoid all inclinations to find *excuses* for students' failures (Johnny's father is in prison, Jill's mother isn't interested in her education).
3. Teachers need to find new and creative ways to assist students in becoming successful (Computers and kids don't fix themselves).
4. Hold the student *accountable* (past tests, future homework, and their consequences).
5. Hold the student *responsible* for their own education, *without blame* (students need to know that they have choices in their lives, that they can take control or they can give control over to others).

Figure 11.1 The teacher should become an expert in looking for strengths in students.

Relationship building has more to do with *effort* than respect. Most teachers talk about respect (or the lack of) in the teachers' break room. They often are heard stating an old cliché, "I will give respect to my students and will demand respect from my students." Unfortunately, this brief cliché is most often all that is said on the subject. Teachers must become aware that respect comes only from effort, not demands. If teachers come to class prepared, organized, enthusiastic, and competent, students will recognize their efforts and give them the respect due, even when the students disagree with what the teachers have to say. Conversely, if teachers come to the classroom ill-prepared, unorganized, and signaling that they would rather be somewhere else, they can demand all they want, but respect will not be given, even when the students agree with the teacher's point of view. Respect must be earned every day.

The very popular movie *Rudy* is about a young man with few natural athletic abilities, who gives everything he has got to give to a football program. He eventually earns the *respect* of all those around him because of his *efforts,* not his abilities. If we may carry this point further, there are, no doubt, those athletes who do not gain their teammates' respect, due to their lack of effort, regardless of their natural abilities.

One important job a teacher has is to look for students' efforts; respect for students will soon follow.

Another theory to build relationships with students is Leon Festinger's (1919–1989) **social comparison theory.** According to Festinger (1954), we become aware of our differences when we compare ourselves with other people. This comparison process is something that occurs without much thought and effort, and begins very early in life. For example, a woman who is pregnant compares her pregnancy to others' or her own previous pregnancies. A baby is born and adults compare size, shape, amount of hair, strength, and health to that of other babies. We tend to describe ourselves in terms of the ways in which we stand

Social comparison theory
Our awareness of the differences that exist between ourselves and others based upon social comparison.

out from (or fit in with) others around us. As we grow and develop, we often are motivated to evaluate our skills, aptitudes, and values by comparing ourselves with other people.

Teachers must be cautious. If during this self-evaluation by one of their students, via comparison to others, the student begins to recognize the many things that he or she cannot do well, or that, for everything he or she does, there is another person that can do it better, the student's self-esteem, self-worth, and self-confidence may begin to suffer. Teachers can play an essential role by reminding students *not* to compare themselves to others, but to recognize the unique individual in each of us. Teachers will be instrumental in creating environments in which acceptance for who people are, tolerance for their differences, and an appreciation of each individual's uniqueness are primary goals, resulting in increased self-esteem, self-worth, and self-confidence for the students. These are the educationally safe environmental issues that are conducive to relationship building.

One way to assess students' self-esteem is to observe whether students expect to be rejected by others, or if they expect to be accepted by others for who they are. Students may have learned by looking into others' eyes that they expect to be rejected. Gradually, over time, these expectations and experiences of being rejected will lower the self-esteem of students (refer to the looking glass self, chapter 1). Conversely, students who have experienced unconditional acceptance by others have gradually, over time, learned that they will be accepted for who they are and will present themselves with high self-esteem. It may be obvious that a teacher cannot raise the self-esteem of a student overnight, but the teacher can make great strides in this effort. The ability to raise students' self-esteem begins with teachers seeing the world from the eyes of the student and then accepting the students for who they are. When students look into the eyes of a teacher who accepts them for who they are, the teacher needs only to get out of the way and watch the students' self-esteem rise.

SUMMARY

Teachers must remind themselves that the privileges students give (idiosyncratic credit) at the beginning of the school year can be lost if they don't continue to earn them everyday. Those teachers who arrive at their classrooms unprepared, uninterested, and preferring not to be there, will soon lose those privileges that were first given.

Relationship building starts with teachers' willingness to self-disclose, establishing and earning trust, and gaining a genuine knowledge of who their students are (referred to as intimacy). Teachers must recognize that without self-disclosure there are no relationships. If only students self-disclose, they soon begin to feel as if they are being interrogated. Teachers must decide in advance what information they wish to share with their students. In deciding what information to share, ethical considerations, sensitivity, age-appropriateness, and sincerity should always be considered.

Relationship building takes time, energy, and trust. Students must learn to trust their teachers in order for relationships to be established. Teachers who keep their word and follow through on their promises, without offering "double talk," are the teachers students learn to trust. Of interest, teachers who jump to conclusions without gathering all the facts are the teachers students trust the least.

Intimacy is when one person is able to see another for who that person really is versus some label, reputation, or stereotype. To truly get to know someone, we must first be willing to accept that person for who he or she is. This requires that we are tolerant of those things that are different from the way we may see the world. Intimacy requires accepting people for who they are, tolerating their differences, and then learning to appreciate people for their uniqueness.

Future teachers must learn to resist the exchange theory. There will be those students who do not wish to give back your enthusiasm, hard work, or interests in topics. It will be only natural for teachers to gravitate toward students who do give back. In resisting this natural tendency, teachers do not fall for the exchange theory's negativity and pitfalls. Teachers must be prepared to give attention and show concern for all students; those interested and those displaying a lack of interest.

After self-disclosing, establishing trust, and getting to know students for who they really are, we turn our attention on the need to actively listen to students. Without active listening, the quality of relationships is severely impaired. Teachers must first seek to understand by using active listening strategies (chapter 4) and then they are in the best position to attempt to be understood.

A concept that needs a great deal of reflection is that we no longer blame students for educational failures. When teachers blame students for academic failures, they are engaged in finding excuses. Once teachers have found an excuse for a student's academic failure, they are no longer responsible for the student's academic progress and can "wash their hands" of the responsibility to find new and creative ways for the student to be successful.

Teachers should note that respect is not something that is given or made demands of; respect is something that is earned through effort. Often a person may disagree with someone that person respects a great deal. This respect is due to the person's efforts, not his or her views, with which a person may or may not agree. This holds true for teachers; students respect those teachers who take their jobs seriously and responsibly, even when the students disagree with their views. Little or no respect is given to teachers who are perceived by students to not care about their responsibilities.

Finally, teachers cannot compare students to each other. This comparison diminishes students' self-esteem, self-worth, and confidence. To increase self-esteem, teachers need only to teach students to recognize and appreciate their own individual uniqueness.

CASE 11.A

Mr. Franklin is one of the "coolest" teachers in high school. He has Myspace and Facebook pages with many student "friends" and allows his students to text him if they need to get hold of him with questions about the homework. Just last night while he was on Facebook, a student saw that he was online and was able to chat with him about questions he had on the assigned homework. If Mr. Franklin and the student hadn't been "friends," he couldn't have offered him the help he needed. Mr. Franklin is careful what he puts on his pages. Although he is of age, he doesn't put any pictures of himself drinking or engaging in questionable activities. However, he does post lots of pictures of himself and his wife and three children. In addition to using Myspace and Facebook to connect with his students, he also uses them both to connect with his friends and family, which means that students might see a side of him they wouldn't normally see in the classroom.

Unfortunately Mr. Franklin is not seen as "cool" by many of his colleagues. In fact, the principal of his school has recently called him into his office to discuss his "digital communication with his students." The principal is concerned about the informal relationships Mr. Franklin has formed with his students and his potential for lacking professionalism.

QUESTIONS

1. Why might Mr. Franklin "friend" students on Myspace and Facebook?

2. What are the benefits of sharing personal information with students?

3. What are some potential drawbacks to Mr. Franklin's approach to connecting with his students?

4. What concerns might the principal have about Mr. Franklin's approach?

5. Imagine you are the parent of a student in Mr. Franklin's class. How would you react to your son or daughter being Mr. Franklin's "friend" on Myspace or Facebook?

6. What are other ways that Mr. Franklin builds relationships with his students?

CASE 11.B

Ms. Kontu is the coach of the drill team in addition to being the social studies teacher. She strives to treat all students equally and to find the inner-learner in everyone. This year she has really connected with her drill team students, however, and has found that those students in particular are more attentive in class, try harder on assignments, and are always prepared to answer questions over the assigned material. It is difficult to not give extra attention to her drill team students, or not call on them more in class because they are motivated students who participate in class.

Ms. Kontu became aware of her favoritism to the drill team members when she overheard a conversation between two of her non-drill team students in which one said to the other, "Know how to get an 'A' on Ms. Kontu's test? Practice your high kicks!" The other student laughed and said, "Yeah, if only I were on the drill team, I'd have the best grade in the class!" This conversation shocked and disappointed Ms. Kontu because she thought she encouraged every student to succeed in her class.

QUESTIONS

1. How does the exchange theory apply to Ms. Kontu's behavior?

2. How does the exchange theory apply to Ms. Kontu's students' behaviors?

3. What can Ms. Kontu do to change the perception among the students not on the drill team?

4. How could social comparison theory apply to the non-drill team versus drill team students?

5. How can Ms. Kontu encourage success with all of her students?

Name: ______________________________

Quiz

Relationship Building Formula

Relationship building starts with _________________ _________________ by the teacher. This activity allows the teacher and students to begin developing reciprocal _________________. Once both of these activities have been established, gradually, over time, we become ___________________________ (we see students the way they see themselves). Once we see students the way they see themselves, we can now learn to accept students for ___________ ____________ __________.

Once teachers have completed the above steps, they are in the best position to have a positive and beneficial relationship with their students.

Relationship building starts with self-disclosure by the teacher. This activity allows the teacher and students to begin developing reciprocal trust. Once both of these activities have been established, gradually, over time, we become intimate (we see students the way they see themselves). Once we see students the way they see themselves, we can now learn to accept students for who they are.

Appendix

Biographies

ALINSKY, SAUL D. (1909–1972)

Saul Alinsky was born the son of a Russian Jewish immigrant. He married and was the father of two children. His wife died in a drowning accident in 1947. Alinsky became interested in group organization during his graduate work at the University of Chicago. He earned his doctorate in the 1930s. Throughout his life he spoke out against discrimination, oppression, and poverty. He fought tirelessly against exploitation of the poor and disadvantaged. He believed that the poor were unorganized and thus lacked the means to realize real equality. To some he was revered as a catalyst for positive social change, but to others he was seen as a meddler and troublemaker. A tribute to his work was given by policymakers in Oakland, California. They outlawed his presence in their town. While in a Kansas City jail (he frequently was arrested), he wrote his first book *Reveille for Radicals.* The controversial book brought praise and contempt. One critic of this text noted, "In some parts of the world fascism has made use of exactly this sort of radical talk." However, it should be noted that during the 1950s, Alinsky was very active in organizing anticommunist labor unions in Italy. In 1971, he published *Rules for Radicals* in which he detailed plans for community reform. Alinsky also announced his plans to establish a national institution for the training of social radicals.

In his obituary, found in *The New York Times*, a week in his life was described. He would sit down with the Canadian Indians on Monday night, help the Chicanos in the Southwest on Tuesday, be in a blue-collar suburb in Chicago on Wednesday, spend Thursday with white steelworkers in Pittsburgh, move Friday to a black ghetto, and be perfectly happy rolling, organizing.

Alinsky believed that organization, not charity, was the solution to the people's social ills. His approach depended on uniting ordinary citizens around immediate grievances and stirring them to protest. Alinsky spoke against violence. Instead, he urged his followers to be practical and use the self-interest of ordinary citizens as the primary force for political participation. For Alinsky, power came from political participation by aroused citizens fighting for their rights.

BERNE, ERIC (1910–1970)

Eric Berne was born in Montreal, Quebec, Canada, and became a U.S. citizen in 1943. Berne's father was a physician. Berne received his B.A. and M.D. degrees from McGill University in 1931/1935. He attended Yale Psychiatric Clinic from 1936 to 1938. Berne attended the New York Psychoanalytic Institute from 1941 to 1943. He served in the U.S. Army Medical Corps from 1943 to 1946, attaining the rank of Major. Berne attended the San Francisco Psychoanalytic Institute from 1947 to 1956.

COOLEY, CHARLES HORTON (1864–1929)

Charles Horton Cooley was born in Ann Arbor, Michigan. His father was a distinguished jurist, professor of law at the University of Michigan, and the leading constitutional lawyer of his time. Cooley was born intelligent, with a fragile physique and a speech impediment. He was described as sensitive, timid, and with a feeling of being inferior. Cooley entered the University of Michigan in 1880, but due to his ill health (some reports have his illnesses as psychosomatic), graduated in 1887. In 1894, he received his doctorate in political economy, with a minor in sociology. Cooley taught economics and sociology at the University of Michigan. He was concerned more with raising questions, presenting different points of views, and suggesting directions than with giving answers.

Coser (1977) described Cooley's performance as an instructor: "The lectures that this slight, nervous, and somewhat sickly looking professor delivered with a high-pitched voice lacking resonance often would not go over well with the undergraduates. Yet, he appealed to a number of graduate students who were inspired by his probing and searching intellect" (p. 316). His students who managed to insert themselves into seminars and lectures were influenced throughout their lives. Cooley did not publish much; rather his impact came from the development of personal relationships with his students. He proposed that the *personality emerges from social influences* and that the individual and the group are complementary aspects of human association. Cooley most often stated, "Self and society are twin-born." In 1917 he was elected president of the American Sociological Society (of which Cooley was one of the founders).

DIX, DOROTHEA (1802–1887)

Dorothea Dix dedicated her life to healing the social ills of those who could not help themselves. Her imprint on people's lives included the mentally ill, underprivileged and unwanted, wounded soldiers, and poor children who could not afford an education. She was guided by the belief that full recovery could be made if the mentally ill were treated and cared for compassionately.

She was described as being awkward and shy, often dressing in hand-me-downs. Dix was described as an invalid with recurring health problems and with a frail frame. She wrote many of her best books while recovering from the effects of tuberculosis. Although she often suffered from lifelong ailments, Epler (1909) reported that Dix had unequal courage; "The tonic of opposition, it always sets me on my feet."

At 19 she opened a school and served the poor children of Boston whose parents could not afford a formal education. Dix was appointed by Abraham Lincoln as superintendent of women nurses in 1861; she remained in this position until 1866. She was known as the "Sister of Mercy" by those who were familiar with her work with the wounded soldiers.

DREIKURS, RUDOLF (1897–1972)

Rudolf Dreikurs was a social psychologist and educator born in Vienna, Austria. He developed psychologist Alfred Adler's system of individual psychology into a pragmatic method for understanding the purposes of reprehensible behavior in children and for stimulating cooperative behavior without punishment or reward. He suggested that human misbehavior is the result of not having one of four basic human needs met: seeking power, desiring attention, getting revenge, and avoidance of failure. His overall goal was that students learn to cooperate reasonably without being penalized or rewarded because they feel they are valuable contributors to the classroom. Dreikurs believed that the central motivation of all humans is to belong and be accepted by others.

FARRELL, ELIZABETH E. (1870–1932)

Elizabeth Farrell's parents were immigrants; her father was from Ireland and her mother was from Wales. Through hard work the family prospered, allowing her to attend college at the Oswego Normal and Training School (which is now the State University of New York at Oswego). Farrell was the oldest of four girls in a family of six siblings. She is best known for her work with "backward" students in an ungraded classroom. Her progressive reforms and visions of what we should be doing took her to the directorship of special education services in New York City. Farrell, more than anyone else, is credited with developing the professional field of special education. She was a founder of what has become the Council for Exceptional Children (CEC), which is the largest and most prominent professional organization in special education in the United States.

FESTINGER, LEON (1919–1989)

Leon Festinger received his B.A. in psychology from City College of New York. He obtained his M.A. and Ph.D. from the University of Iowa (1940/1942). He left New York to study under Kurt Lewin. In 1945 Festinger began work with Lewin as a social psychologist. He felt strongly that he and his colleagues were on to something important. After Lewin's death, Festinger and colleagues moved to the University of Michigan to continue their work. In 1951 he moved to the University of Minnesota, and in 1955 he moved to Stanford University until 1968. In that same year, he returned to New York City at the New School for Social Research.

Festinger was married and had three children, later divorced, and remarried. He loved chess and often wished he had become a professional chess player. At his funeral he was noted for being a scholar until his final breath.

GARDNER, HOWARD (1943–)

Howard Gardner was born in Scranton, Pennsylvania. He is the son of refugees from Nazi Germany. Gardner is married to Ellen Winner and has four children. He has received all of his degrees from Harvard University. Gardner was trained as a developmental and neuron-psychologist. His theory was first introduced in *Frames of Mind* in 1983 (A Tenth Anniversary Edition with new introduction, 1993). He is the author of more than 20 books and winner of numerous honors.

Refer to http://www.howardgardner.com/

HEIDER, FRITZ (1896–1988)

Fritz Heider was interested in how we interpret our own behavior, as well as that of others. The culmination of over 60 years of work is found in his 1958 book titled *The Psychology of Interpersonal Relations.* Heider, the younger of two sons, was born in Vienna. He had the opportunity to work with outstanding scholars at the Psychological Institute of Berlin. Heider received his Ph.D. in 1920 from the University of Graz (Austria). During his career, he conducted research at the Clark School for the Deaf in Northampton, Massachusetts, Smith College, and the University of Kansas (1947). In 1930 he married Grace Moore and had three sons. In his autobiography *The Life of a Psychologist* (1983), he credits his wife for her invaluable contribution to his work. Heider was described as extremely methodical and meticulous in his research. He received numerous awards in his life including the American Psychological Association's Distinguished Scientific Contribution Award in 1965. Heider died at his home in Lawrence Kansas in 1988 at the age of 91.

HOLLANDER, EDWIN (1927–)

Edwin Hollander, most well known for his transactional theory of leadership, received his B.S. in psychology at Case Western Reserve and his Ph.D. at Columbia University. He taught at Carnegie Mellon, Washington (St. Louis), and American University (Washington), and has held visiting appointments as a Fulbright Professor at Istanbul University, an NIMH Senior Fellow at the Tavistock Institute in London, and as a faculty member at Wisconsin, Harvard, Oxford, and the Institute of American Studies in Paris, among others. He also served as study director of the Committee on Ability Testing at the National Academy of Sciences. His most recent appointment has been SUNY as a Distinguished Professor of Psychology at Baruch College and the Graduate Center since 1989. At SUNY Buffalo, he served as provost of Social Sciences and Administration, and was the founding director of the doctoral program in Social/Organizational Psychology.

KOHLBERG, LAWRENCE (1927–1987)

Lawrence Kohlberg was born in Bronxville, New York. His family was wealthy and he attended private schools. After graduating high school in 1945, he joined the Merchant Marines. He served as an engineer aboard a Jewish defense-force vessel attempting to smuggle European Jews into Palestine. After the ship's smuggling operations were discovered, he was held in a British detention camp on the island of Cyprus. This early experience focused Kohlberg's attention on the morality of disobeying authority.

In 1947 Kohlberg entered the University of Chicago, from which he earned a B.A. degree in 1948 and a Ph.D. in psychology in 1958. Kohlberg became an assistant professor of psychology at Yale University in 1959, but returned to the University of Chicago in 1962. In 1968 he became a full professor of education and social psychology at Harvard University's Graduate School of Education. Kohlberg's most influential work was in moral education, reasoning, and development.

Friends described Kohlberg as disheveled in appearance (unruly dark hair topping an angular face) and as disarmingly open in manner and always in motion. He was often absorbed in his work. While doing research in Central America (Belize, 1971), Kohlberg became ill with a disease that was eventually diagnosed as giardiasis, which is caused by an intestinal parasite. Kohlberg suffered intermittent, but often debilitating bouts of nausea and depression for the remainder of his life. In January 1987 he attempted to take his life and was hospitalized. On January 17 he obtained a leave from the hospital where he was being treated, drove to the coast, and committed suicide by drowning himself in the Atlantic Ocean, later to be found in the Boston Harbor. He was 59 years old.

LAING, RONALD DAVID (1928–1989)

A Scottish-born psychiatrist, Ronald Laing received his M.D. from the University of Glasgow in 1951. He served in the British Army as a psychiatrist in the medical corps from 1951 to 1953. Dr. Laing was married twice and had eight children.

Laing's views had far-reaching political, sociological, and scientific implications. He was hailed as a hero to the political left, who articulated a growing impatience with society's status quo. To the political right he was seen as a dissident, a heretic, and a member of the antipsychiatry movement. For example, Laing was convinced that psychotic episodes could serve as a natural healing process if allowed to run their course under the supervision of a trained and sympathetic therapist. The widespread use of chemotherapy and electroshock treatment, he concluded, disrupts the healing process, brutalizes the patient, and serves only to make schizophrenics more manageable and docile for the benefit of overworked mental hospital staffs.

He was observed by some as a social critic, a political poet, an elusive folk hero, and a symbol of nonconformity. He developed his nontraditional theories and treatments in response to his doubts about the traditional ones, which made him "puzzled and uneasy." Laing, himself, would later admit that his own treatments were as inadequate as were the conventional treatments, which he saw as cruel and ineffective.

MASLOW, ABRAHAM H. (1908–1970)

Abraham Maslow's father was born in Russia. Maslow was active in his Latin and physics clubs in high school. He wrote an article predicting atom-powered submarines. He began his college work at the College of the City of New York but transferred to the University of Wisconsin where he received his B.A. (1930), M.A. (1931), and his Ph.D. (1934). He was married in 1928 and had two children. He taught at Wisconsin University, Columbia Teachers College, and Brooklyn College before arriving at Brandeis University. He served as chair of the department of psychology at Brandeis University from 1951 to 1961. He was influenced by Wertheimer (a Gestalt psychologist). Maslow was president of the American Psychological Association in 1968. At the time of his death he was involved in creating new ideas, which would effect immediate social change. His efforts were to combine the philosophies of politics, economics, and ethics, which would be generated by humanistic psychology.

MEAD, GEORGE HERBERT (1863–1931)

George Herbert Mead was a professor of philosophy, but his influence has been primarily in sociology and social psychology. Interestingly, he called himself a social behaviorist. Mead was influenced by the great minds of his time. He graduated from Oberlin College in 1883 in the Classics. He attended Harvard from 1887 to 1888 where he worked with William James, a notable American psychologist, in areas of philosophical and psychological topics. Mead spent three years in Berlin and Leipzig, where he was influenced by Wilhelm Wundt, the founder of psychology. From there he arrived at the University of Michigan in 1891 until 1893. Mead and John Dewey left Michigan for the University of Chicago in 1894 and remained there until his death in 1931. He is said to have exercised a strong influence over his students.

Mead published no full-length statements of his theories. His major contributions were created from edited lecture notes of his students. All four of the books for which he is credited with authorship are posthumously collected and edited works. They comprise a loose accumulation of his notes, fragmentary manuscripts, and tentative drafts of unpublished essays, sketchy developed ideas, and, at times, conflicting statements.

MERTON, ROBERT KING (1910–2003)

Robert K. Merton was a son of Jewish, working-class immigrant parents from Eastern Europe. He was born Meyer R. Schkolnick in South Philadelphia. He was internationally known for his contributions to sociological analysis and considered the founder of sociology of science. He attended Temple College (1927–1931) and Harvard University (1931–1936). He taught at Harvard until 1939, when he became chair of the department of sociology at the University of Tulane. In 1941 he joined the University of Columbia faculty, where he spent most of his career teaching. At the University of Columbia, he attained the rank of University Professor (1974).

ROGERS, CARL (1902–1987)

Carl Rogers was born in Oak Park, Illinois, a suburb of Chicago. He was the fourth of six children. Rogers's father was a successful civil engineer and his mother was a housewife and devout Christian. His education started in the second grade because he could already read before kindergarten. Rogers spent his adolescence on a farm with strict upbringing and many chores. He was to become isolated, independent, and self-disciplined. Rogers received his Ph.D. in 1931 from Teachers College of Columbia University. He was influenced by Otto Rank's theory and therapy techniques. He was offered a full professorship at Ohio State in 1940. Rogers served as President of the American Psychological Association in 1947. He also served as director of the counseling service at the University of Chicago from 1945 to 1957. In 1951, he published his major work, *Client-Centered Therapy*, in which he outlines his theory. Rogers, a humanistic psychologist, is noted for his nondirective approach to psychotherapy.

ROOSEVELT, ANNA ELEANOR (1884–1962)

Eleanor was First Lady of the United States from 1933 to 1945. She was married to her distant cousin Franklin Delano Roosevelt. She was an international author, speaker, politician, and social activist. Eleanor fought for women rights and desegregation. She supported the formation of the United Nations and served as the delegate from 1945 until 1952. Eleanor was known as the "First Lady of the World" due to her work in human rights. She was ranked in the top 10 of Gallup's list of the most widely admired people of the 20th century.

SULLIVAN, HARRY STACK (1892–1949)

Harry Stack Sullivan's life was often a struggle with emotional problems and relationships. Chapman (1976) offers a very comprehensive detail of Sullivan's colorful, at times difficult, at times concealed life. Chapman describes a dysfunctional family coupled with isolation and segregation that impacted Sullivan his entire life. Sullivan's mother was always ill, continuously complaining about the family's poor situation, always unhappy, and showed little affection for her son. Sullivan saw himself as only a "coat rack" on which his mother could hang her illusions. His father was emotionally withdrawn and distant, and offered rare praise for the young Sullivan.

Sullivan spent his youth on a farm in New York, isolated, and lonely without companions. This isolation would continue to be a large part of his adult life. Due to this isolation, Sullivan was fascinated with people and their relationships. He was very aware of the importance of every human interaction.

Sullivan was an excellent student during his public school years (class valedictorian). After being awarded a state scholarship at the age of 17, he quickly flunked out of Cornell. In 1911 he entered the Chicago College of Medicine and Surgery. This college environment was described by Sullivan as "shabby" and a "diploma mill." Sullivan graduated in 1915 but did not receive his diploma until 1917 because of back tuition owed.

Sullivan served as a lieutenant in the Medical Corps during World War I. He worked with veterans at a hospital for the insane who were suffering psychological trauma caused by the war. He would later work in private practice. He was the editor of the journal *Psychiatry;* under his supervision the journal became preeminent in the field of interdisciplinary thinking. He was a professor and chair of the School of Psychiatry at Georgetown University Medical School. At his own request he was buried in Arlington National Cemetery, with full military honors.

Sullivan was seen as charming and creative to his friends and tender and humane toward his patients but scathing in his criticism of psychiatric trainees. Chapman noted that Sullivan taught brilliantly. He was described as thin and elegant, having humor and a commanding demeanor, yet a sharp and biting critic. He had dark and piercing eyes that dominated his face.

TERESA, MARY (1910–1997)

Mother Mary Teresa, born Agnes Gonxha, stood only 4 feet 11 inches tall and weighed less than 100 pounds. But she was never judged by her size when confronting social injustice. She lived among the poor, shared their poverty (starvation, open sewers, disease), and spent her life caring for those who could not care for themselves. Although suffering from tuberculosis, she requested to work with the poorest of the poor. Teresa offered love to the loveless who were sick and dying. She was known for stating, "If you judge people, you have no time to love them" (Beebe, Beebe, & Redmond, 1999, p. 152).

WATSON, JOHN B. (1878–1958)

John B. Watson was born in South Carolina and named for a well-known evangelist of his time. His father, a confederate soldier, was known for his temper and for seldom being at home. His mother was known for being domineering and devoted to harsh liberal Baptist theology. Watson rebelled against his Christian upbringing and defied the evangelical way of life. He would later in his life write of his regret of being baptized.

Watson saw himself as a fighter (although not athletic). He was seen by fellow students as courteous and charming, easily winning friends and support from others. During his young adulthood, Watson experienced a persistent lack of funds. He graduated from Furman University with a Masters in 1899. He was an able student but noted for being argumentative. He left Furman in 1900 to continue his graduate work at the University of Chicago. Of interest, Watson studied philosophy under George H. Mead. He earned his Ph.D. in 1903. He married Mary Ickes in 1904, had two children, and divorced in 1920. His divorce was widely publicized and caused the university to ask for his resignation. He then married Rosalie Rayner, a former graduate student, and had two children in his second marriage. Due to the circumstances of his divorce, academia was now closed to him. Watson's manifesto was published in 1913, titled *Psychology as a Behaviorist Views It.* In all, Watson would publish 35 papers, reports, and books, serve as president of the American Psychological Association (1915), and serve as editor on a number of professional journals.

WERTHEIMER, MAX (1880–1943)

Max Wertheimer was born in Czechoslovakia. He was the younger of two children. His parents were Jewish, but he himself was not affiliated with any religious group. He began his college at Charles University in Prague. He left there to attend the University of Berlin to pursue a degree in psychology. He earned his doctorate in 1904 from Wurzburg (summa cum laude). His dissertation dealt with legal testimony and involved the use of word association for the detection of lies. In 1923 he was married, had four children, and then divorced in 1942. In 1929 Wertheimer moved to Frankfurt and remained there until Hitler came to power. He left Germany for Czechoslovakia, after hearing a speech by Hitler over the radio. He did not want his children to grow up in a country where a man like Hitler could come to power. In 1933 he joined the faculty of the new School for Social Research. He became an American citizen in 1939. He died of coronary thrombosis in 1943.

Wertheimer was noted for his fresh approach to research and his eager curiosity, often leading to new problems for his students to examine. It was said his greatness lay in his ability to fire the imagination and creativity of his students.

Glossary

90/10 Rule Teachers spend 90% of their time looking for undesirable behaviors and only 10% of their time looking for desirable behaviors; this must be reversed.

Adaptors Self-manipulators that are ways of satisfying bodily needs or are habit formed.

Affect Displays Nonverbal gestures that communicate emotional content.

Ambushing Listening to gather information to personally attack someone.

Attention Visual portion of attention; including eye contact and receptive body language.

Attribution Theory Explanation of how we attribute attitudes or causes to other people's actions; either internal (person-centered) or external (situation-centered).

Autocratic Teacher A teacher who teaches by force and punishment, not allowing students to demonstrate creativity in their efforts.

Avoidance and Escape A strategy used by students who struggle academically to avoid and escape the curriculum by acting out and being removed from the classroom.

Balance Theory Observers seek cognitive congruence between the person they are observing and actions the person exhibits.

Balcony View A conflict-resolution technique that involves distancing oneself from the problem in order to take a more objective look at the situation.

Beliefs Ways in which you structure your understanding of reality.

Best Practices The linking of research evidence to classroom practices.

Brainstorming A conflict-resolution tool whereby several individuals come together to create multiple solutions to a problem.

Care-Based Thinking The Golden Rule. Thinking and behaving that requires you do what you would want others to do to you.

Coding The underlying meaning of a nonverbal action.

Cognitive Dissonance Occurrence when people behave in a way that conflicts with their beliefs and values. In response to this conflict, they change their beliefs to decrease psychological discomfort.

Collaboration An interactive process whereby team members develop creative ways to solve student issues; coordinated actions by teachers to create solutions and reach common goals.

Collaborative Style Conflict resolution designed to be a team or joint effort.

Collectivist A culture that focuses on the efforts and successes of the group.

Concentration Focus on verbal and nonverbal messages being sent during a conversation.

Conflict Occurs because of different desires, needs, and goals.

Consultation An activity whereby an expert shares specialized knowledge or skills with others about the issue being discussed.

Context Dependence The effect of first impressions and last impressions are very important and sway how a person or situation is perceived.

Conventional Moral reasoning based on social approval or disapproval from peers or authorities.

Cultural Journey A lifelong examination and experiences of a group of people with shared beliefs, values, symbols, and interpretation.

Culture A group of people with shared beliefs, values, symbols, and interpretations.

Culture Shock Upon entering a new environment, the experience of confusion, anxiety, stress, and the feeling of loss.

Defensive Listening Taking other people's comments as personal attacks.

Democratic Teacher A teacher who allows students to be active members of the education process, who has reasonable expectation for his or her students, and takes responsibility for the education process.

Dependency An undesirable situation in which a student becomes overreliant on a teacher for assistance, reassurance, or confidence building.

Differentiated Instruction The practice of ensuring that each learner receive the methods and materials most suitable for that particular learner.

Ecological Perspective Assumes a mutual relationship exists between the student and the environment.

Educationally Safe Environments Classrooms that are physically and emotionally safe, that encourage and appreciate risk-taking, that offer continuous encouragement, and that promote mutual respect.

Emblems Nonverbal cues that have specific meaning in a given culture.

Empathy Understanding the thoughts, feelings, and experience of another.

Empathy Training Process by which students are taught to take the perspective of others both cognitively and emotionally as a way to decrease aggression and conflict.

Encouragement A form of support that can be given to anyone at anytime. This is in contrast to praise.

Ends-Based Thinking Considering moral dilemmas in terms of the greatest good for the greatest number.

Ethics Moral principles, beliefs, and values by which we determine what is right or wrong.

Ethnocentrism The belief that your culture is superior to others.

Exchange Theory The relationship between two people is a function of what each person gets out of the relationship. If there is no payoff in the relationship, there is no relationship.

Eye Contact Means for eliminating distracting visual information and attending to facial cues during conversation.

Family A self-defined unit with an assumption of love and caring among its members.

Gestalt The whole is greater than the sum of the parts.

Haptics The study of how touch is used in nonverbal communication.

Hindsight Bias The occurrence of interpreting outcomes as expected and obvious all along.

Human Relations Systematic study of the ongoing process of shared interactions that occur among people in all aspects of their lives.

Hypocrisy Expecting from your students that which you are unwilling to do yourself.

Idiosyncratic Credit Exists when a person grants privileges to others because of who the person is or the position the person holds.

Illustrators Typically used to accent or complement the verbal message.

Individualistic Cultures that focus on the achievements and accomplishments of the individuals.

Insensitive Listening Taking the speaker's comments at face value and not considering the full message.

Insulated Listening "Tuning out" or ineffective listening because of a desire to not discuss a topic.

Internalized Conversation The conversation a person has with him- or herself. This interactive process constitutes the "self" according to Mead.

Intimacy The ability to see another person as one sees oneself.

Intimate Space Zero to one and a half feet. Space held for our most personal relationships.

Kinesics The study of bodily movements, including nonverbal communication.

Lack of Understanding Conflict that results from a simple misunderstanding.

Listening Process that entails hearing, attending, understanding, responding, and remembering.

Looking Glass Self Cooley's belief that our "self" develops out of our perceptions of the reactions of other to us.

Meanings Found in people, not in the words they use.

Memory Bias False recall of information to fit our misperceptions.

Meta-Stories Verbal vehicles that can be used by teachers to reach students when other strategies have been unsuccessful. They are designed to deepen students' understanding of concepts and ideas.

Misinformation Effect Remembering wrong information.

Moral Dilemma Conflict that arises when there are opposing points of view on a controversial issue that cannot be resolved.

Moralizer A person who tells others what they should vale and believe in.

Multichanneled Because nonverbal messages are often coupled with verbal communication, you must decide which information you will attend to.

Need for Control Natural desire to feel a sense of control over one's environment. Often the function or reason behind undesirable behaviors in the classroom.

Nonverbal Communication Communication that does not involve spoken or written content.

Objectivity Open and unbiased listening process.

Oculesics The study of eye contact and use of gazes to communicate.

Origin Beginning location of the nonverbal communication (e.g., nervous system versus environment).

Other-Oriented Considering the needs, thoughts, desires, attitudes, and beliefs of others.

Peer Mediation Process in which students are taught to assist others in peacefully negotiating solutions to interpersonal conflicts.

Permissive Teacher A teacher who believes students can do no wrong, and that ultimately they will be valuable members of society without unnecessary guidance.

Personal Conflict Type of conflict whereby individuals involved begin to attack the character of each other.

Personal Space One and a half to four feet. Distance reserved for conversations between close friends and acquaintances.

Postconventional Moral reasoning based upon self-chosen ethical principles.

Preconventional Moral reasoning based on rewards, punishments, or exchange of favors.

Principle-Based Ethics Ethics seen as principles that individuals should voluntarily follow.

Propaganda ideas, facts, or allegations spread deliberately to further one's cause or damage an opposing cause.

Proxemics The study of distance and arrangement of personal space used in nonverbal communication.

Pseudo Listening Giving the appearance of listening, when in fact the listener is not attending to the message.

Public Space Twelve feet and beyond. Distant space often used for observation of behavior.

Quality Communication Requires active listening, empathy, openness, honesty, trust, encouragement, and a genuine concern.

Receptive Body Language Body posture that communicates attentiveness to the speaker.

Regulators Nonverbals used to regulate the flow of conversation between individuals.

Restatement of the Message The process of paraphrasing speakers' message in an attempt to fully understand them.

Role Theory Every role has prescriptions that specify what behaviors are expected from the person who occupies the role.

Rule-Based Thinking Consideration of what the world would be like if everyone acted in the same manner.

Rules of Power Rules develop by Saul Alinsky to help individuals who do not feel they have the power to fight social injustice.

Selective Listening Attending to information that is only of interest or relevant to the self.

Selective Perception Our expectations influence our perceptions. We give extra attention to information consistent with our expectations.

Self Reflection Requires a continual analysis and critical examination of what is going on around a teacher and involves an internal conversation on how the teacher might improve one's teaching.

Self-Disclose Sharing of information about him- or herself that others would not know if the information wasn't given.

Self-Fulfilling Prophecy The ultimate function of SFP is not to *predict* the future, but *make* the future.

Social Comparison Theory Our awareness of the differences that exist between ourselves and others based upon social comparison.

Social Space Between 4 and 12 feet. Space used for impersonal conversations.

Stage Hogs-Conversational Individuals whose intent is to turn attention to themselves.

Stereotyping Placing unique people into inflexible categories.

Strategic Pauses Silence in conversation that allows for comprehension and consideration of the message.

Strengths Abilities, talents, or areas in which individuals excel.

Student Diversity The existence of dissimilar students contributing to the unique experiences found in the classroom.

Team Work Process by which individuals bring forth unique knowledge, skills, and experiences that, when accumulated, provide a more complete and complex understanding of the situation.

Territory The space we claim as our own.

The Self That central inner force, common to all beings and yet unique in each.

Usage Conditions that exist at the time of the nonverbal communication.

Values Things identified by you as being good and bad, right and wrong.

Verbal Villains Those who do not attend to the feelings or emotions of others. Instead they keep others at arm's length and put their own interests in the spotlight.

Virtue-Based Ethics Ethics determined by considering how a caring, virtuous person would behave.

Vocal Cues and Paralanguage Use of pitch, tone, tempo, or rate of speech, and volume to give shades of meaning to the spoken word.

Your Full Attention The greatest compliment you can give a student.

References

Ackerman, D. (2005). An alchemy of mind: The marvel and mystery of the brain. New York: Scribner.

Adler, R. B., & Towne, N. (1999). *Looking out/looking in: Interpersonal communication.* (9th ed.). San Francisco: Harcourt Brace College Publishers.

Alberto, P. A., & Troutman, A. C. (2003). *Applied behavior analysis for teachers.* (6th ed.). Upper Saddle River, NJ: Merrill Prentice Hall.

Alerby, E., & Elidottir, J. (2003). The sounds of silence: Some remarks on the value of silence in the process of reflection and relation to teaching and learning. *Reflective Practice, 4,* 41–51.

Alexander, T. (2000). *Adjustment and human relations: A lamp along the way.* Upper Saddle River, NJ: Prentice Hall.

Alinsky, S. D. (1971). *Rules for radicals: A pragmatic primer for realistic radicals.* New York: Vintage Books.

American Association of University Women (AAUW) (1993). *Hostile hallways: The AAUW survey on sexual harassment in America's schools.* Washington, D.C.: Author.

Archer, R. L. (1979). Role of personal and the social situation. In G. J. Chelune (Ed.), *Self-disclosure: Origins, patterns, and implications of openness in interpersonal relationships.* (pp. 28–58). San Francisco: Jossey-Bass.

Arnett, S. L. (1997). *Taking control through self-determination: The management of personal lifestyles by adults with mental retardation.* Dissertation, Norman, OK: University of Oklahoma Press.

Arnett, S. L., & Burns, S. R. (2008). *Educating the educator: Human relations in the academic world.* Denver: Outskirts Press.

Bailey, J. S., & Burch, M. R. (2005). *Ethics for behavior analysts: A practical guide to the behavior analyst certification board guidelines for responsible conduct.* Mahwah, NJ: Lawrence Erlbaum Associates.

Bandler, R., & Grinder, J. (1975). *The structure of magic 1.* Cupertino, CA: Meta Publications.

Bandler, R., & Grinder, J. (1976). *Frogs into princes: Neuro linguistic programming.* Moab, UT: Real People Press.

Beebe, S. A., Beebe, S. J., & Redmond, M. V. (1999). *Interpersonal communication: Relating to others* (3rd ed.). Boston: Allyn & Bacon.

Beebe, S. A., Beebe, S. J., & Redmond, M. V. (2008). *Interpersonal communication: Relating to others.* (5th ed.). Boston: Allyn & Bacon.

Beland, K. R. (1996). A school-wide approach to violence prevention. In R. L. Hampton, P. Jenkins, & T. P. Gullota (Eds.). *Preventing Violence in America* (pp. 209–231). Thousand Oaks, CA: Sage.

Belle, D., & Burr, R. (1991). Why children do not confide: An exploratory analysis. *Child Study Journal, 21,* 217–234.

Berne, E. (1961). *Transactional analysis in psychotherapy: A systematic individual and social psychiatry.* New York: Grove Press.

Biddle, B. J., & Thomas, E. J. (1966). *Role theory: Concepts and research.* New York: John Wiley and Sons.

Birdwhistell, R. L. (1952). *Kinesics and context.* Louisville, KY: University of Louisville Press.

Bloom, L. (1988). What is language? In M. Lahey (Ed.), *Language disorders and language development* (pp. 1–19). New York: Macmillan.

Brent, R., & Anderson, P. (1993). Developing children's classroom listening strategies. *The Reading Teacher, 47,* 122–126.

Bronfenbrenner, U. (1990). Discovering what families do. In D. Blankenhorn, S. B. Ayme, & J. B. Elshtain (Eds.), *Rebuilding the nest: A new commitment to the American family* (pp. 27–38). Milwaukee, WI: Family Service American.

Bronfenbrenner, U. (1994). Ecological models of human development. In *International Encyclopedia of Education,* Vol. 3 (2nd ed.) Oxford: Elsevier.

Brown, B. B., Von Bank, H., & Steinberg, L. (2007). Smoke in the looking glass: Effects of discordance between self- and peer-rated crowd affiliation on adolescent anxiety, depression and self-feelings. *J Youth Adolescence, 37,* 1163–1177.

Bruner, J. (1990). *Acts of meaning.* Cambridge, MA: Harvard University Press.

Campbell, R. R. (2003). Attributes of good listening. In *Leadership: Getting it done.* Retrieved from: http://web.missouri.edu/~ campbellr/Leadership/chapter6.htm

Caraway, K., Tucker, C. M., Reinke, W. M., & Hall, C. (2003). Self-efficacy, goal orientation, and fear of failure as predictors of school engagement in high school students. In *Psychology in the Schools, 40,* 417–427.

Cardwell, J. D. (1971). *Social psychology: A symbolic interaction perspective.* Northbrook, IL: AHM Publishing.

Cennamo, K. S. (1989). Factors influencing mental effort: A theoretical overview and review of literature. In: *Proceedings of Selected Research Papers presented at the Annual Meeting of the Association for Educational Communications and Technology* (Dallas, TX, February 1–5, 1989).

Chapman, A. H. (1976). *Harry Stack Sullivan: His life and his work.* New York: G. P. Putnam's Sons.

Cooley, C. H. (1902). *Human nature and the social order.* New York: C. Scribner's Sons.

Cooley, C. H. (1909). *Social organization.* New York: C. Scribner's Sons.

Coser, L. A. (1977). *Masters of sociological thought: Ideas in historical and social context.* (2nd ed.). San Diego: Harcourt Brace Jovanovich Publishers.

Daunic, A. P., Smith, S. W., Robinson, T. R., Miller, M. D., & Landry, K. L. (2000). School-wide conflict resolution and peer mediation programs: Experiences in three middle schools. *Intervention in School and Clinic, 36,* 94–100.

Delwiche, A. (2002). *Propaganda: Institute for propaganda analysis.* Retrieved from: http://www.propagandacritic.com.

Dettmer, P., Dyck, N., & Thurston, L. (1999). *Consultation, collaboration, and teamwork for students with special needs.* Boston: Allyn & Bacon.

DeVito, J. A. (1991). *Human communication: The basic course.* (5th ed.). New York: HarperCollins Publishers.

Dove, R. (2005). *Value propositioning: Book on–perception and misperception in decision-making.* Tucson, AZ: Iceni Books.

Dreikurs, R. (1964). *Children: The challenge.* New York: Duell, Sloan, and Pearce.

Dreikurs, R., & Cassel, P. (1972). *Discipline without tears.* (2nd ed.). New York: Hawthorn Books.

Eisenberg, N., Fabes, R. A., Shepard, S. A., Murphy, B. C., Jones, S., & Guthrie, I. K. (1998). Contemporaneous and longitudinal predication of children's sympathy from dispositional regulation and emotionality. *Developmental Psychology, 34,* 910–924.

Ekman, P., & Friesen, W. V. (1969). The repertoire of nonverbal behavior: Categories, origins, usage, and coding. *Semiotica, 1,* 49–98.

Elstad, E. (2006). Understanding the nature of accountability failure in a technology-filled, laissez-faire classroom: Disaffected students and teachers who give in. *Journal of Curriculum Studies, 38,* 459–481.

Festinger, L. (1954). A theory of social comparison process. *Human Relations, 7,* 117–140.

Feyerick, D., & Steffen S. (2009, April 8). "Sexting" lands teen on sex offender list. *CNN's American Morning.* Retrieved from http://www.cnn.com/.

Frankl, V. E. (1984). *Man's search for ultimate meaning.* New York: Simon & Schuster.

Gallese, V. (2003) The manifold nature of interpersonal relations: The quest for a common mechanism. *Phil. Trans. R. Soc. Lond. B, 358,* 517–528.

Gardner, H. (1983). *Frames of mind: The theory of multiple intelligences.* New York: Basic Books, 1985. Tenth Anniversary Edition with new introduction, New York: Basic Books, 1993.

Gazda, G. M., Asbury, F. R., Balzer, F. J., Childers, W. C., Phelps, R. E., & Walters, R. P. (1999). *Human relations development: A manual for educators* (6th ed.). Boston: Allyn & Bacon.

Goddard, R. D., Tschannen-Moran, M., & Hoy, W. (2001). A multilevel examination of the distribution and effects of teacher trust in students and parents in urban elementary schools. *Elementary School Journal,* 102 (1).

Goffman, E. (1959). *The presentation of self in everyday life.* Garden City, NY: Doubleday Anchor Books.

Goldstein, G. S., & Benassi, V. A. (1994). The relation between teacher self-disclosure and student classroom participation. *Teaching of Psychology, 21,* 212–217.

Goldstein, K. (1948). *Language and language disturbances.* New York: Grune and Stratton.

Grice, H. P. (1989). *Studies in the ways of words.* Cambridge, MA: Harvard University Press.

Grinder. J., & Bandler, R. (1976). *The structure of magic* 2. Cupertino, CA: Meta Publications.

Grube, B., & Lens, V. (2003). Student-to-student harassment: The impact of *Davis v. Monroe. Children & Schools, 25,* 173–185.

Hall, E. T. (1959). *The silent language.* Garden City, NY: Doubleday.

Hall, E. T. (1966). *The hidden dimension.* Garden City, NY: Anchor Press.

Hanna, S.L. (2000). *Person to person: Positive relationships don't just happen* (3rd ed.). Upper Saddle River, NJ: Prentice Hall.

Harper, Jr. V. B. (2005). The new student-teacher channel. *The Journal, 33,* 30–32.

Healy, M. E. (1948). *Society and social change in the writing of St. Thomas, Ward, Sumner, and Cooley*. Westport, CT: Greenwood Press.

Heider. F. (1958). *The psychology of interpersonal relations*. Lawrence, KS: University of Kansas Press.

Henley, N. M., (1977). *Body politics: Power, sex, and nonverbal communication*. Englewood Cliffs, NJ: Prentice-Hall.

Hertenstein, M. J., Keltner, D., App, B., Bulleit, B. A., & Jaskolka, A. R. (2006). Touch communicates distinct emotions. *Emotion, 6*, 528–533.

Heumann, J. (1994). Terminology. *TASH Newsletter, 20*, 24.

Hill, A. (1998). *Speaking truth to power*. New York: Anchor Publishing.

Hoffman, L., Hutchinson, C., & Reiss, E. (2009). On improving school climate: Reducing reliance on rewards and punishment. *International Journal of Whole Schooling, 5*, 13–24.

Holden, C. (2004). "Heaven help the teachers!" Parents' perspectives on the introduction of education for citizenship. *Educational Review, 56*, 247–258.

Honig, A. S. (2005). Take time to touch. *Scholastic Parent & Child, 12*, 32–35.

Hupbach, A., Gomez, A., Hardt, & Nadell, L. (2007). Reconsolidation of episodic memories: A subtle reminder triggers integration of new information. *Learning & Memory, 14*, 47–53.

Iannotti, R. J. (1985). Naturalistic and structured assessments of prosocial behavior in preschool children: The influence of empathy and perspective taking. *Developmental Psychology, 21*, 46–55.

Institute for Propaganda Analysis (1939). *The fine art of propaganda: A study of Father Coughlin's speeches*. A. M. Lee & E. B. Lee (Eds.). New York: Harcourt, Brace and Company.

Johnson, D. W., & Johnson, F. P. (2000). *Joining together: Group theory and group skills*. (7th ed.). Needham Heights, MA: Allyn & Bacon.

Johnson, D. W., & Johnson, R. T. (1990). Social skills for successful group work. *Educational Leadership, 47*, 29–33.

Jones, D. (2007). Speaking, listening, planning and assessing: the teacher's role in developing metacognitive awareness. *Early Child Development & Care, 177*, 569–579.

Jones, T. J. (2004). Conflict resolution education: The field, the findings, and the future. *Conflict Resolution Quarterly, 22*, 233–267.

Jussim, L., & Harber, K. (2005). Teacher expectations and self-fulfilling prophecies: Knowns and unknowns, resolved and unresolved controversies. *Personality & Social Psychology Review (Lawrence Erlbaum Associates), 9*, 131–155.

Kahn, W. J., & Lawhorne, C. V. (2003). *Empathy the critical factor in conflict resolution and a culture of civility*. West Chester, PA: West Chester University.

Katzenbach, J., & Smith, D. (1993). *The wisdom of teams*. Cambridge, MA: Harvard Business School Press.

Khoo, P. N., & Senn, C. Y. (2004). Not wanted in the inbox: Evaluations of unsolicited and harassing e-mail. *Psychology of Women Quarterly, 28*, 204–214.

Kidder, R. M., & Born, P. L. (1998). Resolving ethical dilemmas in the classroom. *Educational Leadership, 56*, 38–41.

Kinch, J. W. (1968). Experiments on factors related to self-concept change. *Journal of Social Psychology, 74*, 251–258.

Kohlberg, L. (1976). Moral stages and moralization: The cognitive-developmental approach. In T. Lickona (Ed.), *Moral Development and Behavior: Theory, Research and Social Issues* (p. 31–53). New York: Holt.

Kottak, C. P. (1982). *Anthropology: The exploration of human diversity*. New York: Random House.

Laukka, P., Juslin, P. N., & Bresin, R. (2005). A dispositional approach to vocal expression of emotion. *Cognition and Emotion, 19*, 633–653.

Leathers, D. G. (1986). *Successful nonverbal communication: Principles and applications*. Boston: Allyn & Bacon.

Loftus, E. F., Miller, D. G., & Burns, H. J. (1978). Semantic integration of verbal information into a visual memory. *Human Learning and Memory, 4*, 19–31.

Luft, J., & Ingham, H. (1950). "The Johari window: A graphic model of interpersonal awareness." *Proceedings of the western training laboratory in group development* (Los Angeles: UCLA).

Mairs, N. (1986). *On being a cripple*. Tucson: University of Arizona Press.

Manis J. G., & Meltzer B. N. (1978). *Symbolic interaction: A reader in social psychology* (3rd ed.). Boston: Allyn & Bacon.

Marchand-Martella, N. E., Slocum, T. A., & Martella, R. C. (2004). *Introduction to direct instruction*. Boston: Pearson.

Marcia, J. E. (2002). Adolescence, identity, and the Bernardone family. *Identity: An International Journal of Theory and Research, 2*, 199–209.

Maslow, A. (1968). Some educational implications of the humanistic psychologies. *Harvard Educational Review, 38*, 685–696.

Maslow, A. (1971). *The farther reaches of human nature*. New York: Penguin Books.

Mastropieri, M. A., & Scruggs, T. E. (2007). *The inclusive classroom: Strategies for effective instruction* (3rd ed.). Upper Saddle River, NJ: Pearson.

Mazer, J., Murphy, R., & Simonds, C. (2009, June). The effects of teacher self-disclosure via Facebook on teacher credibility. *Learning, Media, & Technology, 34*(2), 175–183.

Mead, G. H. (1934). *Mind, self, and society: From the standpoint of a social behaviorist*. Chicago: University of Chicago Press.

Mercer, J. (1973). *Labeling the mentally retarded: Clinical and social system perspective on mental retardation*. Sage: Beverly Hills, CA.

Murdock, N., Gartin, B., & Crabtree, T. (2002). *Special education law*. Upper Saddle River, NJ: Pearson Education.

Nastasi, B. K., Clements, D. H., & Battista, M. T. (1990). Social cognitive interactions, motivation, and cognitive growth in logo programming and CAI problem-solving environments. *Journal of Educational Psychology, 82*, 150–158.

NEA, 1975 reference. . . . . I pulled the "code of ethics" off of their National Education Association website. http://www.nea.org/home/30442.htm

Patterson, S. (2009). The effects of teacher-student small talk on out-of-seat behavior. *Education & Treatment of Children, 32*, 167–174.

Piotrowski, D., & Hoot, J. (2008). Bullying and violence in schools, what teachers should know and do. *Childhood Education, 84*, 357–363.

Pittam, J., & Scherer, K. R. (1993). Vocal expression and communication of emotion. In M. J. Haviland (Ed.). *The handbook of emotions* (pp. 185–197). New York: Guilford.

Postle, B. R., Idzikowski, C., Sala, S. D., Logie, R. H., & Baddeley, A. D. (2006). The selective disruption of spatial working memory by eye movements. *Quarterly Journal of Experimental Psychology, 59*, 100–120.

Raymond, E. B. (2008). *Learners with mild disabilities: A character approach* (3rd ed.). Boston: Pearson.

Rex, L. A. (2000). Judy constructs a genuine question: A case for interactional inclusion. *Teaching and Teacher Education, 16*, 315–333.

Rock, E. A., Hammond, M., & Rasmussen, S. (2002). *School based program to teach children empathy and bully prevention.* Paper presented at the Annual Conference of the American Psychological Association (110th, Chicago, IL, August 22–25, 2002).

Rogers, C. (1995). What understanding and acceptance means to me. *Journal of Humanistic Psychology, 35*, 7–22. (Transcript of a talk presented to the Illinois Guidance and Personnel Association 12th Annual Conference in 1956).

Rosenthal, R., & Jacobson, L. (1968). *Pygmalion in the classroom: Teacher expectations and student intellectual development*. New York: Holt.

Rydell, R., McConnell, A., & Beilock, S. (2009). Multiple social identities and stereotype threat: Imbalance, accessibility, and working memory. *Journal of Personality and Social Psychology, 96*, 949–966.

Salinger, J. D. (1971). *The catcher in the rye*. Toronto: Bantam Books.

Salmon, S. (2003). Teaching empathy: The PEACE curriculum. *Reclaiming Children & Youth, 12*, 167–173.

Saunders, M. D. (2001). Who's getting the message? Helping your students understand in a verbal world. *Teaching Exceptional Children, 33*, 70–74.

Scheffler, I. (1974). *Four pragmatists: A critical introduction to Pierce, James, Mead, and Dewey*. New York: Humanities Press.

Seligman, M. (1975). *Helplessness: On depression, development, and death.* San Francisco: W. H. Freeman.

Shadow of Hate (The): A History of Intolerance in America (1995). A film by Charles Guggenheim. Produced by Teaching Tolerance: Montgomery, AL.

Shepherd, K. K. (1994). Stemming conflict through peer mediation. *School Administration, 51*, 14–17.

Sielski, L. M. (1979). Understanding body language. *Personnel and Guidance Journal, 57*, 238–242.

Skeels, H. M., & Dye, H. D. (1939). A study of the effects of differential stimulation on mentally retarded children. *American Association for Mental Defectiveness, 44*, 114.

Skeels, H. M. (1966). Adult status of children with contrasting early life experiences. *Monographs of the Society for Research in Child Development, 31*, 1–56.

Smith, S. W., Daunic, A. P., Miller, M. D., & Robinson, T. R. (2002). Conflict resolution and peer mediation in middle schools: Extending the process and outcome knowledge base. *The Journal of Social Psychology, 142*, 567–586.

Smith, T. E. C., Polloway, E. A., Patton, J. R., & Dowdy, C. A. (2001). *Teaching students with special needs in inclusive settings* (3rd ed.). Needham Heights, MA: Allyn & Bacon.

Steele, C. M. (1999). Thin ice. *Atlantic Monthly, 284,* 44–53.

Steward B. McKinney Homeless Assistance Act (PL100-77, 1987) from www.doe.in.gov/alted/homelesslinkpg.html.

Stogdill, R. (1974). *Handbook of leadership*. New York: Free Press.

Stone, M., & Couch, S. (2004). Peer sexual harassment among high school students: Teachers' attitudes, perceptions, and responses. *The High School Journal,* 1–14.

Sullivan, H. S. (1953). *The interpersonal theory of psychiatry*. New York: W. W. Norton.

Swensen, C. H., Jr. (1973). *Introduction to interpersonal relations*. Glenview, IL: Scott, Foresman, and Company.

Theberge, S. K. & Karan, O. C. (2004). Six factors inhibiting the use of peer mediation in a junior high school. *Professional School Counseling, 7,* 283–290.

Thibaut, J., & Kelley, H. (1959). *The social psychology of groups*. New York: Wiley.

Thomas, C. C., Correa, V. I., & Morsink, C. V. (1995). *Interactive teaming: Consultation and collaboration in special programs*. Englewood Cliffs, NJ: Merrill.

Thompson, F. T., Grandgenett, D. J., & Grandgenett, N. F. (1999). Helping disadvantaged learners build effective listening strategies. *Education, 120,* 130–135.

Triandis, H. C. (1994). *Culture and social behavior*. New York: McGraw-Hill.

Turnbull, A., Turnbull, R., Erwin, E., & Soodak, L. (2006). *Families, professionals, and exceptionality: Positive outcomes through partnerships and trust* (5th ed.). Upper Saddle River, NJ: Pearson Publishing.

Veulgelers, W. (2000). Different ways of teaching values. *Educational Review, 52,* 37–46.

Wagar, W. W. (1963). *The city of man: Prophecies of modern civilization in twentieth-century thought*. Boston: Houghton Miffin.

Walker, V., & Brokaw, L. (1998). *Becoming aware*. (7th ed.). Dubuque, IA: Kendall/Hunt Publishing.

Watson, J. B. (1913). Psychology as the behaviorist views it. *Psychological Review, 20,* 158–177.

Wiggins, J. S., Renner, K. E., Clore G. L., & Rose, R. J. (1971). *The psychology of personality*. Reading, Massachusetts: Addison-Wesley Publishing.

Wilhelm, J. D. (2004). *Inquiring minds learn to read and write: Inquiry, questioning, and discussion strategies for promoting literacy and learning across the curriculum*. Retrieved October 25, 2005 from: http://www.boisestate.edu/english/jwilhelm/Ch7promotingtalk.doc

Wrightsman, L. S. (1977). *Social psychology* (2nd ed.). Monterey, CA, Brooks/Cole Publishing.

Author Index

Subject Index

CPSIA information can be obtained
at www.ICGtesting.com
Printed in the USA
LVHW060017260122
709300LV00002B/2

9 781465 213686